J. Bruce Regan

November 2023

ARE WE NEARLY THERE YET?

'Hear, Land o' Cakes, and brither Scots'

Robert Burns
From 'On the late Captain Grose's Peregrinations Thro' Scotland (Collecting the Antiques of That Kingdom)' (1789)

Robert Burns met Francis Grose at Friars' Carse, Auldgirth, near Burns's farm at Ellisland, in Dumfries-shire, in the summer of 1789, when Grose was collecting materials for *The Antiques of Scotland* (2 Vols, 1789 and 1791).
Burns described his company to Mrs Frances Dunlop, a close correspondent and whom we might today term a critical friend:

'I have never seen a man of more original observation, anecdote and remark… His delight is to steal thro' the country almost unknown, both as most favourable to his humour and his business … if you discover a cheerful-looking grig of an old fat fellow, the precise figure of Dr Slop, wheeling around in your avenue in his old carriage with a pencil and paper in his hand, you may conclude, "Thou art the man!"'.

Any resemblance to the author of this book is entirely coincidental.

Half title page:

Left: A traditional milestone 4 miles from Tomintoul, on the A939, originally a military road built by William Caulfeild. *The Milestone Society*

Centre: A cast-iron milepost with directional 'hands' on milepost, now lost, near Arncroach in Fife. *The East Neuk of Fife Preservation Society*

Right: A cast-iron milepost and older milestone in the Scottish Borders. *Christine Minto and The Milestone Society*

Title page:

Top: A Millennium milepost at Falkland in Fife. *Cosmo Blake and Sustrans*

Left: A traditional milestone between Girvan and Newton Stewart. *Christine Minto and The Milestone Society*

Centre: An impressive restoration of a milepost near Peebles. *Christine Minto and The Milestone Society*

Right: A cast-iron milepost between Forfar and Froickheim. *Christine Minto and The Milestone Society*

ARE WE NEARLY THERE YET?

A journey celebrating Scotland's milestones, inspired by
The Road and the Miles to Dundee

L. Bruce Keith

Published by
Dunnottar Productions Limited
Orchard House
322 Thorpe Road
Longthorpe
Peterborough PE3 6LX

In association with:

Slip Coach Publishing Services Limited
The Trundle
2 Ringstead Road
Great Addington
Northamptonshire
NN14 4BW

and

Priory Ash Publishing
2 Denford Ash Cottages
Denford
Kettering
Northamptonshire
NN14 4EW

Printed and bound in the Czech Republic

Acknowledgements

Writing a book can be a solitary affair. Researching it leads to new and renewed friendships, united in a common purpose or interest. Both activities have been cathartic.

My principal appreciation goes to Christine Minto, in recognition of the years spent touring Scotland on her bicycle, meticulously and methodically recording and photographing milestones, but most particularly for her dedication, patience and genuine enthusiasm to share her knowledge, experience and joyous recollections with me. As the Scottish Representative on The Milestone Society, Christine is a wonderful ambassador for capturing, protecting and enhancing a wider knowledge and appreciation of this aspect of our roadside heritage and encouraging others to benefit from this increased understanding.

Christine introduced me to fellow enthusiasts – to John Riddell, Iain Davison, Carol Haines, Alan and Ruth Thompson, Nigel and Diana Bishop, Dr Adrian Sumner, Christopher Dingwall, Ian Thompson, David Viner and Alverie Weighill, each with their own expansive knowledge of milestones and each willing to share this with me. Likewise, I found kindred spirits in David Courtney McClure from Ayrshire History, in John Beaton and David Jenkins in the East Fife Preservation Society and Paul Monk from the Cromarty Courthouse Museum. Ten years after retiring from Fife Council's Transportation Services Department, Arthur Greene maintains his interest in the milestone heritage within the Kingdom.

On railways, I had the benefit of John Yellowlees's knowledge and indefatigable enthusiasm.

From Sustrans, John Lauder and Cosmo Blake were hugely supportive and informative. May the National Cycle Network and its Millennium Mileposts prosper.

Moreover, I had a wealth of familiar faces to provide encouragement and support. From my friends, the 'railway buffs', I had an invaluable source of reference in Mike Lowson, Colin Shearer, Mike Hogg, Charles Devereux and Tim Roebuck. They were sufficiently generous to contribute a nostalgic, yet honest, Foreword to the book, together with an epilogue. Mike Lowson also subedited the draft text and was ever-patient and good humoured in providing advice on style from his wealth of professional experience. Iain and Heather Matheson and John and Jayne Riddet provided knowledgeable and tempered sounding boards – all useful pointers on my direction of travel along my journey to produce this book. I am very fortunate indeed in my friends.

The professional editorial, design and publishing expertise of Peter Townsend of Slip Coach Publishing Limited and Will Adams of Priory Ash was invaluable, and I am very appreciative of the support of both of them in producing the finished product.

Above all, I do appreciate the support of my wife, Deborah, who ensured that I had completed the annual ritual of painting the shed before retiring to my study to start typing.

I alone take responsibility for any errors that appear. If they do, I hope they are schoolboy howlers, which at least will entertain you.

L. Bruce Keith
Peterborough 2021

Contents

Foreword by members of the annual Boys'
    Walking Weekend   6
Preface   7

1. Early times…   9
2. Mensuration: 'gie him an inch an' he'll tak a mile'   13
    Our milestone odyssey   16
3. The Appliance of Science: mapping our country   17
    Our milestone heritage: The Borders   28
4. The legislative footprint   34
    Our milestone heritage: Dumfries & Galloway   37
5. A journey in time along Scotland's roads: routes to
    progress and prosperity   42
    Trysts and the drove roads   42
    Troops: the military roads   43
    Trade and transport: the Telford era   45
    The turnpikes   48
    Private roads   53
    The 20th century and beyond   53
    Our milestone heritage: Strathclyde, including Glasgow   55
6. A journey in time along Scotland's roads:
    the travellers' tales   72
    Treading where the saints have trod   72
    Troops: on the march   73
    The travellers: on the trail of the early tourist   76

    Our milestone heritage: The Lothians, including Edinburgh   82
7. Promoting milestones   97
    Our milestone heritage: The Kingdom of Fife   99
8. A short musical interlude   105
    Our milestone heritage: Central Region   107
9. Canal milestones   111
    Our milestone heritage: Tayside   115
10. Railway miles   120
    Our milestone heritage: Grampian   126
11. Going the distance: fastest and farthest –
    the top 50 Scots   129
    Our milestone heritage: Highland   134
12. Millennium milestones: putting milestones
    back on the map   143
    Our milestone heritage: The Western Isles   151
13. 'Paddy's Milestone': the story of Ailsa Craig   153
    Our milestone heritage: The Northern Isles   154
14. The Milestone Society   157
15. Journey's end   158

Glossary   162
Bibliography   163
50 top sporting Scots who went the extra mile   165

Index   166

Foreword by members of the annual Boys' Walking Weekend

When a group of close but geographically dispersed friends get together, it's a safe bet there will be no shortage of anecdotes, memories, experiences and a great deal of laughter. That is very much the case with our small group of six who have been colleagues and friends for more than 40 years.

Five of us joined the British Rail Traffic Management Training Scheme on the same day in September 1978. The sixth member, the author of this book, was never a railway employee but his patience in subsequently enduring endless train talk among us, and his knowledgeable contributions to those discussions, have ensured that in our eyes Bruce is now a much-valued 'honorary railwayman'.

He did play a pivotal role in our railway lives, though. He became landlord to Colin in Angus and to Mike H. in Edinburgh, and often a hospitable host as our individual careers spread us far and wide.

In the early 1980s Mike H. and Bruce organised a walking weekend together at glorious Sandwood Bay in Scotland's North-West Highlands. In subsequent years they were joined by Colin and thereafter by the rest of us, too. The Boys' Walking Weekend was born. It is now an annual fixture ranging across the length and breadth of the UK and also to mainland Europe on occasion.

One sure-fire source of amusement on these trips was Bruce's serial insistence that he was going to write a book about his passion for Scottish bridges. It was embedded in his soul as a youngster when accompanying his father, a senior roads and bridges engineer, to many road projects and bridge inspection journeys across Scotland. How we laughed, year after year, when we pressed him for details of progress on this apparently mythical book.

But Bruce had the last laugh. Years of careful research and dedicated writing, often unseen, produced his impressive first book, *Bridgescapes*, which became a notable success. Now cured of our scepticism, we're sure that *Are We Nearly There Yet?* will be a similar triumph. It is a significant and welcome addition to the history and heritage of Scotland's milestones.

It is fitting that we are contributing this Foreword to a book on milestones because we've shared many of the major milestones in Bruce's life. From student days to his work in the Scottish Office; his life-threatening and life-changing road crash; the joy of his marriage to Deborah; the thrill of watching daughter Lauren grow and achieve professional success in her own career; the move from his beloved Scotland to Eastern England; and his rise to become a highly respected land economist, environmentalist and, eventually, published author. It has been quite a journey.

We are delighted to commend this book as an enthralling read about something that previously so many of us took for granted.

Whenever we six meet – three Scots and three Englishmen – the banter is fast-flowing. On each occasion the one guaranteed to deliver the best and often longest anecdotes, and to generate the loudest laughter, is Bruce. During our next Boys' Walking Weekend, or at any other time when we get together either as a group or as individuals, there will be more anecdotes, more memories and many more laughs to come, and Bruce will be at the centre of them all.

It could be asked in the context of how many more stories he has to tell: 'Are We Nearly There Yet?'

From our collective past experience, the answer is absolutely not.

Mike Lowson, Leslie, Aberdeenshire
Colin Shearer, Broughton, Peeblesshire
Mike Hogg, Dunnington, Yorkshire
Charles Devereux, Ely, Cambridgeshire
Tim Roebuck, Maplewood, New Jersey

May 2021

The Boys' Walking Weekend fraternity. From left to right: Tim, Bruce, Mike H., Charles, Mike L. and Colin. For steam railway enthusiasts, the locomotive behind is No 822 *The Earl* on the Welshpool & Llanfair Light Railway in June 2019. *Tim Roebuck*

Preface

That plaintive call, all too familiar to parents embarking on a journey with their children, 'Are we nearly there yet?', rings out as the Wolseley turns left, heading south on the A9.

It's the late 1950s/early '60s. We live in Balloch, a village a short distance from Inverness, and as a child I've made this journey to grandparents living in Dundee and Forfar many times. It was always in a Wolseley car; we had a succession of three of them – a 4/44, a 1500 and a 15/60. They all had leather seats and varnished wooden dashboards, with a small illuminated badge on the distinctive radiator grille, and they were all a similar shade of grey. Prosaic names and a rather dull colour not to become fashionable again until the mid-2000s.

The journey was through some spectacular, rugged and beautiful Scottish scenery. I appreciated it, felt attracted to it, even as a youngster. The road was the old A9, as far as Perth anyway, remnants of which are still visible from the modern highway as it wends its way across Drummossie Muir, through The Slochd and the isolation of Drumochter Pass, before reaching the magnificent greenery of the eastern end of Breadalbane, with the final leg being the rich and fertile Carse of Gowrie.

The journey time was between 4 and 4½ hours, dependent upon season, especially the number of caravans encountered, the prevailing weather conditions and the frequency of 'pit stops', for a distance of approximately 145 miles. In these days the route went through the 'High' streets of Carrbridge, Aviemore, Kingussie, Newtonmore, Dalwhinnie, Blair Atholl, Pitlochry and Dunkeld. No bypasses to these settlements then.

To entertain my sister and me, there were games of I-spy, musical interludes, provided by ourselves – there was no car radio or cassette player – and a rather intriguing 'game' that comprised spotting the next roadside milestone. It was akin to children nowadays being kept occupied identifying and counting the Eddie Stobart lorries encountered during protracted car journeys.

These milestones were traditionally of stone or concrete construction, some cast iron, standing up to 3 feet high, painted white, with the distance from the last town and distance to the next reasonably sized settlement marked in black

Left: Highland journeys, 1958. *J. Forbes Keith*

Below: 'How many more miles, Maa?' *Alan and Ruth Thompson (Arran)*

lettering and numbering. They were a feature of what one might call 'roadside furniture' in these days, and often they were of some considerable age.

My father was a civil engineer – indeed, a roads and bridges engineer – and always looked to add an element of challenge – I would not go as far as to say sophistication – to the 'game'. When we ascertained what distance it was to the next town, he'd ask me to calculate how long it would take us to reach it, if we travelled at, say, an average speed of 40 miles per hour. This 'task' would be undertaken several times during our journey. Certainly a good distraction. And surely an appropriate response to the query 'Are we nearly there yet?'

Fast forward 60 years, and the journey time between Inverness and Dundee is now seldom more than 2½ hours, often less on a quiet day. It's now a much improved road, large lengths of it dual-carriageway and those old milestones replaced by modern road signage. The journey still holds the same sense of delight for me, if not quite the same aspect of adventure, and I often reflect on past travels.

These early car journeys certainly laid the foundation of my interest in my surroundings and nurtured an interest and fascination in the built and natural heritage. Throughout my career as a surveyor and environmentalist I've been exceedingly fortunate to have been professionally involved with the protection and conservation of our heritage assets and natural resources of land and water, and with developments that aim to be sustainable, recognising that we owe it to future generations to leave them that legacy in good shape.

The artefacts that make up this heritage have long held a special place in my affections. This infrastructure, as that is what these artefacts comprise, collectively adds up to more than the sum of their parts, and each is worthy of study, respect and, yes, celebration. Carol Haines, in her book 'Marking the Miles: A History of English Milestones', makes the valid observation that 'every one of them is unique'. Perhaps the milestones encountered in my childhood embedded an interest in measuring distances, so that, in turn, led to a career as a surveyor.

I captured my life-long interest in Scottish bridges and the engineers, architects and briggers who brought us these structures, in my book *Bridgescapes*, published in 2017 to coincide with the opening of the iconic Queensferry Crossing. Since then I've had the pleasure of presenting the book at meetings of history, heritage, civic, landscape and amenity societies and many other interested clubs across Scotland – more than 200

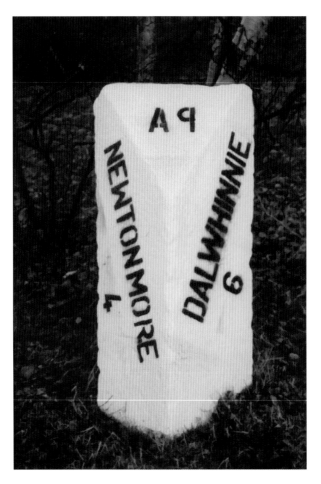

A milestone near Crubenmore on the A9.
Christine Minto and The Milestone Society

of them in fact. The real pleasure, however, has been meeting an eclectic mix of people, each with their own special interest but all with a shared passion for celebrating our heritage. Be it a seeming fixation with AA roadside kiosks or the adoption of a trig point on some remote summit, or an obsession with defensive pillboxes amidst the sand dunes of our coastline, I've encountered them all. To each their own, but for me the historical legacy of such items, be they millstones or milestones, is an integral part of understanding our past. All are valid, and merit celebration.

During the enforced lockdown of the coronavirus pandemic in 2020, many people turned in search of a new project. What could I do while confined to my study, but to turn to something that offered the prospect of some purposeful travel and discovery when the constraints on movement from home were finally eased? What better opportunity than to explore further the history of these old milestones I'd encountered around the roads of Scotland? My journey, metaphorically, had begun…

1
Early times

Before we depart on our journey, however, I'd better let you know that I'm being inclusive in my definition of 'milestone'. I'm also embracing the fingerpost, those timber or, more frequently, cast-iron posts with one or more arms (but called 'fingers') pointing in the direction of named places, often, and essentially for our interest, with the distance alongside. Readers with a narrower perspective on the subject may feel that this is an act of heresy, but be assured that it makes for a more rounded approach to the topic. Moreover, I've the blessing of The Milestone Society, of whom more later, in adopting a more holistic and generic stance. So here goes…

Aside from the childhood plea of 'Are we nearly there yet?', there's an underlying human need, or perhaps just a fascination, even for the most geographically challenged among us, to ascertain where we are, especially in relation to other places. During the heyday of his storytelling triumphs, I always laughed out loud at Billy Connolly's rendition of 'The Crucifixion' in which he relates that 'In those days, no one knew where they were anyway. They used to wander around saying "Where are we? What's the name of this place?" I wish an explorer would come and tell us where we are'.'

If only they'd had a milestone … or a fingerpost.

If you want to find the earliest record in Scotland of any meaningful form of civil engineering, it's always a fairly safe bet to check out what the Romans did. That is in no way dismissing the ingenuity and building prowess of our Neolithic ancestors, who constructed Skara Brae in Orkney in about 3,100BC or the magnificent brochs built in millennia long past.

The Broch of Mousa, in Shetland, is an Iron Age structure from the 1st century BC and is the highest prehistoric building in Britain. But the era of Roman occupation, which is broadly contemporary with the last vestiges of the Iron Age in Britain (our ancestors were relatively late developers), serves us well for exploring the pedigree of milestones as we have substantial evidence of the roads they constructed.

While Scotland was at the extremity of their Empire, the Romans did occupy land as far north as the Central Belt and what is modern Perthshire. The Antonine Wall – in reality a trench and embankment with a wooden palisade on top for most of its length of 39 miles – marked a bit of a northern boundary, although there were forts beyond at Ardoch (Braco), Strageath (Strath Earn), Bertha (Redgorton, near Perth) and Cargill (near Coupar Angus, in Perthshire). There is also speculation that the Romans may have built a fort at Cawdor (Easter Galcantray), near Inverness, with a series of forts and encampments stretching up and round the north-east coast of the country, with evidence of occupation at Stracathro, Raedykes (near Stonehaven), Durno (Inverurie), and several other locations en route. At Kintore there is evidence, mostly from aerial photographs interpreted by archaeologist J. K. St Joseph in the late 1960s and subsequent excavations in advance of residential development and the improvements to the A96, of an extensive (44-hectare) Roman temporary or marching camp. We're taught that Agricola defeated the Caledonian army, under Calgacus, at the Battle of Mons Graupius in about 84AD, but scholars seem undetermined whether the battle site was around Raedykes or Durno, or somewhere else? Whatever the truth,

the Romans appear to have become scunnered with the vagaries of the weather in Aberdeenshire and retreated southwards to the less inhospitable Central Belt.

The Romans constructed a highway immediately to the south of the Antonine Wall, which allowed troops to move quickly between forts. Commissioned in 140AD by the Emperor Antonius Pius, who apparently never visited Scotland, the wall named in his honour was seldom a barrier to hostile Caledonians, and was abandoned in 165AD. The Romans retreated further southwards to the more substantial Hadrian's Wall, which they had started to construct about 20 years before the Antonine Wall. There are more artefacts of Roman occupation in southern Scotland. The legacy of what was Dere Street remains as sections of the A68 with its tell-tale evidence of 'lang strachts' or 'whangs' surviving as integral parts of the modern road from Northumberland through the Scottish Borders up to Edinburgh and beyond, possibly to Falkirk or Camelon, near the fort at Carmuirs. To the south-east of Melrose the road passes Newstead, the site of the Roman fort Trimontium, and there was a significant fort at Cramond, now a suburb of north-west Edinburgh. We know from remains that along these roads linking the forts there were the necessary bridges to afford river crossings, although none survive, and there were isolated buildings, temporary encampments and other structures along the way.

A section of the road to the west of Edinburgh, near what is now the airport, gives us the oldest example of a Scottish milestone. In 1697 Sir Robert Sibbald, on a visit to Ingliston House, came across a cylindrical piece of an old milestone, 25

The Ingliston Roman milestone.
John S. Riddell

inches high and 15 inches in diameter, with Roman text inscribed into a raised panel. He thought it had probably originated at or near Newbridge and dated it to 208AD. However, further pieces of the jigsaw, being the upper part of the stone, came to light later, from which experts revised the probable date to between 140 and 144AD, which supports the time horizon for the Antonine Wall. They also concluded that the stone must have stood at least 1.37 metres above ground level. The inscription, in common with other Roman milestones, pays homage to the Roman Emperor, in this case Caesar Titus Hadrian Antoninus Augustus Pius, including all his titles. Unlike some stones presumed to be milestones but which may rather have been intended as 'Roman Honorific Pillars', it is believed that this stone did feature the measured distance from, or to, depending on one's direction of travel, the Trimontium fort, although that is now lost.

The stone is of old red sandstone, possibly from Arthur's Seat, and, complete as it can be, is now housed in the National Museum of Scotland in Edinburgh.

Another possible piece of the stonework was found, much more recently, in the south gable of a single-storey pantile-roofed building on the east side of the farm steading at West Mains of Ingliston. In a rectangular stone-framed recess at eye level is a grey sandstone slab (11½ inches by 13½ inches) with the figure of a bird standing with spread wings. Although weathered, the body and wings are still clear.

For Robert Sibbald (1641-1722), history and all things antiquarian were hobbies. He's revered, quite properly, today as the founding President of the Royal College of Physicians of Edinburgh and the first Professor of Medicine at Edinburgh University. He also founded the Royal Botanic Garden in Edinburgh. I wonder how often he's remembered for his observational skills of uncovering a Roman milestone?

The Ingliston House of Sibbald's day predates the baronial mansion of the present time. The property has been through several incarnations since the 17th century, and even more owners. Today it belongs to the Royal Highland & Agricultural Society, which runs the Royal Highland Show at Ingliston each June.

Sibbald's discovery of one Roman milestone begs the question, 'Are there any more yet to be found?' Perhaps. In 1726 the Rev William Stukely, who was noted for his scholarly work on both Stonehenge and Avebury, somewhat larger monoliths than most milestones it has to be said, reputedly found a Roman milestone along the Military Way associated with the Antonine Wall. The laudatory inscription was to Antonius Pius. Stukely was a co-founder of the Society of Roman Knights, an organisation whose purpose was the study of Roman Britain. He may have been meticulous about his researches, but he was less careful about his possessions. Stukely lost the milestone, which yet remains unfound. I've been unable to ascertain whether it was stolen or merely mislaid. On either count, it was an act of carelessness or ineptitude. Could it be serving as a doorstep or built into the wall of a house in Kirkintilloch? Who knows? I've another theory....

Dere Street was the 'east coast' route into Scotland, but the Romans also came north on a route not too distant in many respects from the A74(M). Rather than the service stations at Gretna and Annandale Water, they built a splendid fort at Blatobulgium, not a name that has survived the ravages of time. It's called Birren now, and is about 1½ miles from Ecclefechan. The road was a continuation of Watling Street, the cross-country route from Dover to Wroxeter, near Shrewsbury, but then running northward to the east of the Lake District, through Cumbria and up to the Central Belt of Scotland. At some point it joined with the roads running east-west across Scotland, south of the Antonine Wall.

Fast forward to the 19th century and we find ourselves in Braidwood, close to Carluke in Lanarkshire. The 1864 edition of the Ordnance Survey (OS) map shows a milestone, about a hundred yards east of Braidwood House. Although it is not there today, there is contemporary collaborative evidence. In the *New Statistical Account for Carluke (Vol VI, 1845)*, written by the Rev John Wylie in 1839, he includes reference to the proud stone:

'It is supposed to have stood at the side of a Roman Road, passing from Lanark, across the bridge of the Mouse beneath Cartland Crags, through the Lee Valley, across Fiddler's Burn at Chapel, and thence by Braidwood into the main street.'

Furthermore, Francis H. Groome, who edited the encyclopaedic *Ordnance Gazetteer of Scotland Volume 1* (of six volumes) in 1882, wrote that the stone was 'supposed to have been a milestone on Watling Street', but we have no way of verifying this with any certainty. It appears again on the 1898 OS map. Thereafter it was uprooted and destroyed, or relocated?

Was this the same Roman milestone that Rev Stukely found, then lost, in 1726? Perhaps it enjoyed an incarnation in Braidwood and is now a feature in a local garden?

The village of Newstead is reputedly the oldest continually inhabited settlement in Scotland and was certainly an important crossroads in Roman times. Fitting, therefore, that the Millennium should have been marked by a pink granite column, designed in the form of a Roman milestone and erected in the village. The inscription reads:

'TRIMONTIUM
CAPVT VIAE
ANNO DOMINI
2000'

'Capvt Viae' means the head of the road, indicating the place from which the distance on milestones was measured.

Originally mistaken as milestones, a series of highly engraved stones found along the length of the Antonine Wall have since been determined as 'distance slabs'. They were erected by the Legions to record their achievement in building sections of the Wall. There may be many as yet undiscovered, but 15 of these distance slabs are housed in the Hunterian Museum in Glasgow. They are inscribed with two measurements. The slabs from east of Castlehill fort

The Millennium 'Roman' milestone at Newstead. *Walter Baxter, Geograph; Creative Commons Licence*

date from the first phase of construction and carry the distance of Wall constructed shown in paces (1.4795 metres), while those from the Wall lying west of Castlehill bear the mark in feet (0.2959 metres).

One throwback to ancient days was the practice, widespread in Britain in the 17th and 18th centuries, of using Roman rather than Arabic numbering on milestones on many of the early turnpike roads. This ceased after the mid-18th century, but in Scotland there are a few remnants of the Roman numerical system still evident. On Islay, many, but not all, the milestones bear such inscriptions.

A Roman distance marker found near Auchendavy Roman Fort in East Dunbartonshire. The inscription reads 'IMP CAESARI T AELIO HADRIANO ANTONINO AVG PIO P VEXILLATIO LEG XX VAL VICF PER MIL P 111'. This translates as 'For Emperor Caesar Titus Aelius Hadrianus Antoninus Augustus Pius, Father of his Country, a detachment of the Twentieth Valiant and Victorious Legion built [this] over a distance of 3,000 paces'. *The Hunterian Museum in Glasgow*

A traditional milestone, 4 miles from Port Ellen on Islay. *Christine Minto and The Milestone Society*

2
Mensuration: 'gie him an inch an' he'll tak a mile'

These ancient conversions used on the distance slabs on the Antonine Wall are not what one might expect today. One might deduce, therefore, that either the Romans took mighty strides, or they were not taught by Mrs MacQueen at Balloch Primary School. Or perhaps both. However, there is another explanation…

It was the Romans who gave us the 'mile'. The Roman mile consisted of one thousand paces – 'mille passus' as they say in Latin – as measured by every other step; that is, the distance covered by the left foot hitting the ground 1,000 times. Romans marching through unchartered lands would frequently drive a carved stick into the ground after each 1,000 paces. Clearly, robust and energetic Romans had the uncanny habit of creating longer miles than their weaker contemporaries – so some form of standardisation was required. Marcus Vipsanius Agrippa, the second in command to Augustus and a talented engineer and architect, established the standard Roman foot in 29BC, ingeniously by using his own foot, with the calibration of a pace as five feet. An Imperial Roman mile was therefore equal to 5,000 feet. In more modern times, Agrippa's Imperial Roman mile was empirically estimated to have been about 1,617 yards (1,479 metres) in length.

There is one other thing for which we can thank the Romans – the milestone. All roads radiated from the Roman Forum, extending to all parts of the Empire. It is estimated that there were 50,000 Roman miles of stone-paved roads, with perhaps 8,000 of them being in what is now

Britain. At every mile was placed a shaped stone, on which was carved a Roman numeral, indicating the number of miles from the centre of Rome. The datum point was the Golden Milestone (Miliarium Aureum), a marble pillar 4 feet in diameter that had gilded bronze plaques recording the mileages to principal cities of the Empire. Situated in the Forum, it was erected by Augustus in 20BC. Roman Legions had very regulated marching regimes, covering between 10 and 20 miles per day depending on the terrain and whether or not they had oxen with them. Hence every Roman making the return journey to Rome knew the answer to the query, 'Are we nearly there yet?'

Although long gone nowadays, it was the Golden Milestone in Rome that also inspired the Zero Milestone in Washington DC, a monolith in President's Park, a short distance south of the White House, from which point it was intended all distances in the USA should be reckoned. The monument, 2 feet square and 4 feet high, has a bronze 16-point compass rose, with a small pyramid at its centre, the apex of which serves as the National Geodetic Survey benchmark. It was erected in 1923, but so far only roads in the vicinity of the capital city are recorded as measured from this point.

The availability of satnav to all of us now in our cars or on our mobile phones begs the question, 'From where is the measurement taken?' It's variable, often a landmark physical feature or building, but even TomTom isn't consistently specific in its definition. Don't just take it from me

– it's a disclaimer on the website.

We'll see later that the General Post Office in Edinburgh and the Royal Exchange in Glasgow have both served as 'datum points' for distances from the two great cities. In London, it's a plaque behind the statue of King Charles I in Trafalgar Square, the original site of the memorial to Eleanor, the first wife of Edward I. This location is still used today, although the current memorial to Queen Eleanor is a piece of Victoriana, the Eleanor Cross, dating from 1863, situated a short distance away, outside Charing Cross station.

Actually, the story of the Eleanor Cross has a Scottish link too. Edward I was in Scotland when his Queen was travelling northward to meet him in 1290. She got as far as Lincoln, caught a fever and died. Edward commissioned a series of Eleanor Crosses to be erected in major towns on her body's journey back to London for burial, of which three remain today.

Edward I, you'll recall from schooldays I'm sure, had two nicknames. The first, Longshanks, was due to his long legs; the second, the Hammer of the Scots, was earned from his preoccupation with trying to include Scotland within his kingdom. He even stole the Stone of Destiny from Scone Abbey, near Perth. This was the stone on which Scottish monarchs were crowned, an oblong block of red sandstone measuring 26 inches by 16.7 inches by 10.5 inches – so uncannily like a milestone. He placed it in Westminster Abbey in 1296 and it took the British Government until 1996 to return it to its rightful home in Scotland. It's in

Edinburgh Castle now, but in 2024 it's planned to house the Stone in a new museum in the City Halls in Perth, a mere stone's throw from Scone.

Edward I was an expert at falling out with people. Not only did he chafe the Scots, he also battled with the Welsh and the French. And, lest you forget, he also expelled all Jews from England. One of his 19 children succeeded him, as Edward II, to whom Robert the Bruce gave short shrift at the Battle of Bannockburn in 1314.

Some commentators, much more erudite than me, suggest that the term 'milestone' first came into common usage in 1746. That might well be so, although I've been unable to source the reference. 1746 saw the last battle on British soil, at Culloden Moor, with the Jacobites butchered by the Hanoverians led by the Duke of Cumberland – another sorry and bloody story in the nation's history. The site of the battlefield today remains the resting place of those clans loyal to Bonnie Prince Charlie, with the communal graves marked with small stone cairns. They are certainly not milestones, except perhaps figuratively to mark the end of the Jacobite uprisings, which had persisted for more than 30 years.

Interesting stuff, all these different measurements through history, especially for a surveyor like me. For those of you brought up entirely in the metric age, all this must sound a bit like double-Dutch, but it was the staple diet of primary school teaching in the 1960s.

Mrs MacQueen, my Primary Three teacher, would relate, ad nauseam it seemed to her pupils, that one chain measures 66 feet (or 22 yards), so from the formula that 10 chains equate to one furlong and that there eight furlongs to one mile, you can easily deduce that there are 80 chains in a mile, or 5,280 feet (1,760 yards) if you prefer.

Mrs MacQueen was, of course, referring to that trusted surveyor's measuring device, the chain. We've a Welshman to acknowledge for the 'standard' 66-foot-long version. He's Edmund Gunter. Born in 1581, he'd gone to Oxford University to be educated as a Church of England

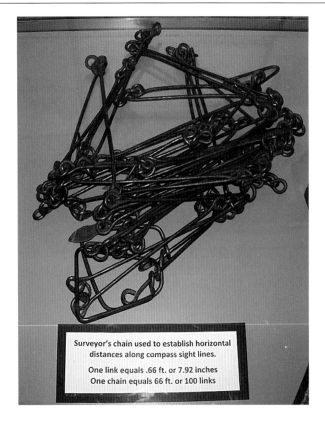

Gunter's chain. *Campus Martius Museum in Marietta, Ohio; Wikimedia Commons*

priest. By the time he'd been ordained he'd 'seen the light', so to speak, finding numbers altogether more inspiring than religion. This turned out to be a blessing for both surveyors and the church, as the one sermon he's alleged to have preached in his 12 years as a student of divinity was described as 'lamentable', while his applied mathematics brought us not only an early slide rule and the chain, but also trigonometry – the fundamental building block of land measurement.

In his excellent book *Measuring America*, Andro Linklater makes the legitimate claim that although the grid pattern of land delineation in the USA was the brainchild of the congressman, author of the Declaration of Independence and

latterly President, Thomas Jefferson (whose father, Peter Jefferson, had been a surveyor and cartographer), the dimensions of the squares, measured in chains, 'owed more to Edmund Gunter than to Thomas Jefferson'.

If you were troubled by decimalisation and metrification, then commiserate with the poor surveyors in the early 19th century. Until the adoption of the Imperial System of measurement in the UK in 1824, the Scots chain measured 74 feet, some 8 feet longer than the English version. A chain can be further subdivided into 100 links – yes, it really was a surveyor's chain in these days. Another surveyor's tool was the rod, comprising 25 links, or equivalent to 16ft 6in. Hence there were 40 rods in a furlong and 320 rods in a mile. To add a bit more potential confusion, a rod was also variably termed a pole or a perch, the last from the Ancient Roman unit of a 'pertica'. I thought it would come back to the Romans eventually.

But it doesn't end there. Although the Scots system of mensuration was introduced by King David I (1124-53), there are no surviving records until the 15th century, by which time the system was well established, albeit variable in different parts of the country. The Scots did use feet and inches akin to the English versions, but instead of the yard (or yaird) the Scots had the ell as a base unit of length, which was 37 inches long. The Barony ell, however, was 42 inches long, and was used as a basis of land measurement in the Four Towns area near Lochmaben. There are also records of a fraudulent inch, calculated as 1/42nd of an ell.

The Scots ell was standardised in 1661. If you want to see what an ell looked like, visit The Ell Shop in Dunkeld. Dating from 1775, the shop is named after the ell-stick attached to one corner of the front elevation. This instrument was once used to measure cloth and other commodities being sold in the adjacent market place.

Across in Fettercairn, the shaft of the 17th-century Kincardine mercat cross stands in the village square and is notched to show the

The Dunkeld ell – on the corner of the building. *Gordon Hatton*

mile of 1,760 yards. Although the Scots mile had become obsolete by the first quarter of the 19th century, it took three attempts to abolish it, and many of these other confusing units of measurement, legally. First by an Act of the Scottish Parliament in 1685, again by the Treaty of Union with England in 1707 and, finally, by the Uniform Weights & Measures Act of 1824, a piece of legislation aimed at stopping 'great confusion and frauds'.

In 2002 South Ayrshire Council decided to combine its historical links with Burns and the increasing focus on exercise and keeping fit by creating a 'Measured Scots Mile' along the seafront at Ayr. The route is between two car parks, with start and finish posts and quarter-mile markers, and is a flat surface, so those in wheelchairs need not feel neglected. For those who like purpose to their exercise, beyond fitness, the views across Ayr's sandy beach, with Arran, Kintyre and the Cumbraes over the Firth of Clyde, are a helpful distraction.

measurements of an ell. It would be an easy, but lazy, association to suggest that the town of Edzell, some 5 miles from Fettercairn, had its rather unusual name in some way derived from the 'ell'. However, the current Edzell used to be Slateford, and was renamed after an earlier and abandoned hamlet about a mile and a half to the west when the Earl of Panmure developed the present Edzell in 1818. In reality, the name Edzell is probably derived from the Gaelic 'Elgill'.

Just to convince you that measurement in Scotland was never straightforward – and my wish is not to confuse you further – 6 ells made up a fall (pronounced faw). A fall equated to a Scots rod, or raip (rope). Yes, back to the omnipresent rod again.

So there were inevitably 320 falls in a Scots mile. But perhaps this is all taking the measurement of distance to ridiculous lengths.

If one thing is certain, it is that quantifying distance has varied considerably over time. There really was the 'lang Scots mile', referred to by Robert Burns in 'Tam O' Shanter':

'…While we sit bousing at the nappy,
An' getting fou and unco happy,
We think na on the lang Scots miles…'

Although itself somewhat variable, a Scots mile was reckoned to be an average of 1,984 yards (or 5,952 feet), compared to the English

The half-mile post marks halfway on the 'Lang Scots Mile' at Ayr Esplanade. The motto on the post reads 'Walk the Mile, Lose the Inch'.
Lindsay M. Keith

Are miles here to stay? There has been rapid movement in recent years to move from the imperial to the metric system of measurement. I've been fortunate to have driven long distances touring Australia, New Zealand, South Africa and Canada and several mainland European countries, where kilometres are the standard unit of measurement and the signage gives places ahead in kilometres (km). Even India and the Philippines are metricated. Odd, therefore, that the UK and the USA have retained miles as the travel-speak. It is perhaps stranger that Myanmar, which has gone to the effort of changing its name from Burma, not only retains miles, but has milestones by the roadside giving distances not only in miles but also in furlongs.

Our milestone odyssey

There are a variety of ways to present the story of milestones on our roads. In *Bridgescapes* I introduced bridges in chronological order in a journey through Scottish history. With milestones, since they are representative of journeys, let's select a few in each part of the country on a geographical basis and note those where either the stone or the immediate vicinity has a story to tell. Fingerposts are another way of indicating distance, but also direction, and are properly included within the broad definition of milestones and waymarkers.

A map of Scottish counties might be a good start, although we know that local authorities have been subject to several iterations of reorganisation since the Act of 1973 was implemented in 1975.

Our journey takes us on a tour of the worthy milestones in each region of the country, with each region having its own section, interspersed between the chapters. Each geographic section uses a 'purple' text for ease of differentiation, with the information on each region presented on an 'old pre-1975 county' basis.

Scotland
Counties 1890 - 1974

A map of Scottish Counties, 1890-1974. *Wikimedia Commons*

3
The Appliance of Science: mapping our country

Mapmakers have played a key role over many centuries in recording not only the geographical but also the historical references that inform our understanding of the past. They are databases, providing a wealth of information from which we can interpret our heritage.

A map published in 1583 is one of the earliest records of the Scottish coastline. It was the work of Alexander Lyndsay, a Scottish coastal pilot, in association with King James V's partial circumnavigation of the country in 1540. So it took a long time to produce. By the 1580s Timothy Pont (c1560-c1627) had made a start on his epic map-making exercise that resulted in Scotland's first atlas.

Pont was a cartographer who, it is claimed, 'personally surveyed … and added such cursory observations on the monuments of antiquity … as were proper for the furnishing out of future description.' He died with the task almost complete. His maps were published in Joan Blaeu's *Atlas of Scotland* in 1654 and Pont's originals are held in the National Library of Scotland in Edinburgh.

It was a Scot, John Ogilby, born in Kirriemuir in 1600, who produced what was heralded as the first road atlas of England and Wales. Ogilby had a colourful, if only intermittently successful, career as an impresario and translator before he became the cosmographer and geographic printer to Charles II and published the *Britannia … a Geographical and Historical Description of the Principal Roads thereof* in 1675. The survey was plotted using an odometer and compass and was a landmark in accurate road descriptions. He produced 100 colour strip maps on plates, at a scale of 1 inch to the mile. The disappointing feature from the Scottish perspective is that having titled his great work *Britannia,* only one of the plates, number 62, extended into Scotland,

and that only as far as Jedburgh and Kelso, in describing the road between Carlisle and Berwick. You'd have expected more of a Scot.

When Robert Sibbald, whom we met earlier unearthing a Roman milestone, was appointed Geographer Royal in 1682, his first resolve was to have a proper map prepared of the whole country. He was as good as his word. The following year, John Adair (1660-1718) published a prospectus in Edinburgh for a 'Scottish Atlas', stating that the Privy Council of Scotland had engaged him, a 'mathematician and skilful mechanic', to survey the shires of Scotland. He did set out with good intent, mapping the coast of Scotland from 1686, but due to financial difficulties besetting his surveying activity and the loss of much of his work in a fire in 1811, only 12 manuscripts survive, at varying scales, covering the Lothians, Stirling, Fife, Kinross and southern Perthshire.

Detailed maps were being produced at this time by the great estates. Good land management dictated that knowing what was where and doing what became essential to driving agrarian improvements in land and buildings and ensuring that rents were properly assessed on a per acre basis and, of course, collected. Land ownership interests championed the production of accurate plans, and the skills of land surveying and cartography became an integral part of the land management profession. Funnily, that's also how my career as a chartered surveyor started back in the 1970s. Back in the mid-18th century, getting someone with

Pont's map of Alyth, c1595. *Christopher Dingwall*

a solid background in land measurement to take on the task of mapping Scotland could produce results.

William Roy (1726-90) was just that man. The son of an estate factor in Carluke in Lanarkshire, William had learned about making maps from his father. He'd moved to Edinburgh as the assistant quartermaster in the Board of Ordnance's office when his senior officer, David Watson, delegated him a task that was to propel Roy's career. The Board of Ordnance was the body responsible for military infrastructure and mapping. William Augustus, the Duke of Cumberland and third son of King George II (and, paradoxically, the cousin of Bonnie Prince Charlie) had led the Hanoverians to a bloody victory at Culloden in 1746 and the genocide that followed (he wasn't called 'Butcher Cumberland' lightly). Once the Jacobites had been quelled, he commissioned the Board to produce a comprehensive map of Scotland. It wasn't completely comprehensive, it has to be said, as it comprised the mainland areas but the islands were excluded. So 21-year-old William Roy set about his exercise of producing what turned out to be a uniquely important cartographic document – a snapshot of Scotland (well, less the islands) in the mid-18th century.

Bedevilled by the curse of a shortage of resources, for the Board of Ordnance had only four engineers as late as 1748, Roy started out on his Military Survey single-handedly to survey the land, starting around Fort Augustus. Thereafter he was assisted by six surveying teams, each with six men. Quite remarkably they had completed the survey of the Highlands by 1752, and southern Scotland, south of the Forth and Clyde, completed by 1755. Roy was also somewhat of a Roman enthusiast and while in the Central Belt undertook a detailed survey of the military antiquities along the Antonine Wall.

Roy's survey was not based on triangulation. Rather it relied on a set of measured traverses along important features, using a surveying compass for measuring angles, called a circumferentor. For measuring distances, he used chains – but bizarrely ones measuring either 45 feet or 50 feet in length, and not the standard 66 yards. I hope he remembered which one he was employing at any time, otherwise his measurements would be 'questionable' to say the least.

The teams surveyed linear features such as roads, rivers and lochs with instruments, but other landscape features such as towns and village, enclosures and woodland and relief were sketched in by eye or copied from existing maps. Survey work was undertaken in the summer months,

while the autumn and winter were spent back in the Board's drawing office in Edinburgh preparing the composite map, known as the 'original protraction'. A great achievement.

Not in any way wishing to downplay this undertaking, there were some shortcomings. The map did not provide latitude or longitude references, nor was it to a standard scale, and the orientation was towards magnetic North. The approximate scale was 1 inch to 1,000 yards (roughly 1:36,000) and showed detailed landscape, relief, hydrology and land cover using symbols to illustrate trees, tilled land, moorland and sands, with the effective use of colouring. Roy himself acknowledged that his 'map' was rather a 'magnificent military sketch, than a very accurate map of the country' in which 'no geometrical

Roy's map of Alyth, c1747. *Christopher Dingwall*

exactness is to be expected, the sole object in view being, to shew remarkable things, or such as constitute the great outlines of the country' (Roy, 1785).

By then promoted to the rank of major-general, William Roy was appointed practitioner engineer in 1755 in recognition of his endeavours producing the *Military Survey of Scotland*. Following Roy's death, the documents were kept in the British Museum, but are now in the British Library. To ensure their longevity, they were scanned in the 1980s.

There is a memorial cairn to Roy in Carluke. Inscribed upon it the visitor learns:

Here stood Miltonhead the birthplace of Major-General William Roy 1726-1790 from whose Military Map of Scotland made in 1747-1755 grew the Ordnance Survey of Great Britain.

In 1776, following extensive practical survey work, George Taylor and Andrew Skinner, originally surveyors from Aberdeen, published their *Survey of the roads of Scotland on an improved plan*. It's arguably Scotland's first 'road atlas', and shows some 3,000 miles of roads on a series of 61 plates with maps at a scale of 1 inch to the mile. Some of the early milestones are recorded. Funded by the Commissioners for the Forfeited Estates, the idea was to produce a volume designed to be folded into a portable accessory for the growing number of travellers visiting Scotland. The information is now all digitised. I wonder what Taylor and Skinner would have made of that technology? Although the maps sold for 12 shillings, the venture proved not to be the financial success they envisaged. By 1780 we find that both of them had emigrated to Ireland, then North America, producing maps on their travels. Their manuscript map of New York is now in the British Museum.

In describing milestones, reference is made on several occasions to the use of maps in finding them on the ground. We've Ordnance Survey's diligent work to acknowledge for this archive

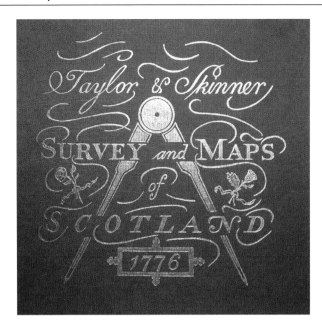

The Taylor & Skinner maps are housed in the National Library of Scotland in Edinburgh.

source. The OS 6-inch maps record the milestones. Up until the 1883 edition the principle was that distances were recorded on the map. That resulted in perhaps five or even six distances appearing, appended to the milestone symbol (MS) in minute writing. From 1883 the policy for milestones and posts that gave distances to more than two places was to record on the map only the distances to the two nearest places. In addition to the milestones on roads, the OS maps also recorded milestones on canals and railways. An amazing archive.

We must not leave Scottish maps without paying due respect to Edinburgh map-maker Bartholomew. Founded in 1826, the firm was renowned for its maps at a scale of half an inch to 1 mile, produced and marketed with cyclists, motorists and tourists very much in mind. The series was frequently updated and produced in different editions, being highly coloured to represent contours and features such as roads and railways. Between 1911 and 1928 the firm had

An example of one of Taylor & Skinner's maps (Perth to Fort George). *John S. Riddell*

an arrangement with the Cyclists' Touring Club whereby members were encouraged to submit any revisions they found while using the maps.

But the firm's output did not stop at Scotland, or indeed Great Britain. In 1920 John George Bartholomew produced the Second Generation of *The Times Survey Atlas of the World*, the preparatory work undertaken by the Edinburgh Geographical Institution. Bartholomew died that year, but what a legacy he left the world in his atlas: he named the continent Antarctica. Before he started using this name in 1890, it was generally unnamed as people thought it was very cold and lacked any meaningful resources. The Third Generation, produced by Bartholomew between 1955 and 1959, was a five-volume set of elephant folio atlases comprising 120 plates in eight colours. Quite a pedigree for an atlas whose 15th edition was published in 2018.

These half-inch Scottish maps, usually 29 or 30 covering Scotland (62 sheets for Great Britain), were the 'foundation' to my exploration of my native land as a teenager in the early 1970s. I had the full set of maps produced in 1971 – indeed, I still do.

The maps were available in either paper or cloth versions, both folded. From 1898 Bartholomew also produced a 'dissected and folded' version, with the map dissected into equal manageable parts, before being mounted on linen with a small uniform gap between the pieces. This allowed the map to be folded many times without loss of the details on the fold lines – a major advantage when a large map is used frequently in the field. In 1898 the paper version was priced at 1/- (one shilling, or 'one bob' for those of you of my vintage, 5p for younger readers) and 2/- for cloth. The dissected and folded version was priced at 2/6d (half a crown, or 12.5p). By 1920, presumably because of more modern printing technology, they were still excellent value at 1/6, 3/- and 4/- respectively. When I bought my set, or more likely received them as a joint Christmas and birthday present, in 1971, they were 6/- (30p), 8/- (40p) and 20/- (£1) respectively. The maps

metamorphosised into the national 1:100,000 scale maps and were generally out of print by the late 1990s, by which time Bartholomew had merged with Harper Collins Publishing. After 169 years in various locations in Edinburgh, the company relocated to Bishopbriggs, near Glasgow, in 1995. All of the Bartholomew maps are now held in the National Library of Scotland in Edinburgh.

Perhaps one of the greatest advances in capturing and interpreting mapped information was created through the combination of photography and aviation. The idea of taking a camera with you in an aircraft first found a practical and tactical use during the First World War when the British (and probably the Germans too) deployed hand-held cameras in sorties over the Western Front. The technique proved invaluable in stealing a march, metaphorically at least, over your enemy's position and supply chain. By 1918 some 2.5 million aerial photographs had been taken.

After the Armistice, Francis Wills, an observer in the Royal Naval Air Service, and Claude Grahame-White, an aviator who had made the first night flight in 1910, established the first commercial aerial photography company, based in Hendon. Arriving in Scotland in 1927, throughout the 1930s Aerofilms Ltd revolutionised the way we look at our country, capturing on film landmark events and key industrial features, such as the shipyards on the Clyde. The collection of more than 100,000 photographs of Scotland from the air is held in the archives of Historic Environment Scotland, a rich treasure trove of historic and geographic information.

Born out of military conflict, aerial photography had revolutionised intelligence gathering. So just as the British garnered information on key sites in Germany, so the Germans amassed photographically referenced knowledge of our shipyards and sprawling factories. Much of the aerial photography of the Clydebank shipyards and the 'secret' establishments such as those in

Benbecula was taken by the Luftwaffe.

After the Second World War the use of aerial photography in land-use planning came into its own. The Ordnance Survey Photo Mosaic of Scotland, taken between 1944 and 1950, provided a landscape view of the country, including detail on its urban topography and land use. It was invaluable, too, as a resource for planning the development of the hydro-electric power schemes in the Highlands and Dumfries & Galloway, the afforestation of vast swathes of upland, agricultural improvement schemes, the development of new road networks, and the expansion of our towns and cities and, indeed, the creation of new towns across the Central Belt. In 1945 the Air Photo Division was established in the OS, utilising surplus aircraft and personnel demobbed from the RAF. 'Operation Revue', as it was called, flew 500 sorties in Scotland, producing more than 280,000 photographs. The Spitfires and Mosquitos used in the exercise were specially adapted to take the photographic equipment, and two wing-mounted cameras allowed stereoscopic images. All these were then painstakingly pieced together to create 221 mosaics, each drafted at a scale of 6 inches to the mile (1:10,560), following OS National Grid sheet lines. Each sheet covers a ground area of 25 square kilometres. In total the coverage extends to 2,130 square miles (5,525 square kilometres), all now also housed in HES's archive.

The chap who was fortunate enough to immerse himself in all this data during in his career at Historic Environment Scotland, James Crawford, has made a series of excellent television programmes, *Scotland from the Sky*, for BBC Scotland, which captures, and quite rightly enthuses, about the very practical use of this legacy. A 'must see' for any budding historian, geographer, surveyor or planner – in fact for anyone with a fascination for Scotland.

Another wartime-related episode is worthy of recall, as it has a strong bearing on our milestone heritage. I refer on several occasions in later chapters to the practice of councils being required to remove milestones and waymarker signs after the outbreak of the Second World War, under the Defence of the Realm Act. The idea was to hinder the Germans if and when they invaded the UK. It all sounds a desperate waste of effort, almost like an episode of *Dad's Army*. The truth is – it really was a waste of time, resource and effort.

The Germans had this intelligence already. One inch and half-inch OS maps of Scotland, captured by the German Army in the 1930s, were reprinted by the Germans as part of their preparations for a possible invasion. In the case of the 1-inch maps, it was the Popular Edition from 1921-30. In each case the Germans did not revise the topographical detail, but they did metricate the maps (from 1:63, 360 to 1:50,000 and from 1:126,720 to 1:100,000 respectively) and gave them all updated titles, marginalia and legends. They were produced in 1941 as *karte von Schottland*. That's what you call being prepared. With this level of intelligence in your backpack, who needed milestones? The National Library of Scotland has 70 of the original 92 sheets at 1:50,000 and a complete set of the 34 sheets at 1:100,000 scale.

We rely heavily on Ordnance Survey grid references to identify the location of milestones and benchmarks shown on its world-class set of maps. We take these for granted, but to discover the origin of this system we need to travel back to the late 18th century again. In 1784 we encounter once more our military mapmaker William Roy, as he embarks on the Trigonometrical Survey of Great Britain, which was the precursor to the Ordnance Survey established in 1791, the year after Roy's death. The original markers at each end of the 5-mile-long baseline used in the measurement in the triangulation exercise by Roy in 1784, and upon which all OS maps were subsequently based, were two canons. One was at what is now aptly named Roy's Grove in Hampton, and the second, 5 miles distant, is at a point near Hounslow Heath on what is now the Northern

Perimeter Road at Heathrow Airport. The precision achieved was startling. The measurement was accurate to within 3 inches over the 5 miles.

Extensive, but detailed, survey work continued over 60 years, setting out the 'geodetic line' – the minimum distance line that can be drawn between any two points using the triangulation methodology and the trig points that are now familiar landmarks on the summits of our hills and mountains. And in the 1840s the Ordnance Survey conducted Scotland's First Primary Levelling Survey. For this we have to thank Colonel Sir Henry James RE (1803-77), described as 'perhaps the Ordnance Survey's most eccentric and egotistical Director General'. He wasn't to be promoted to DG until 1854, a role he occupied for the ensuing 21 years, but he had been in charge of the Edinburgh office from 1850, giving an emphatic nudge to the survey work in his *Abstracts of the Principal Lines of Spirit Levelling in Scotland*, although it would be 1861 before the survey was eventually published. The originals are in the National Library of Scotland.

The network of trig points, which provide sites for triangulation of the whole of the UK, date from the re-triangulation exercise of Great Britain, conducted between 1935 and 1962. With advances in GPS, they are functionally obsolete nowadays. Many have been adopted by members of the public, however, who undertake to maintain them, necessitating a bit of a hike with a tin of white masonry paint every few years. Although the formal adoption procedure has been abandoned, it remains a worthy cause, and a practice fortunately adopted by members of The Milestone Society for some excellent examples of milestones.

Using a series of benchmarks, the survey records height above Ordnance Datum. On mainland Britain benchmarks are the physical manifestation of ODN (Ordnance Datum Newlyn), forming the reference frame for height above mean sea level. On the ground, there is a network of approximately 190 Fundamental Benchmarks (FBMs), and from these the tens

of thousands of benchmarks were established. On the offshore islands there are local mean sea level datums. If you're really keen to see examples of Fundamental Benchmarks in Scotland, then I suggest that Lamberton Moor/Mordington (immediately north of the border with England at NT 9519 5853) or the FBM just off the A785 near Dunlop in Ayrshire (at NS 4161 4962) may satisfy your curiosity.

A benchmark is a horizontal mark that surveyors chisel in stone structures – in very many cases these are milestones – into which an angle-iron can be placed to form a 'bench' for a levelling rod. This mark ensures that a very high level of accuracy is attained on repositioning the levelling rod in future surveys. Fundamental! Any surveyor who replies 'near enough' when asked the question 'Are we nearly there yet?' should be debarred. Mind you, the young surveyors of today have laser and Global Positioning Systems (GPS) technology to ease their toil. Nowadays, the Ordnance Survey's National Grid is defined by the European Terrestrial Reference System 1989 (ETRS89) coordinates of the OS National GPS Network, together with the definitive OSTN15 transformation. The buzz words are now 'geospatial data', which is any data with a locational component. There's a UK Geospatial Commission, which uses Geographical Information Systems (GIS) to analyse the data by converting it from an incomprehensible bank of numbers into colourful layers draped over maps, making it easier for the non-expert to interpret. I've witnessed some of the capability of this use of technology when attending FIG (International Federation of Surveyors) Conferences around the globe in recent years. It's impressive stuff and I can wax lyrical about this transformation of cartography. However, for a lad who spent countless hours trying to master a slide rule and logarithm tables, and grimaced whenever the maths teacher mentioned sine, cosine and tangents, the 'how you do it' remains quite beyond my ken.

In case you're thinking 'there must be a

Benchmark Society for folk with like-minded interests in all things related to Ordnance Datums', you'd be right. Look no further than The Charles Close Society for the study of Ordnance Survey maps, established in the name of Colonel Sir Charles Close, who held the office of Director General of the Ordnance Survey between 1911 and 1922.

In my early training to be a chartered surveyor, I was introduced to the theodolite, both theoretically at university and in practice, marking out sites for development or producing reduced-level plans of field drainage systems. The theodolite, complete with tripod stand and levelling staff, became part of the young surveyor's 'toolkit' although, to be fair, the instrument was normally a somewhat less sophisticated Dumpy Level. The difference between this simple level and a theodolite was that the latter also measured angles in the vertical plane.

Until I started the research for this book I'd never looked up 'theodolite' in an encyclopaedia, but I'm glad I did. Evidently, the first use of the word is in a surveying textbook, *A Geometric Practice named Pantometria*, by Leonard Digges. He wrote this in 1571, so it must have been out of print by the time I went to university in 1973. In all my 40-plus years as a qualified chartered surveyor, 'Pantometria' is a new word to me, although I can recall (but won't on this occasion, for fear of being embarrassed) several episodes when using a theodolite out on a windswept hillside that were more akin to a 'Panto-mime'.

The theodolite took on its modern, accurate role as an instrument of measurement in 1787, with the introduction of Jesse Ramsden's 'great theodolite'. Ramsden's instruments were used in the Principal Triangulation of Great Britain. Theodolites are basically optical instruments, and it is little surprise that the original mathematical and scientific instrument makers were opticians. Several of the leading figures in this field in the late 18th and 19th century were Scots. Not much of a surprise, really, but it may be helpful

to cite a few of the most prominent. John Miller (1746-1815) was already an established instrument-maker in Edinburgh, having been trained in London by George Adams, a protégé of Jesse Ramsden. What a grounding to have in theodolites! In 1789 John took on his 15-year-old nephew, Alexander Adie (1774-1858), and by 1803 they were in partnership, operating from premises in South Bridge and Nicholson Street. This early period coincided with an upsurge in surveying activities in Scotland, and theodolites, levels and measuring chains featured strongly in the firm's advertising. In 1818 Adie invented and patented the sympiesometer (a marine barometer used widely on ships for the next century), and the firm supplied lenses to Charles Darwin and Sir David Brewster. As if that did not keep them fully occupied, Adie and his son were both opticians by Royal Appointment, serving both King William IV and Queen Victoria.

Alexander Adie's grandson, Alexander James Adie, would become Manager of the Edinburgh & Glasgow Railway in 1863, another feat of

engineering we'll encounter later in our journey.

Over in Glasgow, another optical instrument-maker, Islay-born James White (1824-84), struck up a close working partnership with Sir William Thomson (Lord Kelvin), the founder of the Atlantic Telegraph Company and pioneer engineer on the first transatlantic cable. Operating from Cambridge Street in Glasgow, the partnership started making instruments for Thomson, who was Professor of Natural Philosophy at Glasgow University, but also built and supplied brass transit theodolites of the highest quality. A second Glasgow-based instrument-maker, Alexander Ferrie-Mabon (1856-1934), continued the tradition of painstaking accuracy in the products his firm produced at its premises in Renfrew Street and West Campbell Street. In addition to making scientific instruments, including theodolites, Mabon specialised in producing scale engineering models, one of which is displayed in the Vienna Technical Museum.

This book is chiefly about linear measurements, but I couldn't leave the practice of surveying without referring to another world first in measurements, with its genesis in Scotland – attempting to determine the mean density of the Earth. In the early 1770s the Astronomer Royal, one Nevil Maskelyne (1732-1811), commissioned the surveyor Charles Hutton to find a mountain on which detailed measurements could be made to feed into a calculation of the density of this planet. Maskelyne proclaimed that the experiment would 'do honour to the nation where it was made'. For Englishman Maskelyne this somewhat backfired. Both Whernside in Yorkshire and the Bencathra-Skiddaw massif in Cumbria were considered, but discounted, in favour of the almost conically shaped and relatively isolated mountain named Schiehallion, in central Perthshire. It's a significant landmark between Loch Tay and Loch

Antiques Atlas brochure: a George III 5-inch altazimuth double telescope theodolite by Miller and Adie, Edinburgh.

Rannoch, and the summit is 3,553 feet above sea level, so certainly a 'Munro'. Coincidentally, Schiehallion is also located at almost the latitudinal and longitudinal centre of Scotland, not that this had any bearing on the experiment. Lest you're thinking you've heard the name Nevil Maskelyne elsewhere, you'd be correct. There was a magician of the same name, who also invented the penny-coin-operated pay toilet, but he was a distant relation only. Our Maskelyne was not into illusion or paying a penny to spend a penny; he traded in theory and practice.

The experiment involved measuring the miniscule deflections of a pendulum due to the gravitational attraction of a nearby mountain – to wit, Schiehallion – with the volume of the landmass effectively subdivided into a series of individual vertical prisms, then painstakingly computing the volume of each prism and summing to provide a total. From this assessment, Maskelyne believed he could gross up the sum to calculate the density of the Earth. Charles Hutton conducted the survey, with a multitude of measurements providing reduced levels at points all over the mountain's topography. In doing so, he gave us another surveying measurement, the contour line, linking points of equal height above the Datum Point, and illustrated cartographically as a series of equally spaced contours.

I'm unaware of whether Charles Hutton did many of the calculations himself. Presumably he had a team of enthusiastic comptometers back in the office going through what was a detailed but somewhat laborious and repetitive task of number-crunching the data. The survey commenced in 1774 and, not surprisingly, took two years to complete and conclude the calculations. Surely during this protracted process at least one of the comptometers must have opined 'Are we nearly there yet?'

So what was Maskelyne's conclusion? His calculation gave a density of the Earth as 4,500kg·m^{-3} (kilogrammes per cubic metre). In case you don't have the modern thinking on this to

hand, and why should you, the highly sophisticated methodologies and computer programmes currently available estimate the Earth's density to be approximately 5,515kg·m^{-3}, so Maskelyne's mathematical and arithmetic skills in 1776 were within 20% accuracy. Quite an achievement.

Not that the Scottish part of the story stops there. Henry Cavendish repeated the Schiehallion experiment in 1798, this time calculating the density to be 5,448 (+/- 33) kg·m^{-3} – that's within 1.2% accuracy of the 2020 calculation.

In 1811 John Playfair resurveyed Schiehallion, with a better understanding of the mountain's geology and rock strata. He produced a figure of 4,560 to 4,870kg·m^{-3}.

Not to be outdone, Henry James (of the Ordnance Survey) decided to repeat the methodology used in the experiment, but on a different landform. Again, he chose a Scottish candidate, the volcanic plug that is Arthur's Seat in Edinburgh. The year was 1856. He'd probably moved from Edinburgh by that time, but obviously there was a substantial Ordnance Survey office in the city, so the travel and subsistence costs of the surveyors would be low. James's calculations arrived at a figure of 5,300kg·m^{-3}, so, again, pretty accurate.

The advent of Global Navigation Satellite Systems (GNSS) technology brings us into a wholly new territory, so to speak, on land mensuration, in all three dimensions. Trilateration is, of course, a cousin of triangulation, but involves the observation of distances rather than angles to determine position. It's the 21st-century version of ascertaining 'Are we nearly there yet?'

One application, close to home for us Scots, is the measurement of the height of our highest mountain, Ben Nevis. It is the highest mountain in the British Isles, and the last time I stood on its summit, albeit several decades ago, I firmly believed I was at 4,413 feet above sea level (that's 1,344 metres in metric-speak).

The height had then most recently been calculated by a team of 20 surveyors from Ordnance Survey in 1949 as 1,344 metres. They

lugged 200lb of equipment to the summit of the mountain and her surrounding peaks, pitched camp, and carried out multiple surveys over 20 days. At nightfall, when the marker lights were visible, they secured the angles between the peaks and calculated the height at 1,344 metres.

In 2016 a team of three Ordnance Survey surveyors, using GPS technology, calculated the height at a mere few centimetres more than the 1949 survey, but with 'rounding up' the official height became 1,345 metres.

Commenting on the 1949 survey, Angus Hemmings, one of the three surveyors from the 2016 team, said:

'What it did do though, was give me a greater sense of respect for the 1949 surveyors. It took the surveyors 20 nights, because they only had three clear nights in that period to get it right. To do the best possible job it had to be run with military precision, everything they did had to be timed to perfection. Their effort and accuracy is remarkable.'

But what is a mountain? It would appear a simple enough question to answer, but, just as many specialist topics have developed their own 'speak', so the terminology for categorising 'mountains' has its own nomenclature. In the British Isles it's generally accepted that in order to be classified as a mountain the feature must be at least 2,000 feet (610 metres) above mean sea level. Height, however, is not the only criteria. With the exception of Munros (all Scottish summits over 3,000 feet (914.4 metres)), which are deemed 'mountains' in their own right, all mountains require to have a topographical prominence above 30 metres (98.43 feet). Prominence means relative height, or top, or re-ascent between neighbouring peaks. This complies with the International Climbing & Mountaineering Federation (UIAA) definition of an 'independent peak'. While the classification in the British Isles uses a quantitative metric of topographical isolation (for example, the distance to the next point of equal height), the concept is embedded in the qualitative definition of a Scottish Munro, and the requirement of 'sufficient separation' determined by the Scottish Mountaineering Club. There are 282 Munros plus 227 Munro Tops, being subsidiary summits.

Further, in Scotland only:

- A 'Real Munro' has a prominence of more than 150m (490ft) – there are 202 of them.

- A 'Metric Munro' has a height in excess of 1,000m (3,300ft) and a prominence of either more than 200m (660ft) – there are 88 of them – or a prominence of more than 100m (330ft) – there are 130 of them.

- Then there are Murdos. These are Munros with a prominence of more than 30 metres – there are 442 of them.

- Then there are Corbetts. These are Scottish mountains between 2,500 and 3,000 feet with a prominence of at least 500ft (152.4m) – there are 222 of them. In addition, there are 454 Corbett Tops, with a prominence of between 100 and 500ft (30.48 and 152.4m).

- Then there are Grahams. These are Scottish mountains between 2,000 and 2,499 feet with a drop of at least 490ft (150m) all round – there are 219 of them. In addition, there are 776 Graham Tops with a prominence between 30 and 150 metres.

- Then there are Donalds. These are hills in the Scottish Lowlands that are more than 2,000 feet and have a prominence of 30 metres. The criteria were simplified in 1995, resulting in 118 New Donalds, of which 89 are Donald Hills and the remaining 29 are Donald Tops.

Straightforward? It doesn't end there. There are also a range of summit definitions that are universal, as far as the British Isles is concerned.

- We've 'P600 Majors', which have a topographical prominence of at least 600m (1,969ft) regardless of absolute height or other features. There are 82 'Majors' in Scotland, of the British Isles total of 129. Moreover, Ben Nevis has the greatest topographical prominence. Of the 282 Munros, 54 are also Majors.

- Then we have Marilyns. These have a prominence of more than 150m (490ft). Good examples are Ben Lui, near Tyndrum, and Stac an Armin. Most of us will have heard of Ben Lui, but I'd hazard that few will be familiar with Stac an Armin. It's remote, by any count, being a sea stack in the St Kilda archipelago. At 196m (643ft), it's the highest sea stack in the British Isles. That's high. By comparison, the very impressive Old Man of Hoy in the Orkney archipelago is 137m (449ft), which is not of sufficient stature to be classified as a Marilyn. There are 2,011 Marilyns in the British Isles, of which 1,219 are in Scotland.

Among the other weird and wonderful classifications of mountains and hills in the British Isles, we also encounter HuMPs, Simms and TuMPs, but let's leave it there, shall we? There will be other books to tell you about some of the equally odd English names, such as Furths, Hewitts, Nuttalls, Wainwrights, Birketts, Carns, Binnows, Deweys and Hardys.

Writing a book about linear measurements suddenly seems a lot less complicated…

Although Scotland is a relatively small country, it has a mainland coastline extending to 7,330 miles. This increases to 11,660 miles (at High Water Mark) when you include more than 920 islands, of which 118 are inhabited. No wonder Scotland has a long and proud association with

maritime matters, and, in its heyday, enjoyed a world-renowned tradition of building very substantial ships. Actually, that's somewhat of an understatement. In the 19th and 20th centuries about 30,000 ships were built on the River Clyde, including the liner QE2 in 1968. In the early 1900s a fifth of all the ships in the world had been built on the Clyde. It's appropriate, therefore, in our quest for milestones to include nautical miles and the measurements associated with them.

Firstly, a nautical mile was historically defined as 1 minute (a 60th of a degree) of latitude along any line of longitude. It is now refined into the international system of units (SI) as 1,852 metres, which is equivalent to 6,076 feet, or 1.1508 statute miles.

All new or redesigned ships require to undergo sea trials before they are released to their owners. One of the critical tests is the maximum speed test carried out over a measured mile. Nowadays GPS allows this to be done effectively, but until the advent of this technology it was a much more practical test, necessitating highly defined procedures, over a 'Measured Mile'. Scotland has had several such miles, all of which are worthy of note.

The first Measured Mile in Scotland was established on the Clyde in 1841 as the Gare Loch Measured Mile (GLMM). It was marked by the Mill Burn, near Mamore at the northern end, and by the Meikle Burn, near Burremman, towards the south, and was created for the purpose of testing Thomas Assheton Smith's *Fire King* paddle steamer. Twenty years later Robert Napier, the Scottish engineer, had the Mile recreated by the Institution of Shipbuilders & Engineers for trials of the transatlantic steamer *Scotia*, with impressive results. She went on to win the Blue Riband in 1863, a prize awarded to the passenger liner that crosses the Atlantic westbound with the highest recorded speed while in regular service. The GLMM was later used as two half-miles, with one half subdivided into quarter-miles. In 1952 the GLMM was re-established by the British Ship

Research Association for trials of the jet-propelled *Lucy Ashton*, with the posts repositioned to improve the accuracy of the Mile, but its use was discontinued after 1980.

The Measured Mile at Skelmorlie was initially somewhat longer, at rather more than 13 miles. Originally sea trials were conducted with the vessel steaming at full power over a '13.6666 nautical mile' course between the lighthouses at Cloch and Cumbrae Head. The exercise was known as 'Running the Lights'. Tables produced at the time show that at 14 knots the run would take 58 minutes 34 seconds; at 20 knots the time was reduced to 41 minutes. Initially there was a return run, by which time the tide, wind and weather could all have changed, so the test was reduced in length. The points for measurement became the steamer pier at Skelmorlie and the Skelmorlie Hydropathic Hotel, south of Skelmorlie Castle. This measured 6,080 imperial feet, which came to be regarded as the most important Measured Mile in Britain – that was the original 'nautical mile'. The Skelmorlie Measured Mile was notified in the 'Notice to Mariners No 36' on 4 July 1866, and installed by the 'Father of Shipbuilding on the Clyde', Robert Napier.

The unlit beacons marking the mile were described as 'a single pole, 45-feet high, with arms 10-feet long forming a broad ('V' and inverted 'V') angle 15-feet from the base, the whole being painted white'. Once the 'V' and inverted 'V' were aligned, they formed an 'X', at which moment the tester's stopwatches would be started or stopped. From the precise time recorded for the run, and the known distance between the beacons, the results were read off from standardised time and distance tables published in almanacs. If I'd known about ready-reckoners when I was child on those car journeys from Inverness to Dundee, how much easier life would have become.

The Skelmorlie markers used to be recorded on OS maps, but no longer. The system operated for 120 years, but was revived in July 2016 for the speed trials of *Catriona*, then the newest ferry to be made for the CalMac fleet.

Over on Arran, a Measured Mile was established by the Admiralty in 1916, at the height of the First World War. It comprised of two consecutive miles, marked by three sets of pylons or beacons on the north-east of the island, between South Sannox and Corloch. The northern mile measures 1.8544 kilometres, while the southern is 1.8514 kilometres. At the end of the Second World War Polish soldiers were tasked with clearing the site, and they cut down the posts, a fact discovered only when Britain's last battleship, the 51,000-ton HMS *Vanguard*, began her sea trials. The posts were very quickly re-erected. When the liner *QE2* returned to the Clyde in 2017, marking the 40th anniversary of her launch, one of the procedures she observed was a full-power run over the Arran Mile, recreating part of her original sea trials in 1968.

Established by the Admiralty in 1940, the Loch Long Measured Mile (LLMM), near Coulport, allowed the Clyde shipyards to conduct speed trials, especially of the motor torpedo boats, during the Second World War. It was re-established by Yarrow Shipbuilders in 1959 as two half-miles for the speed trials of the company's pusher tug *Gonzola* and her train of eight barges. The LLMM no longer exists. Similarly, the Ardmaleish Measured Half Mile on the east Kyle of Bute, again dating from 1940, has been removed.

The Parklea Measured Mile, east of Port Glasgow, was erected by the Denny Hovercraft Company in 1963 for testing its D1 hovercraft. The posts, 18 feet in height, were painted bright yellow but are no longer visible.

All of these Measured Miles are 'doon the

RMS *Mauritania* passes St Abb's Head on her sea trials. *Tyne & Wear Museum, Wikimedia Commons Licence*

watter', which one might expect from the proximity of the shipbuilding yards. However, there is a well-known Measured Mile on the east coast too. A set of four Admiralty Distance Poles situated above the spectacular cliffs near St Abb's Head are used to good effect by the shipbuilders on the English River Tyne.

The RMS *Mauritania* was the largest ship in the world when it was launched in 1906. Built in Northumberland for the Cunard Line, she undertook her speed trials on the St Abb's Head Measured Mile in 1907.

In December that year, on her maiden voyage, she captured the eastbound Blue Riband, followed by the westbound two years later, holding both speed records for the next 20 years. She probably passed the Admiralty Distance Markers and the lighthouse at St Abb's Head for the last time in 1935, on her voyage to be scrapped in Rosyth Dockyard.

Another Measured Mile is very worthy of mention – on Loch Ness. On 29 September 1952 John Cobb (born 1899) lost his life on Loch Ness while piloting a jet-powered speedboat in an attempt to break the World Water Speed Record. He was no rookie. Already the three-times holder of the World Land Speed Record (1938, '39 and

'47), he had earned the moniker 'The Fastest Man Alive'. His 1947 record, achieved in Utah in the USA, was 394.19mph, not surpassed until 1963.

His speedboat, *Crusader,* was travelling in excess of 200mph when it hit an unexpected wake on the water and disintegrated. A memorial, erected by the locals of Glenurquhart, stands by the roadside. Cobb's body was recovered on the day of the accident, but the wreckage of *Crusader* was only raised from the bed of Loch Ness, at a depth of more than 650 feet, in 2019.

Others have had more success in achieving records on Loch Ness, however. In 1966 Brenda Sherratt became the first person to swim the length of the loch. It took her 31 hours and 27 minutes. Definitely merits a 'shivery bite', that one. In 1974 David Scott Munro from the Ross-shire Caberfeidh Water Ski Club became the first person to water-ski the length of Loch Ness. In fact, he did it twice, from Lochend to Fort Augustus and back; he covered the 48 miles in 1 hour and 17 minutes, an average speed of 37mph.

Please don't underestimate Loch Ness. At 23 miles in length, it's the second largest Scottish loch, but reaches 755 feet in depth and contains more water than all the lakes in England and Wales combined.

Since we're into measurements in this book, I should refer to a depth of 755 feet of water as 126 fathoms. A fathom was originally defined, somewhat empirically, as 'the span of a man's outstretched arms'. Not the most precise or consistent standard for measuring anything on which you then rely to keep your boat afloat. In practice, a fathom has varied slightly in size, depending on whether it was defined as one-thousandth of a nautical mile (6.08 feet) or as a multiple of an imperial yard (i.e. 3 feet times 2). In days gone by the way to measure the depth of water was to drop a weighted line, duly calibrated, over the side of the boat and measure off the depth when the weight hit to seabed. Indeed, that is how Samuel L. Clemens derived his nom de plume 'Mark Twain' (two fathoms), from the measuring of the depth of the Mississippi River. It's also the way depths shown on most of the Admiralty charts were derived. With the advent of sonic devices, the process has now become a lot more sophisticated. There's an instrument for measuring depths called a fathometer, and it uses sound as the key, by means of measuring the echo sound transmitted back to the bridge on the ship from the seabed. There are some impressive depths around Scotland's shores. For example, where the Highland Boundary Fault traverses the Firth of Clyde between Arran and Bute, a distance of only 5 miles, the depth of water is 1,050 feet, or rather 175 fathoms.

Back on dry land and on the road again…

The first motorway in Scotland was in Fife. It was the approach road to the Forth Road Bridge, opened in 1964. It was followed in November 1965 by the Harthill Bypass, now between Junctions 4 and 5 on the M8. There are now 403 miles of motorway, from Gretna Green to Perth, and as with so many things in life I've pleasure in confirming to you that as far as distance measurement on motorways is concerned, there are

The start of John Cobb's measured mile.
Des Colhoun

distinct differences and nuances between Scotland and England.

Let's take the M74/A74(M) heading northwards from the border, where it changes nomenclature from the M6, as an example. In theory, all motorways in the UK have marker posts at 100-metre intervals, numbered in kilometres and tenths. Prior to the 1970s these markers were at 110-yard spacings, numbered in miles and sixteenths (half a furlong). As 110 yards equals 100.584 metres, there was little practical difference in their locations. Since 2007, on most English motorways these marker posts are supplemented by Driver Location Signs at 500-metre intervals. These are not used in Scotland.

The original post markers are thought, but not evidenced, to have increased numerically as the motorist drove northwards. This is as per the original junction numbering. The zero point was Draffan. The present system, however, dating from 1986/87 when Phase 2 was opened, increases travelling southwards, along the M74 and thereafter on the northern section of the A74(M), as far as Johnstonebridge at Junction 16. The zero point on the northern extension was observed, in 2011, to be on the Port Eglinton Viaduct in Glasgow, midway between the crossings of Pollockshaws Road and Eglinton Street, although quite why is a mystery, at least to the author. In the gap between this point and where the road meets the M8, the posts are numbered in a unique local system beginning with the letter 'x'. I wonder what Stanley Baxter would have made of that, with his 'Parliamo Glasgow' sketches?

South of Johnstonebridge the numbering is as per the London-based system used on the M1 and M6, with the Kirkpatrick Fleming to Gretna section (Junctions 21 to 22) being a late conversion.

The marker posts on motorways provided a very good reference point for reporting an accident or other emergency. With the arrival of mobile phones, you'd have thought that the need for roadside emergency telephones would diminish, but they are still a necessary adjunct to road safety. The battery could go flat, or you could have an archaic mobile phone like mine, which is as temperamental as its owner and displays a marked reluctance to receive or transmit any signal when most relied upon.

There are two systems of emergency telephone operating on the M74/A74(M). The dividing line is at Nether Howcleuch, between Junctions 14 and 15. To the south, presumably connecting to the police in Dumfries, they are marked 1, 2, etc, sequentially southwards, each one preceded by 'E' or 'W' to indicate the eastern (southbound) or western carriageway. North of Nether Howcleuch the phones connect to the police in Glasgow, but follow the English numbering system, although, again, with a twist. Each phone has a four-digit number followed by an 'A' or 'B' for the carriageway, and the last three digits of the number represent the distance in units of 0.1km. Normally this would mean a single relationship between the number on a phone and that on the nearest marker post. That would be too logical. On the M74 there is a systematic difference of about 9km, which would imply that the distance for the phones were measured from a point near Renfrew on the M8.

I mentioned that Charles Hutton brought us the contour, from his preparatory work on Schiehallion. In the last decade of the 19th century, a series of 'Contour Road Books' were published by Gall & Inglis, the first of this genre being the Scottish book, published in 1896. Each book comprised a series of elevation plans of the roads, with measurements and descriptive letterpress – with a diagram of the road in profile, a description of it, a list of gradients, and details of the exact points from where the milestones had been measured. Harry R. G. Inglis cycled all the Scottish routes himself, so assuring a high standard of accuracy.

Indeed, in the 1897 edition comments were included on the accuracy of the milestones, thus:

118 Glasgow to Irvine Milestones measured from the commencement of the Pollockshaws road – correct.
120 Glasgow to Strathavon Milestones measured from the Glasgow Cross – fairly accurate.

Sometimes things got rather complicated:

99 Ayr to Carstairs Milestones measured from Ayr Town Hall to Cumnock, then from Cumnock Church to Wellwood. Here those from Ayr via Mauchline continue to the County Boundary, when the numbers and positions of those from Cumnock are resumed. After Douglas they are irregular.
9 Edinburgh to Moffat Milestones. To Leadburn as previous route, thence deficient until Romanno Bridge, after which they are correct. This set, however, is measured from Grassmarket, Edinburgh, via Howgate. The 20th and onwards is 207/8 from G.P.O.'

And, occasionally, even Mr Inglis is not sure:

62 Dumfries to Carlisle Milestones measured from Greyfriars Church Dumfries, to Collin; thereafter to the Border (where the milestones measured from Glasgow are met) they are seemingly measured from Carlisle, Market Place.

We're used nowadays to the road and pavement surfaces having embedded within them studs or other markings – 'cat's eyes', coloured reflective lights, raised concrete squares to assist the blind – but you'll also come across them in the centre of some towns. Arbroath was an example, where the line of studs placed in the road outside the Town House marked the point from which mileage distances were calculated. Most will now have become buried under resurfacing schemes, but look out for them.

So, how many milestones are there in Scotland? Not the sort of question I'd like to be asked to win the star prize on *Who wants to be a Millionaire?* Canmore, Historic Environment Scotland's system for recording structures of architectural and historical importance, lists 1,177 sites with milestones. Of cast-iron mileposts alone, Canmore records 162, which includes those on railways, and 37 mileplates, but of the 199 such artefacts, 78 are 'lost'. Of 40 cast-iron mileposts that are 'Listed' by HES, three were reported as 'missing' in 2019. Clearly there must have been many thousands of mile distance markers, and this can be confirmed by reference to old editions of Ordnance Survey maps, where the symbols 'MS' (for milestone) and 'MP' (for milepost) are a regular feature. Many,

indeed most, of these have been the victim of road widening schemes or highway developments, were lost during the last war or have become redundant or neglected for other reasons, but years of research and cycling round Scotland from Portpatrick to Shetland, Stornoway to Berwickshire, have resulted in a database with over 2,300 recorded as still in situ. For this I acknowledge here, and elsewhere in the book, the outstanding endeavours of Frank and Christine Minto and fellow members of The Milestone Society. The reader will be much relieved to learn that my book is not an

encyclopaedic account of every last milestone. Sorting the wheat from the chaff to present some of the very best and most interesting examples, which intend to celebrate Scotland's rich heritage and heighten our enjoyment of our Scottish travels, has been an enlightening and educational exercise in its own right.

Our milestone heritage: The Borders

Before we even reach Scotland, there's a treat in store – the last distance marker in England. Just 10 metres south of the border, in a layby on the A1, lies a plaque that is too good to miss. Laid in late 2019, it's a disc of a diameter of approximately 1.2 metres with not only the compass points marked, but also the distance to northern European places, most strikingly Svalbard in the Arctic Ocean in northern Norway. Until 1925 Svalbard was known as Spitzbergen, and it's 2,584 kilometres from where you're standing in Northumbria. For the traveller arriving in Scotland, the plaque advises that it's another 73 kilometres to Edinburgh and 319 kilometres to John o' Groats. These distances are, of course, as the crow flies, and not by road.

The early attempts to modernise the administration of the road network in Berwickshire were spectacularly unsuccessful. The Berwick Roads Act of 1753 was ineffective in introducing any innovation, and the statute labour system persisted. In 1772 there was a second attempt. The Berwick Turnpike Act made all the right noises, but no turnpikes were created. It wasn't until the Berwick Roads Act of 1787 that the first of the county's turnpikes was established – the Eastern District Trust. This was part of the

The Borders.
Wikimedia Commons

Whither Svalbard? *John S. Riddell*

The Scottish/English border at Carter Bar (A68).
Ken Diamond collection, The Milestone Society

Great Post Road from Edinburgh, 18½ miles of which lay within Berwickshire. Tolls were erected at Dunglass, Grantshouse, Ayton and Lamberton. The route was not too distant from the current A1. Subsequent Acts in 1805, 1811 and 1832 extended

the term of the Eastern District Trust as required and provided for major road improvements and realignments. The Trust also oversaw the building of some major bridges along this steeply indented coastal fringe, including Pease Bridge, which was the highest bridge in the world when it was opened in the late 1780s.

By the 1830s there were at least eight turnpike trusts operating in Berwickshire, covering 166¾ miles of road. These were the Eastern District Trust, the Greenlaw Trust (aka the Western District Trust), the Middle Trust, the Deanburn District Trust, the Cornhill District Trust, the Dunse & Westruther Trust, the Whiteburn & Kelso Trust, and the Coldstream Bridge Trust. And then there were the statute labour roads – according to the Report of 1859, there were 457 miles of such roads in Berwickshire at that time.

The A1 route from Edinburgh to Berwick is traditionally referred to as the Great Post Road. However, following an inspection of the routes from Newcastle to Edinburgh by Thomas Telford, his recommendation in favour of the A697/A68 route meant that from 1830 until 1838 the London to Edinburgh mail coach ran by the Greenlaw Mail Road. As a consequence, the Eastern District Trust, which operated the Great Post Road, lost £328 per annum in mail tolls commutation, without compensation. The Mail Road became the principal route for all through traffic, resulting in revenues that were double those of the Great Post Road. However, the times they were a-changing. In 1846 the North British Railway Company had opened its Edinburgh to Berwick line. Under the North British Railway Act of 1844, the railway company was required to acquire half of the Eastern District Trust's bond debt, as postponed creditor with no expectation of repayment. No compensation was paid to the Greenlaw District Trust, which was the obvious greater loser. No investment is guaranteed.

But what remains of the milestone legacy…?

Not all milestones are obvious. It often needs care to spot one. On the Kelso to Hownam road,

just south of Kelso, is a milestone almost sunken out of sight.

Others are more obvious, including one on the A698, between Jedburgh to Hawick, a short distance south of Minto.

When I say a short distance, I mean a stone's throw. That's a metaphoric term of measurement, of course, as it's dependent not only on the size and weight of the stone but also the strength of the thrower. But we find the planned estate village of Minto on the north side of the River Teviot, which the A698 follows between Jedburgh and Hawick. Designed by William Playfair for the Earl of Minto in the 1830s, it's the recently restored peel tower called Fatlips Castle that perhaps draws the most attention, given its unusual name.

Evidently, tradition has it that a gentlemen arriving at the castle had to kiss each of the women he met during his stay.

Above: A milestone on the A698 between Jedburgh to Hawick. *Christine Minto, The Milestone Society*

Since I've mentioned Minto, so winning plaudits from our Milestone Society friend, it would be churlish not mention that but a few short miles north-west of Minto lies Riddell and the impressive country estate of the same name near Lilliesleaf. Thus I've found favour with our other Milestone Society friend, John Riddell, as there

Left: An old milestone beneath a hedge on the A699, east of Roxburgh Newtown, 4 miles from Kelso. *Iain Davison, The Milestone Society*

is a mileplate, inscribed 'Riddell 1', on the track through a field near the East Lodge Plantation. It is shown on the OS map of 1897 and still stands today.

Not all milestones are where one might expect to find them. At Bow Farm Cottages, on the A7 near Stow, is a milestone stating that it's 27 miles to Edinburgh. In fact, the milestone was originally sited 500 metres further east along the A7, at which time it was 1 mile within the Midlothian county boundary. It found its way to the garden some 40 years ago, 'for safekeeping during roadworks'. The milestone is marked on the OS 6-inch 1st Edition, surveyed in 1853. The A7 was the turnpike road from Edinburgh to Galashiels, operated by the Lasswade & District Trust. The present route lies to the east of the Gala Water, whereas the earlier route lay to the west of the river.

A milestone of the Blaydon design (Smith Patterson & Co) on the B6397 in the village of Smailholm. *The Milestone Society*

'Riddell 1'. *John S. Riddell*

Another example of the old and the even older. *Christine Minto and The Milestone Society*

Others just about manage to disappear under vegetation, like this milestone on an unclassified road in front of the Keeper's Cottage at West Printonan, in Eccles Parish. The inscription reads 'K 10/ D 6' where 'K' stands for Kelso and 'D' for Duns. *The Milestone Society*

The garden milestone at Bow Farm Cottages, near Stow. *John S. Riddell*

Peeblesshire (Tweeddale)

For a unique example of a roadside milestone that has captured the care and protection of a local society, 'ye may gang faur an' fare waur' than visit Peebles. On the A703, going north from Peebles towards Edinburgh, there are nine milestones.

Peeblesshire county sign. *Ken Diamond collection, The Milestone Society*

These are probably the largest to be encountered anywhere in the country, which have been reinstated, replaced, repaired and maintained by the Gutterbluids Society, of which more later.

The stones are of concrete construction, made by the local firm of L. Grandison in the 1920s to replace the original turnpike stones. The lettering and pointing hands are of metal, a unique combination. The stones have been strengthened with concrete supports and metal brackets, and include the inscription 'Peeblesshire', a tradition adopted by several local highways authorities in that era. The distances include furlongs, expressed as a fraction of a mile.

Under the Defence of the Realm Act, the stones were removed during the Second World War, some of them hidden in a trench dug behind the stones. Three of them were subsequently reported 'missing', turning up later in local gardens. In the 1990s the Gutterbluids Society undertook the highly successful restoration project – an excellent example of a local community preserving an important element of our roadside heritage.

So what is the Gutterbluids Society?

The Scottish word 'gutterblood' means 'a

The road to Peebles from Leadburn (A703) has very distinctive milestones. *Christine Minto, The Milestone Society*

low-born person'. Hardly flattering, but the term 'gutterbluid', regarded by some as unique to Peebles, is used to describe one who was born in the town. I've checked his passport and my very good friend Colin Shearer is certainly a 'gutterbluid', and proud of it. According to J. L.

Brown and I. C. Lawson in their book *History of Peebles 1850-1990*, it had been said that the 19th century was the century of the 'Gentlemen's Club', and certainly this could be true of Peebles. 'In addition to the Gutterbluid Club formed in 1823, the following were active during the period: the Incomers Club, the Peeblesshire Society, the Edinburgh Peeblean Club, and so on.' The Gutterbluids Club survived until the outbreak of the First World War; it was resurrected in 1974 as the Peebles Gutterbluids Society.

Berwickshire

Berwickshire county sign. *Ken Diamond collection, The Milestone Society*

The old A1, from Dunbar to Berwick-upon-Tweed, has been realigned several times over the years. There's even word that it will be dualled for its entire length, but don't hold your breath.

The milestones erected along the A1 by Berwickshire County Council date from between 1896 and 1908 and have what's termed a 'pipe shaft' and a thin head, with face perimeters and raised rim. The Berwickshire heads are noticeably less bulbous than their East Lothian counterparts.

A milestone on the A1 near Burnmouth. *The Milestone Society*

The 'lighthouse shaft' design was used on the milestones on the network of minor roads that weave across Berwickshire. The use of italic lettering is also a feature in this county.

Ayton Castle is the first substantial building you encounter on a train journey heading northwards after departing from Berwick-upon-Tweed. A red sandstone baronial mansion dating from the 19th century, the original peel tower was a stronghold of the Home family. When Mark Twain visited in

An example of the use of italic lettering on the A6105. *Christine Minto, The Milestone Society*

1873 he was so taken with the fireplace mantel in the dining room that he purchased it. The mantel is now in the author's museum in Hartford, Connecticut. And the castle had its own private milestone.

In the Canmore (Historic Environment Scotland) records, the 'old milestone' (1856) on the Castle South drive is described as a 'square pillar type with chamfered edges, top partly rounded … inscribed with a large "7"'. The distance from Berwick is now 5.6 miles, but 7 by the original Ayton to Cocklaw Old Post Road route. Whether this is a private milestone for prestige reasons or the original 7-mile marker on the turnpike road, relocated to the castle for preservation, is uncertain. However, the Berwickshire map of 1771 shows '7' on the old route immediately east of the church across the river, 200 metres south of the present location.

On the A6089, in what was Roxburghshire, Ettrick and Lauderdale, lies Nenthorn. Its medieval name was Naithansthirn, but that really is a mouthful. Here we find a good example of a replacement fingerpost that does justice to its predecessor.

The 'modern' fingerpost at Nenthorn, complete with decorative finial. *Iain Davison. The Milestone Society*

At the entrance drive to Spottiswoode House on the A697 near Westruther are East and West Clock Lodges. Built in 1796, both lodges have tall battlemented screen walls at one end, onto each of which a later member of the Spottiswoode family added a clock and two distance panels. West Cottage provides distances to locations throughout Scotland: Dalkeith (24 miles), Edinburgh (30),

Falkirk (54) and Glasgow (72) on one, and the more distant towns of Crieff (84), Perth (70), Aberdeen (136) and Inverness (185) on the other.

On the East Lodge the distances are all to

West Clock Lodge at Spottiswoode. *Iain Davison, The Milestone Society*

English destinations – some very far distant, like Portsmouth (422 miles) and Plymouth (567). Quite why these naval ports are featured is unclear, but perhaps the owner of Spottiswoode responsible was a Navy officer?

Before leaving the Borders, a salutary tale for milestone enthusiasts – things ain't always what they appear at first glance. Advertised for sale on the internet in 2019 was what claimed to be a 'vintage milestone marker', and it certainly looked like an historic cast-iron V-shaped milepost. To the expert eye of Milestone Society member Robert Caldicott it didn't quite seem 'genuine'. It was slightly squat in shape and had an intriguing embossed rose motif on the front face, with no obvious explanation. The key lead was the 'MELROSE' name on the front face, with an '18'

on each of the side faces. The initial conclusion was that it had originated 18 miles from the town of Melrose in the Scottish Borders and presumably removed from the roadside many years before.

The distance panels at East Clock Lodge, Spottiswoode. *Iain Davison, The Milestone Society*

Robert went to investigate with the vendor, who lived in Nuneaton, who helpfully advised that he'd acquired the 'milepost' some two years previously at a car boot sale near Aberystwyth, Wales.

Iain Davison and John V. Nicholls, Society stalwarts, took up the research within an 18-mile radius of Melrose. The Melrose Historical & Archaeological Association also checked local records. Both concluded that the milepost was an 'imposter', and speculated that it probably was the name of a private property, perhaps a guest house, with house name and street number. And, most probably, nowhere near the historic town of Melrose. But if you know differently, please let the Society know.

4
The legislative footprint

Is there any aspect of our modern lives that is not regulated in some way? Probably very little, and by and large an ordered society does need governance to succeed.

We cannot expect to find our system of not only measurement, but also signage, other than weighed heavy in statutory provisions, so it's worth a look at the principal legislation that has developed as the history of travel and transport has evolved over time.

According to a Report from the Commission on Public Roads in Scotland in 1859:

'…there appears to have been no general legislative provision on the subject of roads in Scotland until the Act (of) 1617 gave powers to the Justices of the Peace to mend highways and passages to or from any market town or seaport.'

The breadth of such roads was to be '20 feet at the least' – which must have been their equivalent of a motorway. The statutory provisions were renewed on similar terms in 1661, and in 1669 provision was made to levy tolls on bridges and ferries.

Maintenance was carried out under 'statute labour', whereby locals were obliged to provide up to six days of a man and horse every year for the first three years, reducing to four days annually thereafter. This system remained in force on 'statute labour roads' until the General Statute Labour Act of 1845, which replaced personal service with an annual monetary payment to be expended on the roads.

Turnpikes first gained statutory provision in Scotland in the Turnpike Road Act of 1713, entitled 'An Act for upholding and repairing the Bridges and Highways in the county of Edinburgh'. It provided for the erection of turnpikes and the levying of tolls.

In England, the monies received in tolls were primarily applied to the payment of interest on the debt – the capital sum incurred in the construction of the road. There were other sources of funds for upholding the road. In Scotland, with its distinct and different legal system, and where other sources of funding did not exist, the repair of the road was the 'first and preferable burden upon the trust' for the toll income. The payment of interest on the debt was contingent on the surplus available after the costs of maintenance of the road had been met.

It was the General Turnpike Acts of 1744, 1766 and 1773 that made the use of milestones and fingerposts compulsory on turnpike roads, but it was the 1750s before any real advance was made on Scottish turnpikes – the history of this era is covered in a later chapter – and lasted until the late 1880s. Just as the advent of the railways in the 1840s put paid to the canals, then the inter-city coaches, so the railways eventually saw off the turnpike system of road charging.

Turnpike roads were established by individual Acts, although several roads in a locality were often included in a single statute. For example, the Midlothian Turnpike Act of 1751 established the Midlothian General Trust (aka Edinburghshire until 1890) and delegated responsibility to eight District Trusts to manage the radial turnpikes. Subsequent mergers saw the number of trusts reduce to four.

1751 also heralded the establishment of turnpike trusts for West Lothian and Stirlingshire

The Hammerhead Toll, east of Auchtermuchty (1871). *Fife Folk Museum in Ceres*

under the Post Roads (Scotland) Act, which paved the way, so to speak, for the Edinburgh to Linlithgow to Falkirk to Glasgow turnpike. This was the 'northern route' (the A803 equivalent), with a fork from Falkirk to Stirling. The route between Edinburgh and Glasgow via Kirk o' Shotts, equivalent of the A71, B7105, A705, B7066 and A775, became the 'southern route' and was turnpiked in 1764. In 1778 the route via Newbridge and Bathgate, equivalent to the A8, A899 and A89, became the 'middle way'; this latter was eventually measured to be a few hundred yards shorter than the 'southern route'.

The Turnpike Roads (Scotland) Act of 1831 was a General Consolidating Act covering all turnpikes. It stipulated that tollbars should be erected at intervals of 6 miles and reiterated the requirements to install milestones, with guideposts at junctions. Any person damaging or removing such stone or post was liable to a fine of £5.

'An Inquiry Report to the Commissioners into Matters relating to Public Roads in Scotland' in 1859 recommended that the turnpike system had passed its use-by date. Subsequently, in 1878 (yes, it took a long time then, too) the Roads & Bridges (Scotland) Act established the County Highway Trusts for 'main roads', which were to be maintained by local rates. It took until 1883 to wind up the turnpike trusts and 'de-turnpike' the roads, with all tolls repealed.

The Local Government (Scotland) Act of 1889 transferred responsibility for maintaining roads to the County Councils, so in effect marking the final demise of the turnpike system and their legal requirement to erect milestones. The 1889 Act regularised in statute the 33 Scottish counties, which remained almost intact until local government reorganisation took effect in 1975. The largest county, by area, was Inverness-shire at 2,695,094 acres, but Argyll was not far behind at 2,067,034 acres. Four further counties had areas in excess of 1.2 million acres. Should this fascinate you as much as it does me, I'll recount that Ross & Cromarty extended to 1,977,254 acres; Perthshire was 1,586,577 acres; Sutherland was 1,297914 acres; and Aberdeenshire was 1,246,585 acres. At the other end of the scale, Clackmannanshire was only 34,838 acres.

The Motor Car Act 1903 was a very significant piece of legislation for this new form of transport. As well as introducing vehicle registration, driving licences (no test, just pay 5 shillings), the crime of reckless driving and, following a bitter parliamentary debate, raising the speed limit from 14 to 20mph, the statute also passed road sign responsibilities to the relevant highway authority within the then United Kingdom of Great Britain and Ireland. Although no specifications were set in the statute, guidance was given in a 1921 circular that road direction signs should have upper-case lettering 2½ or 3 inches high on a white background, and white supporting poles. It also recommended that the name of the highway authority be included somewhere in the design.

The Ministry of Transport, then a UK Government department, was formed in 1919 and set out to review the road systems, for which it had inherited responsibility. The following year the County Surveyors' Society was invited to consider and provide recommendations for standardisation. An extensive consultation exercise was undertaken with motoring organisations, safety groups and local authorities. The Society's report recognised that in many areas and on various sections of road these were still the only guide to traffic as regards direction and distance. It was proposed that a standardised system be introduced that would include either amending the mileposts to correct the mileages or repositioning them so they were in the correct position for the mileages stated.

According to the National Archives, both the AA and the RAC failed to provide any substantial comment on the topic of milestones, so when the MoT produced its final report on 23 February 1921, there was no reference to milestones. It was to be a dozen years before any meaningful attention was paid to standardisation.

Mandatory standards were eventually issued by the Ministry of Transport in 'The Traffic Signs (Size, Colour and Type) Provisional Regulations' for Great Britain in 1933. This required poles to be painted with black and white bands, the lettering to be of a different typeface, and the fingers to have square ends – removing further the obvious association of a pointing digit.

Road signing was next comprehensively reviewed in the United Kingdom in the early 1960s by the Government-appointed Worboys Committee, and the 1964 Traffic Signs Regulations brought in the signing system largely remaining in force today. While the 1964 regulations did encourage local authorities to remove and replace traditional fingerposts with the new designs, it

The cover of the Warboys Report of 1963.
Ministry of Transport

was not made compulsory to do so. Regulations did not, however, permit new fingerpost-style signs to be erected until a design was permitted by the Department for the Environment in 1994 (in the 'Traffic Signs Regulations and General Directions').

Of particular note was that the design did not allow for mileages of more than 3 miles to be expressed with the use of halves and quarters. New fingerposts, therefore, have been required to round the previously more accurate distance measurements. Is this an example of dumbing-down, or merely a pragmatic move?

The concern over the visual effects caused by a proliferation of signs along Scotland's roads has been heard repeatedly for many years. In 2006 Transport Scotland published 'Road Furniture in the Countryside: Guidance for Road and Planning Authorities and Statutory Undertakers'. The aim, the report stated, should be to maintain adequate levels of information while also respecting the quality of rural scenery. In common with many reports, there's advocacy for a critical audit approach, but two conclusions are reached regarding signposts that are apposite to our interest in milestones and way-markers. Firstly, avoid

combining traditional signposts with modern components, as these are rarely compatible. Secondly, wherever possible use traditional elements, restoring damaged or worn parts such as broken fingerposts.

Evidence of where the errors highlighted in the first recommendation are all too apparent can be seen in the accompanying photograph of the signage outside the old tollhouse at Bridge of Feugh, near Banchory.

The Report quotes Dame Sylvia Crowe, the President of the Institute of Landscape Architects, who stated that the objective should be 'the fewest

Left: The former tollhouse at Bridge of Feugh with modern signage. *Richard Slessor*

Below: 'A rose between two thorns': the juxtaposition of the old Fettercairn milestone at Bridge of Feugh tollhouse. *Christine Minto, The Milestone Society*

possible signs of the smallest adequate size in the clearest and simplest form'. Dame Sylvia Crowe said that in 1955, the year I was born, and it is surely as relevant today as then.

Mention is made on several occasions throughout this book to the removal of milestones and direction posts during the Second World War. This was in an effort to make it more difficult for any invading German troops to determine their location. I'd draw the line at suggesting that it was in an effort to disorientate them for, as we know, any self-respecting invaders would arrive armed with their own maps.

But the legislative provision for the removal of milestones was not conceived in 1939. In fact, the Defence of the Realm Act dated from 1914 and came into effect on 8 August, only four days after war with Germany had been declared in the first great conflagration. It was a piece of emergency legislation, enacted without debate, which allowed the Government to exercise a wide range of powers during wartime to ensure the defence of the realm and security of the nation.

On Friday 31 May 1940 a short article entitled 'Signposts to be removed' was published in the *Daily Express*, and undoubtedly other newspapers, with the story:

'Sir John Reith, Minister of Transport, announced last night that highways authorities had been instructed to remove signposts and direction indicators which would be of value to the enemy in case of invasion. The work was put in hand on Wednesday.'

Our milestone heritage: Dumfries & Galloway

The Midsteeple building in the centre of Dumfries dates from 1707, a contemporary of the Acts of Union of the Scottish and English Parliaments. The 'town house' is one of several buildings constructed in the local red sandstone and it is here that Robert Burns's body lay awaiting his funeral in 1796. Burns, of course, had commented wryly on the Acts of Union, saying that Scotland was 'bought and sold for English gold' by 'such a parcel of rogues in a nation'. But it's the outside of the Midsteeple that catches our eye, for there is not only a metal 'bed of a yard measure', but also a cast-iron distance plate, probably both dating from 1827. The distance plate gives mileages to the local towns such as Castle Douglas (18), Annan (16) and Portpatrick (84), the latter emphasising the fact that the distance to the western end of Galloway is some 10 miles further than that to Glasgow (74 miles). The most remarkable entry, however, is the distance to Huntingdon – 272 miles – only a short hop, skip and a jump over 20 miles from where I now live, in Cambridgeshire. Why would someone in the middle of Dumfries in the late 1820s wish to know the distance to Huntingdon? From early times there was a bustling trade in Irish cattle at Smithfield Market in London. The route the drovers took was from Portpatrick to Dumfries, then southwards. The last major cattle gathering point before London was at Huntingdon, and to

Dumfries & Galloway. *Wikimedia Commons*

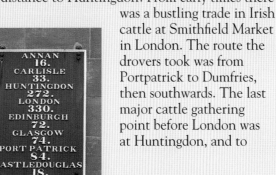

The distance marker on Midsteeple, Dumfries. *John M. Riddet*

this day the livestock market in Dumfries is in Huntingdon Road. The mail coach between London and Portpatrick travelled the same route. If you search the AA's distance calculator website, the road distance quoted between Dumfries and Huntingdon is 272.2 miles, a quite remarkable endorsement of the surveyor's skills in 1827.

It's not unique though. There's a similar distance marker on the elevation of the Douglas Arms Hotel in Castle Douglas, also dated 1827 and quoting the distance to Huntingdon et al. There's a photograph of this one on the front cover of this book.

As with most of the cast-ironwork in this area, these markers are the product of J. Afflect's foundry in Dumfries.

Wigtownshire

This old county was the first in Scotland to be mapped by the Ordnance Survey at the 6-inch scale, between 1843 and 1847, so we have comprehensive pre-1850 cartographic records. Milestones were evident on the road between Newton Stewart, Glenluce, Stranraer and Portpatrick; this would be the A75 nowadays, as far as Stranraer, and the plates on the remaining milestones may be originals. Those on the road from Stranraer to Ballantrae and on to Girvan, the coastal A77, have inscriptions cut into the masonry, many with a black band beneath. The other road having milestones at that time forms the third side of the triangle, between Newton Stewart via Barrhill to Girvan, probably mostly the B7027 then, but nowadays the A714. Some of the older stones refer to 'Newton Steuart', the former spelling, but I have not encountered any with the town's relatively short-lived interim name, Newton Douglas.

Above: An example of a Wigtownshire granite milestone, on the B733, a short distance to the west of the Bronze Age standing stones of Torhouse stone circle, with Wigtown ('W') shown as 3 miles and Glenluce ('G') via Kirkcowan as 14 miles. *Christine Minto, The Milestone Society*

With many more milestones shown on later maps, it seems that these probably date from the late 19th century. Many are on unclassified roads that form a network across the Rhinns of Galloway and The Machars. Usually triangular in cross-section, they invariably show the destinations by

Left: Note the old spelling, 'Newton Steuart', on this black-banded milestone on the road to Girvan (in Ayrshire). *Christine Minto, The Milestone Society*

a single initial letter, painted black on a white background, and occasionally with an arrow. The individual stones vary considerably, however, with some being tall and thin, others short and stumpy.

Kirkcudbrightshire

Although there were many more miles of turnpike road in Kirkcudbrightshire than in the neighbouring Wigtownshire, recent maps indicate that Kirkcudbrightshire County Council was less assiduous about reinstating its milestones in the late 1940s. A pity, perhaps, because maps from 1845-50 indicate that this county had a significant legacy of milestones along its greater length of turnpike roads. Those along the future A75, from Dumfries through Castle Douglas and Gatehouse of Fleet to Newton Stewart, were particularly interesting, some giving the distances to two, others three and some four destinations, including London. The cumulative distances show discrepancies, but that's down to realignments. The milestone at Caulkerbush on the A710, the coastal road between Dumfries and Dalbeattie, via New Abbey, merely states '16'. That's from Dumfries, if you measure back.

These milestones may well have marked the route to Stranraer and Portpatrick. The one that is located a mile from Portpatrick gives the distance to London – 415 miles. For those with less ambitious travel plans, Stranraer is 7 miles and Dumfries 83. If you think that this old milestone records the greatest distance from London, there is a surprise in store when we reach Golspie, as illustrated.

There are also milestones showing the distance to the railway station. Due to the terrain, the station was sometimes located out of the town or village. From Gatehouse of Fleet, for example, there is a milepost showing the station as 5½ miles distant, up into the hills. These milestones are D-shaped and were erected by the railway company to encourage the use of the train rather

Portpatrick milestone. *Christine Minto, The Milestone Society*

than the winding, slower coach roads. Milestone Society member Alverie Weighill has found a complete set of six of these stones on the road from New Abbey to the former station at Killywhan, now a row of houses off the A711 near Beeswing. Similar stones are found on either side of Loch Ken, linking Dalry and New Galloway to the railway, and along the coastal route to Dalbeattie.

On the old road from Newton Stewart to Barrhill in South Ayrshire (B7027) is the small hamlet of Knowe. Now comprising a handful of properties only, it lies on the Southern Upland Way, but once commanded an AA/Royal Scottish Automobile Club village sign, which nowadays

can be viewed in the museum in Newton Stewart.

I can understand the weary traveller arriving at Knowe in bygone days and finding that having walked the 9 miles from Barrhill, he still has 8 more to complete before he reaches Newton Stewart. How many travellers on reaching Knowe would be interested, I ponder, to learn that they are 393¼ miles from London?

The cast-iron, three-armed milepost at Haugh of Urr dates from the late 1920s and has been

The AA/RSAC sign at Knowe.
Newton Stewart Museum, Christine Minto

Listed Category C. Made by Smith Patterson Company Limited of Blaydon (near Newcastle-upon-Tyne), it is a tapered post painted in black and white stripes with ring shafts and a conical finial. The foundry's name is in raised lettering near the base of the post and the white-painted cast-iron arms have chamfered corners, black raised lettering and black painted edges. The distances are shown as 'Haugh of Urr ¼', 'Dalbeattie 3½' and 'Urr Church ½'.

The five best surviving examples of this type of free-standing milepost in Dumfries & Galloway have been selected for statutory Listing in recognition of their attractive design, historical importance and present scarcity. The milepost at Corsack is identical to that at Haugh of Urr, while the other three – at Loch Head (near Elrig in Wigtownshire), Kirkland (near Moniaive) and Old Bridge of Urr – are variations on a theme. The Loch Head fingerpost, complete with hoop finial inscribed 'Scottish Automobile Club', provides the traveller with a great assortment of distance information: Kirkcowan via Drumwalt 9½, Mochrum 2½ and Port William 4½; Elrig Village 1¼, Port William 4¼ and Glenluce 13¼; and Kirkcowan via Malzie 10 and Wigtown 8½. What a choice! The only slightly disappointing element to this sign, to the pedant at least, is that it's very likely that the original arms were replaced in the late 20th century.

The fingerpost at Loch Head, Wigtownshire.
Billy McCrorie

Dumfries-shire

Dumfries-shire county sign. *Ken Diamond collection, The Milestone Society*

A milestone on the B724, between Annan and Dumfries. *Christine Minto, The Milestone Society*

Across in Annan, the milestones use the local red sandstone, as do most local buildings and Robert Stevenson's bridge in the town. Most of this series of milestones have been painted white; the accompanying photograph shows an unadulterated stone, although the comparative clarity of the information is obvious when contrasted with the 'Dumfries 6, Annan 11' milestone also shown here.

The milepost at Gretna, on the B721, was erected by the Mail Turnpike Trust in the 19th century.

West of Teviotdale and Eskdale, Craik Cross Hill straddles the boundary between Dumfries & Galloway and the Borders. The commanding views from atop its 1,480-foot summit provided an excellent site for a Roman signal station along this section of the old Roman road. A modern milestone provides an attractive feature on the road from Beattock.

Views for a loftier elevation are in the hills around the village of Wanlockhead; at 1,531 feet above sea level, it's the highest village in Scotland. Famed for its mining – principally lead, although zinc, copper and silver were also mined locally – the rich seams also yielded the world's purest gold. At 22.8 carats, no

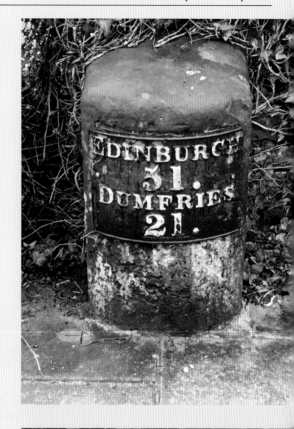

Above right: A milestone in red sandstone outside the Moffat Arms Hotel, on the A701. *Mike Hogg*

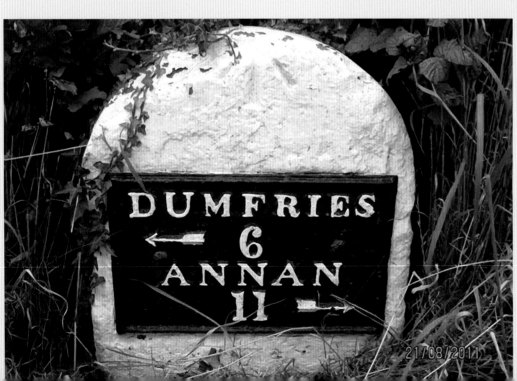

Right: A milestone on the A709 at Priestgate, near Lochmaben – note old spelling of Lockerbie. The vestiges of the white paint are visible. *Christine Minto, The Milestone Society*

wonder it was used in the Scottish Crown, now housed in Edinburgh Castle. Driving the B797 leading to Wanlockhead and beyond from the A76 at Mennock is a motorist's delight. There are three milestones on this stretch, two of them with no legend, but the one at the village has '47' inscribed on the top. There's no indication where from, but a check on the 'distance finder uk' website determines that it must be Glasgow. Edinburgh is 44 miles.

The B729 runs from Holywood (with one 'l'), just north of Dumfries on the A76, to join the A702 east of Moniaive, with the square block milestones having a number inscribed on the slightly sloping top. Only '6' and '7' are missing, although several are inconspicuous. Near Dunscore there is a tollhouse at the appropriately named Throughgate, which is splendidly called Macphail Drover's Toll Tower House. A 'gate' or 'gait' in the Scots tongue is a road, path or, in a town, a street, while 'gate mail' is a road tax or toll paid for the right of passage.

The modern milestone on the old Roman road to Craik Cross Hill. *The Milestone Society*

5

A journey in time along Scotland's roads: routes to progress and prosperity

Trysts and the drove roads

It's usual to assume that the early roads in Scotland were those used by drovers making their way to the market with their livestock – predominantly cattle and sheep – or the passage of troops engaged on some military exploit. Some, however, are older than you might imagine…

From medieval times, the trade in cattle, sheep and horses, and the livestock products, had become an increasingly important part of the economy. Certainly in the monastic period, post-Roman but predominantly from 900AD until the wider European Protestant Reformation in the mid-16th century, most of Scotland lying below the Highland Boundary Fault Line (Helensburgh to Stonehaven), but extending north into Aberdeenshire and round to Morayshire, had an extensive network of tracks and paths to facilitate the significant agrarian activity of the multiple monasteries and friaries then operating. To apply the term 'track' to these routes is probably not a disservice, and that would be true in most rural areas until the late 17th century.

That isn't to say that relatively significant engineering infrastructure was absent. The Brig o' Balgownie, with its elegant Gothic arch over the River Don, dates from 1320, the year 51 Scottish nobles signed the Declaration of Arbroath. In Dumfries the Auld Brig, the oldest surviving multiple-arched stone bridge

in Scotland, dates from 1432, and Devorgilla, the mother of John Balliol, had erected its predecessor, a wooden structure, in 1291. By 1717 the splendid Carr Bridge was conveying packhorses across the River Dulnain; it is the oldest surviving stone arch bridge in the Highlands. The word 'carr' has nothing whatsoever to do with motorised transport – it is the Old Norse word for 'boggy area', of which there are many in Scotland.

The drove roads of yesteryear grew out of the increasing trade in livestock, with drovers bringing their cattle and sheep, bred and reared in the Highlands, to markets in the Central Belt through the glens and valleys, and round, and in some cases over, the upland terrain. The map of Scotland shows how extensive this network of drove roads had become by the 18th century. The principal market, or tryst, was in Crieff, but by 1770 all roads led to Falkirk. It is estimated that more than 2,000 drovers brought 150,000 head of cattle, sheep and horses to trysts held in Falkirk on the first Tuesday in August, September and October, which serviced the spring-born livestock.

Mid Calder, in what is today West Lothian, was a major crossroads in the 19th century, with livestock moving southwards from Falkirk, and dissected by the turnpike road (now the A71) between Edinburgh and Glasgow. Thieves Road was the name given to a track heading south from Little Vantage near Harperrig Reservoir, across moorland to a pass in the Pentland Hills called Cauldstone Slap, through which cattle

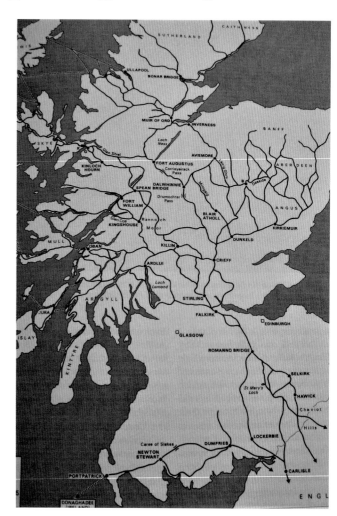

The drove roads of Scotland. *Ian Scott, Falkirk Local History Society*

were driven to West Linton and thence to market at Peebles and their English buyers. Sheep from the Borders made the journey in reverse from West Linton mart – well, perhaps not in reverse, as that would be too much to expect of any self-respecting sheep.

Some old stones found at Linton Burnfoot, near Morebattle in Roxburghshire, may hark back to when this was an important trade route south through the Cheviot Hills, but also subject to the hostilities between the families of Border reivers on both sides of the national divide in the late Middle Ages. The parish is supposed to have formed 'one of the principal thoroughfares betwixt the two kingdoms', and in the mid-19th century it was remarked that 'a narrow aperture between two hills along the verge of Linton Loch appears to have been regarded as an important pass, and there are still obvious marks of its having been once closely guarded.'

In 1603 two nations had been united, at least by a single monarch, when James VI of Scotland became James I of England. It's often said that HM The Queen believes that the world, or at least the decreasing part of it over which she is sovereign, smells of paint. Given scant advance notice of her arrival, there's an operative, one of her subjects, a few yards ahead busy giving the walls a lick of fresh paint, so they say.

It seems it was ever so. Owen Silver, in his excellent book *The Roads of Fife*, relates the controls exercised over local road administrators to improve the condition of the roads for the visit to Scotland of James VI and I in 1617. There was strenuous activity in some areas to create a great impression. In Berwickshire, for example, not only was the highway improved but buildings and other developments constructed that gave an aura of prosperity. Similarly, from Falkland to Perth a 16-foot-wide highway was the standard decreed, although whether it was achieved all the way through Auchtermuchty, Strathmiglo and Arngask is not recorded. When, in 1628, Charles I sought to emulate his father's visit to Scotland,

he expressed the wish 'that the high wayes may in lyke maner be made readie for our passage.' Although the Privy Council issued orders for the highways 'to be perfyte', and claimed that the work had been done, it then persuaded the King that there was no money in the budget for his expenses that year. The visit was delayed until 1629, then again until 1633, his coronation year as King of Scotland. While fresh instructions on road repairs and improvements were issued on each occasion, there is no evidence that any work was ever carried out.

Troops: the military roads

The first extensive road-building programme in Scotland was wrought out of rebellion.

Desperate to quell further Jacobite risings, especially that in 1715 and a second attempt in 1719, the Royalists commissioned General Wade to construct roads to facilitate access through the Highlands linking a series of forts being built along the Great Glen and the barracks at Ruthven, near Kingussie. Until the roads were complete it was said to be impossible to move military equipment much further north than Newtonmore or Kingussie, so the infrastructure was a basic supply chain need.

There's no point beating about the bush. The Wade roads had a purely military objective. No economic development measure here, and certainly not a philanthropic gesture. The National Anthem of the so-called United Kingdom spells it out, albeit in a verse not quoted in polite circles:

Lord grant that Marshal Wade
May by thy mighty aid
Victory bring.
May he sedition hush,
And like a torrent rush,
Rebellious Scots to crush.
God save the King!

In 13 years Wade constructed roads along the southside of Loch Ness (Inverness, down the Great Glen to Fort William); Dunkeld to Inverness through the Pass of Drumochter; Crieff to Aberfeldy and Tummel Bridge; and Dalwhinnie to Fort Augustus via the Corrieyairack. The last-named is the most impressive, a major feat of engineering across rugged terrain.

Wade's roads were generally 16 feet

A milestone, albeit much more recent, on the road at Errogie, above the Falls of Foyers on the south side of Loch Ness. *Christine Minto, The Milestone Society*

wide, constructed by the military at a cost of approximately £90 per mile. He constructed some 250 miles of road and 40 bridges, normally quite simple stone arches, but others, like his bridge at High Spean and the grandiose Tay Bridge at Aberfeldy, significant architectural structures. To put that in context, in the case of the latter he engaged William Adam, the doyen of the Scottish architectural dynasty, at a total build cost of £4,095 5s 10d. His more basic bridges were costed at less than £200 each. The road construction was basic but represented a vast improvement on the drove roads.

As one commentator quipped:

'Had you seen these roads before they were made
You would hold up your hands and bless General
Wade.'

The tourist-type history books often celebrate Wade as the great road-builder, but it was his successor, William Caulfeild, appointed in 1732, who built more miles of road and significantly more bridges.

Over the ensuing 35 years, Caulfeild was responsible for 900 miles of road and more than 600 bridges. This included the road linking Tyndrum and Fort William across Rannoch Moor, with its spectacular series of zig-zags known as the Devil's Staircase, but now made easier, for the motorist at any rate, with the more leisurely A82. Then Caulfeild turned his attention to the road from Dumbarton to Inverary, via Arrochar, over the Rest and be Thankful from the shores of Loch Lomond at Tarbet. That's now predominantly the most southerly end of the A82 and the A83. In 1755 he constructed the road from Fort Augustus westwards through Glen Shiel and across the hill to Bernera, near Glenelg, although this was remade by Thomas Telford in the 1820s. Caulfeild's other great Highland roads were from Blairgowrie northwards to the Spittal of Glenshee, down to Braemar; the road then forked, with a branch along Deeside via his new bridge at

A map showing Wade and Caulfeild roads. *Thincat*

Invercauld, while the other continued northwards passing Corgarff and Tomintoul to Grantown-on-Spey, and finally to Inverness.

Other roads in the east included the route from Fettercairn over the Cairn o' Mount to Alford, Huntly and Fochabers. On the Ordnance Survey 1-inch map of 1958 there is a milestone marked on the very minor road from Dulsie to Cawdor, part of Caulfeild's road-building efforts in the mid-1750s. It's located at the settlement of Bruachmary,

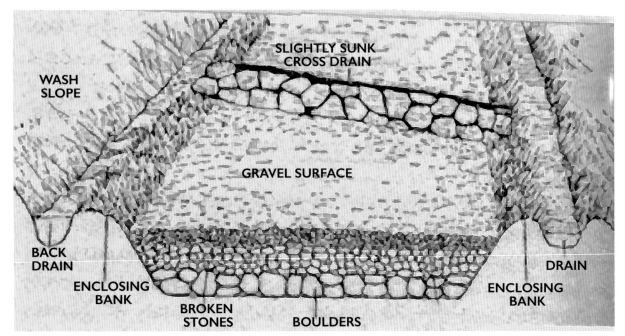

A cross-section through a typical Wade road construction with an open-paved cross drain. *Dr William Taylor in 'The Military Roads in Scotland'*

An old Highland milestone on the B9008 at Inveraven (Moray), approximately 1 mile south of the A95 – later than Caulfeild, however. *The Milestone Society*

just off the side of the road, and is a large stone, roughly milestone-shaped, with no visible markings. There are no other milestones marked on that 10-mile stretch of road. A mystery? I'm not so sure. Dr William Taylor in his authoritative volume *The Military Roads in Scotland* mentions that the final act of construction of the roads was to place 'milestones and markers'. However, there is scant evidence that milestones were used, or, if they were, they have not withstood the test of time. Markers, on the other hand, do occur, and many remain to this day. Their purpose appears to have been as distance markers, celebrating the completion of, say, a 5-mile section of road by a Regiment. At the Well of the Lecht, for example, near Tomintoul, the stone indicates that this part

of the road was built by 'Five companies of the 33rd Regiment, Honourable Lord Charles Hay, Colonel'. The stone is dated '1754', and by the end of that year the road, including the bridge over the Spey at Grantown, was completed.

Similarly, the marker stone on the Wade road between Slochd and Sluggan at Inverlaidnan is thought to be a 5-mile marker post. The Grants owned Inverlaidnan Estate and Bonnie Prince Charlie is said to have stayed at the house in 1746, and would have benefited from the new roof, the original having been extensively damaged in a fire in 1736. He'd have used Wade's road, somewhat ironically, to continue his journey through Slochd Pass. This was a particularly steep section of the military road, being substantially replaced by James Donaldson's road in 1803.

Other evidence of marker posts includes one at Laggan Farm, south of Strathyre, commemorating the efforts of the 4th Regiment of the King's Own Royal Regiment. However, as it is dated 1769 these efforts were on maintenance and repair of the road rather than initial construction. It would seem, therefore, that a few economies may have been made on milestones, but distance markers, akin to those that the Romans installed on the Antonine Wall nearly 1,600 years earlier, were erected.

And why would the Royalist troops want milestones anyway? Imagine a company of squaddies making its way back from a day's march to the camp at Ruthven Barracks, along the side of the Insh Marshes, the flood plain of the River Spey between Kingussie and Kincraig, on a summer's evening – and under hostile attack from the most ferocious Scottish clan. But not the MacPhersons, wielding their claymores. No, *Diptera nematocera* of the *Caratopogonidae* clan – the dreaded Scottish midge! Never underestimate the capacity of this insect to cause horrendous irritation and suffering. Weighing one eight-thousandth of a gram and with the fastest wingbeat speed of any animal, the female members of the clan inflict misery on unsuspecting souls as they go about

their daily business. Clouds of them descend upon you – there is no escape. There is a population of 180,750 trillion of them inhabiting Scotland – an estimate, as I'm reasonably confident that no one has counted them all individually. But their bite is the only blight on an otherwise blissful evening stroll. If you're a Royalist soldier, however, the last thing you want to be alerted to as you march through a horde of midges, fretting 'Are we nearly there yet?', is that it's another 3 miles until you reach the relative safety of the barracks. Hence, no milestones.

Before we move forward from the achievements of Wade and Caulfeild, although it is often less well appreciated than his Highland endeavours, it's worth noting that Caulfeild also gave us the road from Bridge of Sark, near Gretna Green, westwards to Portpatrick, via Dumfries, Castle Douglas, Newton Stewart and Stranraer. That is what today is largely the A75. Again the road has its origins in a military requirement, which, in the 1760s, was to facilitate getting troops to Ireland. Nowadays it's a key transport link, being part of the Euro-route 18.

Trade and transport: the Telford era

As any property owner will know, assets need to be maintained. This has always been the issue for highways authorities, and it was no different in the past. As early as 1758 Kirk Sessions resorted to fining parishioners for misdemeanours to raise funds for urgent road and bridge repairs. At Struan, one John Robertson 'gave a joist for the bridge … valued at 14sh Scots, which the Session takes to account in so much of his fine for fornication with Ann Robertson in Auchinleeks.'

In 1786 John Knox – an Edinburgh bookseller, not the Presbyterian tormentor of Mary Queen of Scots – wrote of his travels in the Highlands:

'It is hardly agreed upon by travellers which is the line of the road, everyone making one for himself.

Even sheep follow better routes, understanding levels better and selecting better gradients.'

By 1790 much of the considerable effort of Wade and Caulfield in constructing roads had been overtaken by disrepair and lack of maintenance. In the Highlands only 600 miles of the roads remained usable, and some of that scarcely so.

And it wasn't much better in the Lowlands and Southern Uplands. On the toils of travelling by highway, Robert Burns announced:

'I'm now arrived – thanks to the Gods!
Through pathways rough and muddy:
A certain sign that makin roads
Is no this people's study.

Yet, though I'm no wi' scripture crammed,
I'm sure the Bible says
That heedless sinners shall be damn'd
Unless thay mend their ways.'

Charles Abercrombie (1750-1817) was a pioneer in his field. He left a legacy of many miles of new and improved roads in Perthshire, Angus, Aberdeenshire and Ayrshire. His crowning glory, though, is Union Street in Aberdeen, completed in 1805.

If Scotland was to grow and prosper economically, it needed investment in a modern infrastructure. The dawning of the new century saw a fresh impetus to investment in canals, roads and later railways, which formed the basis of much of the network systems we enjoy to this day.

In 1803 the Commissioners of Highland Roads & Bridges was established. This body immediately took control of the maintenance and repair of roads from the military.

Thomas Telford had arrived – 'The Colossus of Roads', 'Pontifex Maximus', or whatever title you wish to bestow. Telford, the shepherd's son from Westerkirk, born in 1757 and founding President of the Institution of Civil Engineers, was to transform the UK, and much of his

activity would bring enormous benefits to the Highlands. Construction of the Caledonian Canal, incorporating Neptune's Staircase, a series of eight locks, and improvements to the Crinan Canal, secured new means of transporting goods and people and a much-needed stimulus to the economy. He built Pultneytown, a new town and harbour at Wick, for the industrialisation of the herring fleet. He also built 32 Parliamentary churches, together with 41 manses (in case you wonder why there were more manses than kirks, it's because some parishes already had a kirk, but nowhere for the minister to live). And, of course, over the 60 years that the Commission functioned, he and his protégé and successor, John and Joseph Mitchell, built 930 miles of new road and 1,117 bridges.

Telford also introduced innovations in construction. He experimented with more scientific approaches to both road and bridge building, looking at the thickness of the broken stones used to form the foundations and the compacted course (a surface dressing comprising 'a good depth' of gravel), as well as the gradient of the slopes and the use of a camber on the finished road surface to aid drainage. He took account of potential traffic movements and the consequential wear and tear on the surface and the need for planned maintenance. In much of this he was leading the development of new practices and adopting a thoroughly professional approach to civil engineering. Who better to be the first President of the Institution of Civil Engineers? He was also putting into practice what that great Scottish economist and philosopher and key figure of the Scottish Enlightenment, Adam Smith from Kirkcaldy, had espoused in his magnum opus *The Wealth of Nations*: 'Good roads are the greatest of all improvements.'

The accompanying diagrams show the development of different road construction techniques. We're considering Telford here, and will encounter McAdam later, but John Metcalf (1717-1810) also had involvement in our story.

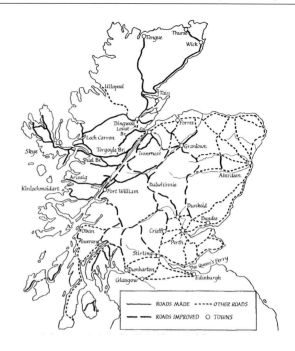

The Parliamentary roads – construction 1803-28, maintenance 1814-62. *From 'Roads and bridges in the Scottish Highlands: the route between Dunkeld and Inverness, 1725-1925' by G. R. Curtis, Proc Soc Antiq Scot, 110, 1978-80, 475-96*

He was a Yorkshireman, known as Blind Jack of Knaresborough on account of him being blind from the age of six years as a result of smallpox. He built about 180 miles of turnpike road in the north of England and became known as one of the 'fathers of the modern road'. He was an accomplished fiddler and diver and during the 1745 Jacobite rebellion he was enlisted in the Government troops. He didn't see action (well, he was blind) but was, rather, engaged in moving guns over boggy ground. He must have been busy because there was a lot of boggy ground to cover on the trek north.

In the 35 years in which Telford was active in road building in Scotland, he not only improved some original Wade and Caulfeild roads by realignment, widening and improvement, but also

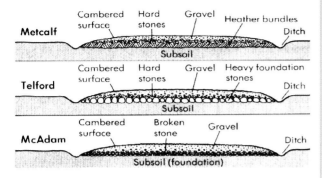

Cross-sectional drawings of road construction techniques. *From 'New Ways Through the Glens' by A. R. B. Haldane*

constructed many new roads and routes, which facilitated easier and speedier travel between settlements and along trade routes. Tables 1 and 2 show the extent of the principal highway development in the Highlands and Islands. It should also be recognised that Telford's other major road in Scotland was what is now the M74/A74 (M) between Glasgow and Carlisle, which was the principal land-based trading route between Scotland and England.

Telford's roads were funded by a new financial model. The Government paid 50% of the total cost, while local landowners were expected to donate the requisite land and raise the other 50%. It was a complex, impractical proposition, so most of the money ended up coming from an early form of council tax, administered by the county councils.

Telford's legacy in Scotland includes some of his finest bridges. His first bridge in his native land was at Tongland, near Kirkcudbright, in 1805, but there soon followed his masterpieces at Dunkeld (1809), Craigellachie (1814) and, one of his last, Dean Bridge, over the Water of Leith in Edinburgh. With the exception of Bonar Bridge, all of Telford's bridges survive to this day, albeit Craigellachie is bypassed by its more modern incarnation.

Table 1: Significant upgrades to existing routes

Current number	From	To
A82	Glasgow	Inverness
A83	Tarbet	Inverary
A86	Spean Bridge	Kingussie
A87 (part)	Invergarry	Kyle of Lochalsh
A887	Invermoriston	Bunloyne
B846	Tummel Bridge	Aberfeldy
B852	Dores	Foyers
B862	Inverness	Fort Augustus
A93	Blairgowrie	Balmoral
A939	Balmoral	Grantown on Spey
A938	Carrbridge	Grantown on Spey
A980/A93	Alford Bridge	Potarch Bridge
B9176	Alness	Struie Hill
Arran: A841	Brodick	Kilbride
B880	Brodick	Blackwaterfoot
Jura: A846	Feolin Ferry	(very different from modern road)
Islay: A846	Bridgend	Towards Port Askaig
A847	Bridgend	Portnahaven
Skye: A87	Kyleakin	Uig
A850	Carbost	Dunvegan
A851	Broadford	Armadale
A863/A864	Sligachan	Dunvegan
B886	Fairy Bridge	Stein

Table 2: Significant new routes

Current number	From	To
A815	Strachur	Ardentinny
A816	Kilmelford	Kintraw
A819	Dalmally	Inverary
A826/A896	Loch Carron	Shieldaig
A827	Lix Toll	Killin
A830	Fort William	Arisaig
A831	Beauly	Tomich
A836	Tain	Tongue
A861	Corran Ferry	Kinlochmoidart
A862	Inverness	Dingwall
A890	Auchtertyre	Auchnasheen
B836	Loch Fyne	Loch Riddon
B839	Ardno	Lochgoilhead
B851	Daviot	Inverfarigaig
B8004	Banavie	Gairlochy
B8005	Gairlochy	Loch Arkaig
A9	Dornoch	Thurso (via Helmsdale/ Wick)
A95	Aviemore	Craigellachie

He was something of a perfectionist, as one might expect. He always sought to achieve the best design, whether in a bridge or in a milestone. Unable to unearth a quotation from the great man on milestones in Scotland, I ventured to other major projects that he led. He made a huge contribution to the infrastructure of England and Wales too, of course, including the first publicly funded long-distance road-building project in Britain since the Romans. This was the road between London and Holyhead, and thence by ferry to Dublin, which incorporated his Menai suspension bridge. Determined to mark each of the miles with a milestone, he went looking for a design he could match. Exasperated, he wrote:

'I never saw a proper milestone that I could copy; I looked for three years all over England trying to find out one as a pattern, and after all that could not find out one that looked like a decent milestone.'

Undaunted, he designed his own, built from

an identical stone throughout, a carboniferous limestone sourced from quarries at Red Wharf Bay, meeting his requirements as to hardness of consistency and lightness of colour. The milestones were large, standing some 4ft 6in above the ground, with a distinctly shaped gable end. A cast-iron plate was affixed, with distances marked. Excellent. Telford's only failing in his own key performance target was that, of the potential 265 milestones, it appears that only 120 were laid to the original design.

The turnpikes

Turnpike roads are the next step in the evolution of our road network. And, importantly for our interest, are where we first encounter the milestone in a modern context.

It was the Turnpike Act of 1766 that made milestones compulsory on turnpike roads. These roads were built by private enterprise under licence from the Government and maintained by tolls on those who used them. Before this Act, milestones were put up occasionally, often as charitable acts and commemorations. Many Turnpike Act stones still exist. They are usually 2 to 3 feet high, with the initial letter or abbreviation of the nearest market town shown on two faces, and the distance from it.

The first Turnpike Act in Scotland was in 1713, for the county of Edinburgh, to raise money from traders for upkeep and improvement. Actually, Scotland trailed England in adopting the turnpike system; the first Turnpike Act south of the border had been passed in statute exactly 50 years earlier. It took a while to catch on, too. The first phase in expanding the network of designated toll roads began in 1750 with plans for the initial radial routes out from Edinburgh to Glasgow, London and the north. 1751 saw the Edinburgh to (South) Queen's Ferry road designated as a turnpike road, with (North) Queen's Ferry to Perth (the Great North Road) following in 1753. The Edinburgh to Glasgow road, via Falkirk, was designated in

1752, and the following year the more southerly route via Livingston. Going south towards Carlisle, the Edinburgh to Dumfries road, via Carlops, was designated in 1753. That year saw 17 roads in Scotland become turnpikes, 12 of them being in what would become known as Strathclyde.

There was another lull in turnpike designation for 11 years until the 'turnpike boom' between 1764 and 1789. This period saw the enactment of 18 further Turnpike Acts, many designating several roads within a county under a single statute. A county trust was established in Ayrshire in 1767, then for the counties of Peebles (1771), Lanark (1772) and Dumfries (1777). Although the Great North Road had been a turnpike since 1753, it wasn't until the 1789 and 1790 Acts that provision was made for turnpikes in the counties of Perth, Stirling, Fife and Forfar. Even then, not all the proposals came to fruition; in Fife, for example, as many as 25% of the proposals did not materialise.

Concerns were also raised about the routeing of roads, the design and engineering techniques employed to counter the challenges of gradient and drainage and, not least, the specification of materials used in their construction. In many ways the turnpikes were the 'motorways' of the 18th and 19th centuries. The aim was to provide rapid transport routes between cities and major towns, by the easiest means possible. They often took detours from the direct line to avoid steep gradients and other physical obstacles to speed, or where towns charged 'local tolls'. We find a good example of that latter reason in East Lothian, where the turnpike road heading eastwards from Edinburgh was routed through Athelstaneford, bypassing the much larger settlement of Haddington for the simple reason that it chose to charge a local levy.

For this part of our transport history we have another Scot, or rather Scottish family, to acknowledge – the McAdams.

John Loudon McAdam (1756-1836) was born in Ayr, the 10th son of minor nobility, his mother being the niece of the 7th Earl of Dundonald.

He had a very different childhood from that of Thomas Telford, but his father's business, the Bank of Ayr, failed, and he died when John was 14 years old. John was sent to New York to work for a wealthy uncle and, following the American Revolution, made his own fortune as a merchant dealing in army surplus materials from the war. Unfortunately for McAdam, he'd made the wrong decision on whose side to back during the war. As a loyalist, he backed the loser, so he had all his assets seized before he and his American wife and two children were put on a ship back to Scotland. He did, however, appear to have sufficient funds to purchase an estate at Sauchrie, near Maybole, and he set about re-establishing business interests in an ironworks and in the production of tar-based products from coal.

Like his slightly younger contemporary, Charles Macintosh (1766-1843), also a Scot, McAdam's name lives on in our language for what he 'invented', or probably more accurately 'created'. But let's clear up a common misconception here and now. It isn't tarmacadam. His interest in tar-based products was actually his only connection with tar.

In common parlance, the word 'macadam' means a hard smooth road surface over which vehicles, carriages and wagons, in these days, could travel as fast as horses could draw them. As devised, the construction consisted simply of a layer of small, broken stones resting directly on the sub-soil. He was precise. In 1811 he stated that 'Every piece of stone put into a road which exceeds an inch in any of its dimensions is mischievous.' According to a later pronouncement, he obliged surveyors working for him to carry pocket scales so they could weigh sample stones, any exceeding 6 ounces being too large. Stones that were broken to the right size were angular rather than round, so that under the weight of traffic they consolidated to provide the surface required. This was achieved without tar, or, indeed, any other binding material.

McAdam's earliest engagement with the turnpike trusts was his appointment to the Carrick

John Loudon McAdam, from an engraving by Charles Turner. *Wikimedia Commons*

(Maybole) District Turnpike Trust as a young man, but as his experience in road construction became more widely acknowledged he did what so many Scots do, myself included. He went to England. He was appointed surveyor to the Bristol Turnpike Trust in 1815, and in the subsequent two years produced papers that argued comprehensively for raising the road surface above the surrounding ground level, properly graded and cambered surfaces to aid drainage, and the use of the crushed stone specification. These recommendations, contained in *Remarks on the Present System of Road-Making* and his *Practical Essay on the Scientific Repair and Preservation of Roads* defined methods that were both cheap and durable. Together they represented the greatest advance in road

construction since Roman times, and became known as 'macadamisation', or just 'macadam'.

I hope that clears that up. It's a popular misconception.

If John Loudon McAdam's chief contribution was to road construction techniques, his three sons, William, (Sir) James Nicoll and Loudon, and indeed their children in turn, developed the profession of road surveying as distinctly a management rather than a creative engineering role. Each of the McAdam sons became a general surveyor of turnpike roads. By 1823 the family had been appointed to 75 surveyorships. Most of these were south of the border, but J. L. McAdam himself, by then in his 70s, won six commissions in the neighbourhood of Perth, his final surveyorship being awarded in 1833 on the Perth and Blairgowrie road.

During his last 10 or so years, old man McAdam adopted the rather pleasant habit of spending the summer months in Scotland – indeed, he had a home in Moffat. This fitted well with visits to the various trusts, probably providing advice, for he had a much younger colleague, John McConnell, who handled most of the day-to-day work in the north. Two agreements with Perthshire trusts provided for a specified number of visits each year, four in one case, increased to six later. However, they did make it clear that McAdam need not attend on every occasion – McConnell would do instead. Sounds like a great deal. I've been fortunate, too, in that my talks to clubs and societies the length and breadth of Scotland have given me the opportunity to 'come home' frequently in my retirement years.

There are lessons, though. In 1832 McAdam and McConnell were involved in a quarrel over a proposal by the North Queensferry and Perth Trust to appoint them as surveyors, over a local candidate, on about 40 miles of the Great North Road. Complaints about the condition of the road and the cost of upkeep led to their dismissal, albeit five weeks after McAdam had died. It's wise to ensure, where he's proven to be competent, that

the local man gets a fair kick at the can. However, it's also important to note here that McAdam's rivals in Perthshire and Lanarkshire where our friends Telford and his assistant Mitchell, who had most of Scotland, at least the northern part, already sewn up. Whatever the decision of any public body, what's essential is that proper governance is in place, a lesson as resonate today as back then.

But to return to the history of turnpike trusts…

Turnpikes sought to meet the challenge of providing good roads for the growing economy and the resultant demand for improved communications for trade and personal travel. The concept was to recover the costs of building and maintaining roads through the collection of appropriate tolls. The funding for the turnpike roads, and associated bridges, was raised by using the conversion money from the former statute labour system (days of labour had been converted to a monetary value); by subscription (where the lender was paid interest on his loan or a proportion of the toll); or by a person making it at their own expense and receiving a proportion of the conversion money from each parish through which the road ran. The difference in approach between English and Scottish practice in the primary use of toll monies was discussed earlier. There were no doubt pros and cons to both systems, as in most methodologies used to fund infrastructure.

In any event, it was always intended that the toll system would be a temporary arrangement. Tolls could be removed once all finances had been repaid and the roads were in good condition. This, of course, never happened. 'History repeats itself' is oft quoted as received wisdom. Well, fast forward to the 1990s and the UK Government's preoccupation with the Private Finance Initiative (PFI) to fund public infrastructure projects. Skye Bridge was the first major capital project funded by PFI in Scotland. Its opening in October 1995 brought with it years of protestation from locals and more widely concerned individuals and pressure groups. At £5.90 for a car to cross the

500-metre-long bridge, it was the most expensive toll per metre travelled in Europe. Ably led by a colourful, but principled, character, Brian Robertson, aka Robbie the Pict, and the group's secretary, Andy Anderson, the Skye and Kyle Against Tolls (SKAT) made its strong feelings of resentment known by staged protests, including paying the toll in pennies and driving a flock of sheep across the bridge. The protests may have resulted in 14 days in prison for Andy Anderson, but the cause did not go unheeded. In 2004 the Scottish Parliament paid £27 million to buy out the contract, and toll collection ceased with immediate effect. With more than that amount collected from drivers in the previous nine years, the protestors' argument that it had already paid for itself was certainly vindicated. Interestingly while we're on the subject of tolls, the action in Skye heralded a new dawn in bridge tolls in Scotland. Those on the Erskine Bridge were abolished in 2006, followed by the Forth and Tay Road Bridges in 2008, under the Abolition of Bridge Tolls (Scotland) Act.

But what happens where there is no bridge, but rather a ferry? Obviously this is a vital means of transport and communication to and from the islands. That's where the concept of 'virtual miles' arises, on which is calculated the 'Road Equivalent Tariff', which island residents pay for travel via ferries in Scotland. The fare is based on what would have been the cost of driving the road mileage between, say, Stornoway and Ullapool, had a road been capable of existing. And it's not a 'stick a finger in the air' approach either. In 2011 the Halcrow Group prepared a Report to the Scottish Government, entitled 'Assessment of the impacts of the Road Equivalent Tariff Pilot'.

In the late 18th century and 19th century, the turnpikes created by Act of Parliament under a single piece of legislation often provided for the formation of a series of trusts, usually within the same county. The overarching rules of governance were provided for in General Turnpike Acts, covering a wide range of aspects from the operation of a trust to the exemptions from tolls that might apply. There were such General Acts in 1758 and 1823, but the principal statutory provisions were contained in the Act of 1831.

By way of example, the turnpikes in Ayrshire are uncannily well-documented, thanks to excellent record-keeping but also to the diligent researches of local historians like David Courtney McClure.

The Turnpike Act of 1766 provided for the creation of trusts in Ayrshire, with responsibility for 24 roads, extending in total length to about 255 miles. These were predominantly in the north of the county, north of a line drawn between Ayr and Cumnock. Of particular interest to us is that the Act also provided for milestones to be erected along these roads.

It was another seven years before the southern part of Ayrshire benefitted from the turnpike system. A further 38 roads were built under the 1774 Turnpike Act, and there were further Acts benefitting the county of Ayr: in 1805 (adding 35 roads); 1809; 1818 (particularly central and southern Ayrshire); 1827; and yet again in 1847. As the road between Girvan and Portpatrick was extensively used by the Army, the Government paid for its construction, but its future maintenance would be the responsibility of the local administration.

The tariffs for tolls were contained in the Acts and the actual location of toll points agreed at committee meetings. Tolls were let annually at public auction, advertised in local newspapers.

As an example of the tolls levied, those given in the 1774 Act included:

Coach, chaise or hearse drawn by 6 horses, mares, geldings or mules: 8/-; reducing on a scale down to 1s 6d for 1 horse;
Wagon, wain or cart or other carriage drawn by 6 horses, oxen or other beasts 12/-; reducing on a scale down to 1/- for 1 horse;
Every sledge without wheels: 1/-;
Every drove of oxen or meat cattle 1s 6d per score and so in proportion for any greater or less number;
Every drove of calves, sheep, lambs, hogs or goats: 10d per score and so in proportion for any greater or less number.

Exemptions included pedestrians, soldiers on the march, mill journeys, going to church (ministers were always exempt), and the carrying of lime, manure and hay.

The tollkeeper's lot was not an easy one, regularly having to turn up at any hour to open the gate. They sought to supplement their income through several means, often by being granted a licence to supply wine and spirits, a welcome relief, no doubt, to travellers. One story, from the Irvine to Ayr turnpike, tells of Hugh Donald of Loans, near Troon, who took a glass of whisky out to the driver of a gig while his two companions warmed themselves by the fire. On getting no response from the man, Donald took a closer look, only to find it was a corpse, wrapped in a top coat. His companions were Resurrectionists, who had just dug him out of his grave.

By the latter part of the 19th century the responsibility for highways was in the hands of a miscellany of different bodies, and varied across the country itself.

The Report of the Commission on Public Roads in Scotland provides us with a valuable insight into the road system in the Scotland of 1859. It collected and collated information on the lengths of each category of road, on a county-by-county basis, and the costs incurred in the maintenance and repair of this infrastructure. Table 3 provides a summary of this information on mileage per category of road. The mileages quoted have been rounded from the furlongs and yards recorded in the Report. So, in 1859, there were 21,318 miles of public road in Scotland, of which 26% were turnpiked (including the Parliamentary road in Caithness), with 1,060 tollgates. Zetland is the historic name of Shetland, officially until 1974.

The annual expenditure on maintenance and

management of each class of road was analysed by the Commission. The findings were that the average annual cost for turnpike roads was £25.11s.0d per mile (£25.55), excluding the costs of upkeep of tollhouses and gates; for military and Parliamentary roads £10.6s.2½d per mile (£10.31), and for statute labour roads a mere £6.3s.0d per mile (£6.15). It has to be said, however, that the costs varied considerably between counties and projects, and the average expenditure on statute labour roads, in particular, was seldom sufficient to ensure that the roads were being maintained in a proper state of repair and to safeguard its reputation against criticism for having a predetermined objective, one is left to presume that the Commission did garner evidence. Indeed, the third part of its Report, documenting the written evidence, makes for interesting and at

Table 3:

The road network in Scotland in 1859

County	Total (miles)	Turnpike (miles)	Military (miles)	Parliamentary (miles)	Statute labour/ county/ parish (miles)	Comments
Aberdeen	2,288	436		16	1,836	
Argyll	1,320		80	131	1,109	Islay (92) and Colonsay (15)
Ayr	1,354	714			640	
Banff	663	145		2	516	
Berwick	620	163			457	
Bute	139			17	122	Includes Arran (17)
Caithness	231	136		54	41	Parliamentary road also shown as turnpiked in the Report
Clackmannan	75	37			38	
Dumbarton	280	134			146	
Dumfries	1,170	370			800	
Edinburgh	600	429			171	County
Elgin	484	88	27	9	360	
Fife	736	406			330	
Forfar	977	192			785	Includes Dundee
Haddington	436	141			295	
Inverness	1,157	11	149	383	614	Includes Skye, Harris, North and South Uist and Barra
Kincardine	500	103			397	
Kinross	111	62			49	
Stewartry of Kirkcudbright	760	249			511	
Lanark	1,332	416			916	
Linlithgow	235	76			159	
Nairn	170	22		21	127	
Orkney	0					No figure recorded
Peebles	230	123			107	
Perth	1,667	502			1,165	
Renfrew	501	200			301	
Ross & Cromarty	776			210	566	Includes Lewis
Roxburgh	757	217			540	
Selkirk	183	50			133	
Stirling	508	164			344	
Sutherland	510			96	414	Plus the Scourie to Lairg road (30 miles) built in 1847 and maintained by the Duke of Sutherland
Wigtown	430	51			379	
Zetland	118				118	98 miles on Mainland; 28 miles on Yell
Totals	**21,318**	**5,637**	**256**	**939**	**14,486**	

times amusing reading. It seems that folk with a beef about a certain topic were as likely to put pen to paper then as they are to invoke social media nowadays.

The Commission was instructed to 'assume that the objectionable nature of the tolls and the expediency of their removal, are admitted'. Nevertheless, the principal grumbles against tolls, and the turnpike system in general, included:

- The wont (lack) of any consistent or fixed principles
- The careless and perfunctory manner in which the Turnpike Acts were passed, 'without any proper check or control, have led to much confusion and perplexity'
- The heavy expense of obtaining and renewing Turnpike Acts
- The construction and maintenance of tollhouses, gates and steelyards (for weighing carts and loads)
- The annual advertising and letting of the toll-bars
- The profits accruing to the tacksmen
- The salaries of the collectors where tolls are let
- The risk of loss from percolation
- The fruitful sources of litigation presented under such a system

And that's not all…

Not only was there inequality in the operation of the tolls for the community as a whole, but also by those who used the roads.

The Report took a firm, but fair, line in reaching this measured conclusion:

'The somewhat trite maxim, that "those who use the road should pay for it" has been frequently mentioned to us in justification of the toll system; but the persons who rely on this plan, either forget, or are blind to the fact, that it is practically impossible by means of toll, to make all, or nearly all, those who use the roads, pay for such use. The whole of the space intervening between the

toll-bars is open to use without payment. We have instances in which no toll is exacted for distances of twelve, fourteen or seventeen miles, and it is notorious that large portions of many turnpike roads are used daily by parties who contribute little or nothing by payments at turnpike gates. And besides those who actually use the roads, there are many who rarely travel, and who yet individually derive great benefit from those turnpike roads, to which they contribute nothing.'

The case is rested.

In fact, almost certainly the biggest driver in the demise of the turnpike system was the advent of the railways. They sounded a death knell by offering a faster, more efficient means of transport for goods and passengers, so reducing very substantially the income turnpike trusts were able to generate.

But the way the road system was managed, and the manner of funding, needed a fundamental overhaul, too.

In an effort to bring some consolidation and structure to the road network, and resulting from a recommendation from the Commission, an Act of 1878 provided the statutory basis for the creation of county road boards. Over the ensuing decade the turnpike system was wound up and responsibilities passed to the new county councils established under the Local Government (Scotland) Act 1889, which remained almost intact until 1974/75, since when there have been several restructuring and reorganisational changes.

The Commission's Report also recommended that each of the county road boards appoint a county surveyor and set out, in some detail, both the job description and the qualifying character qualities required for the role:

'A considerable amount of special ability is requisite on one whose duty is to lay out new lines of road, advise and execute important improvements, prepare plans and specifications for bridges, masonry, and earthworks of all

descriptions, adjust and superintend the execution of contracts, exercise a close and vigilant inspection of sub-surveyors and workmen, and, generally, whose intelligence and experience may enable him duly to discharge the varied and important duties of his office.

Nor is professional ability the only requisite for such an officer; it is no less desirable that he should be a person of such status in society as shall enable him to feel and exhibit an adequate degree of independence, and with whom parties of all ranks may co-operate with comfort and satisfaction … it is imperatively necessary that he should possess great firmness, as well as an earnest determination faithfully and fearlessly to discharge his duty. Sound judgement and good temper are required in the ungracious proceeding of having sometimes to decline the wishes of influential parties and to refuse approval of works which have been negligently or insufficiently performed.'

There's a personal link here to the post of county surveyor, created under the 1878 legislation. My father, Forbes Keith, had been Divisional Road Surveyor and Bridge Engineer for Inverness County Council during my formative years. After a spell of five years in the Ministry of Transport in Edinburgh, designing Scotland's motorway systems, he was appointed County Road Surveyor for Stirling County Council in 1968. When reorganisation came along in the mid-1970s, he had to apply for 'his job', which had been retitled to Director of Roads in the newly created Central Regional Council. Fortunately, he was successful and that kept him busy through to retirement in 1984.

Reading the Commission's descriptor for a county surveyor as being 'a person of such status in society' would have brought a wry smile to my parents. When they purchased our home in Stirling, our new neighbours, Atholl and Stewart Watson, who became firm family friends, misheard my father's job title and announced to others that their next door neighbour was the Countess of Ayr!

Private roads

Notwithstanding the growth in the number and extent of public roads in Scotland in the 18th and 19th centuries, many of the roads and tracks were in private ownership. But they were not all in isolated locations or sub-standard. For example, Granton Road in Edinburgh was a private road, designed by Robert Stevenson, the lighthouse engineer, and belonging to the Duke of Buccleuch. It was described in the New Statistical Account for Scotland of 1845 as 'one of the finest roads in Scotland, both as regards to its breadth and construction'. And the Duke charged a toll to use it, as evidenced from the 'ticket' reproduced here.

Granton Road gave access to Granton Harbour, built in the 1830s, when the need for a major deep-water harbour was recognised by R. W. Hamilton, the manager of the General Steam Navigation Company, operator of a fleet of passenger steamers. Leith was at that time only partly developed. The Duke of Buccleuch owned the land and Stevenson provided the engineering design expertise. Queen Victoria and Prince Albert landed at Granton in the Royal Yacht, the *Royal George*, in 1842 on their first state visit to Scotland.

Granton was to become very important as a major transport hub. The Duke of Buccleuch and Sir John Gladstone, father of the Victorian Prime Minister, also constructed a new harbour at Burntisland, 5 miles to the north across the Firth of Forth. With railway connections in place, the Granton to Burntisland roll-on/roll-off train ferry became the first such means of transport in the world. It opened in 1849 and operated until the Forth Bridge was completed in 1890.

Given that the Duke of Buccleuch was the largest private landowner in Scotland, it is not surprising to encounter him in several guises. Among these he was a well-kent face on Turnpike Trusts, acting as trustee on at least three in the hinterland of Edinburgh alone – namely Cramond,

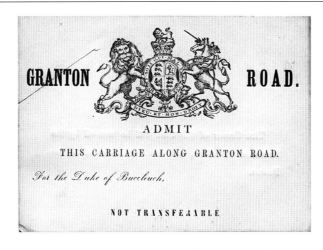

A pass for Granton Road in Edinburgh, granted by the Duke of Buccleuch. On the reverse the card was printed with 'The corner of this card will be torn off by the Person at the Gate, and the Card returned to the Bearer'.

Lasswade & District, and the Post Road Turnpike Trust.

The 20th century and beyond

The 20th century was the age of the motor car. From early beginnings, just before the closing of the Victorian era, the motor industry witnessed the innovation of mass-production and mass-ownership in a globalised economy and the problems generated by traffic congestion. Towards the end of the 20th century the threats of climate change had heightened worries about emissions, calls for decarbonisation and a concerted effort to search for innovative and alternative fuel technologies.

It is worth reflecting that Scotland played an important part in the early history of car production. Scotland's first motor car was built by George Johnston in Springburn, Glasgow, in 1895. Indeed, on 26 January 1896 he was convicted of driving a horseless carriage of his own design on the streets of Glasgow 'at an hour when locomotives are not allowed there'. His fine was 2s 6d – or 12.5p in new, but not equivalent, monetary terms.

Seeing potential in this form of transport, George became managing director of a syndicate, funded by Sir William Arrol, who had built the Forth Bridge, and opened a factory in Camlachie, in the east end of Glasgow, manufacturing vehicles.

Arrol-Johnston's other vehicles included an oil-fuelled, steam-powered tram in 1895, and an electric motor car, to be used for removing the city's refuse, in 1899. Both were built for Glasgow City Corporation.

Before leaving our short history of Scottish roads, it's worth recalling how the road numbering system we all take so much for granted today came into existence. For throughout our journey discovering milestones, reference will be made to the road number on which it is situated, or to give a geographical proximity, as so many of the roads have been realigned over the centuries.

In 1921, 100 years ago, the Ministry of Transport instituted the scheme of road classification that became operational from 1922 and remains so today. The first class, or 'A', roads connected London and, in Scotland, Edinburgh, with large provincial towns. The second class, or 'B', roads comprised roads connecting the minor towns with the first-class roads and with each other. Each 'A' and 'B' road was allocated a number. The whole of Great Britain was divided into nine zones. Starting with the Great North Road (the A1) to Edinburgh, the other roads radiating from London to Dover, Portsmouth, Bath, Holyhead and Carlisle, became the A2, 3, 4, 5 and 6 respectively. In Scotland, the roads radiating from Edinburgh became the A7 to Carlisle, the A8 to Glasgow/Gourock and the A9 to Inverness, eventually Thurso. Each road takes its initial number from the zone in which it starts and even if it crosses into another zone it still retains its initial number.

In Scotland, the motorway system is numbered

Scotland gets on the motoring map with the Arrol-Johnston. *Britain by Car*

motorway along its length, neither does the A68 Edinburgh to Jedburgh road; the M68 is actually in Lancashire, being the Middleton Link opened in 1972. However, it is now part of the M62, which used to be the M66. The A96 road between Aberdeen and Inverness does not have a matching motorway either. The M96 isn't even open to the public – it's the section of road used for training purposes at the Fire Service College near Moreton-in-Marsh in Gloucestershire. Straightforward?

Transport Scotland publishes statistics annually on all manner of transport matters. According to the latest statistics in *Transport Scotland No 38*, in 2019 there were 56,591km of public road in Scotland. That's 35,369 miles – based on 1km = 5/8th of a mile – thus representing a 66% increase in the extent of the road network since the Commission's records of 162 years earlier. It is also almost 15% of the UK total (241,700 miles/386,720km), if these sort of statistics grab your imagination. Of these Scottish roads, only 3,961km (7%) are trunk roads (of which 16.3% are motorways and a further 20.8% dual carriageway). These trunk roads are managed centrally by Transport Scotland. The bulk of the public road network is managed by local authorities. The non-trunked 'A' roads account for 7,357km (13%), so 80% of the total network is minor roads, being classified 'B', 'C' or 'Unclassified', extending to 45,273km. These are, of course, only the 'adopted' roads. Scotland is the richer for this wonderful web of country roads and urban streets.

More than a quarter of the total trunk road network, and one-seventh of the country's road network, is within the area of the Highland Council. Around 10% of the Scottish road network is within the Aberdeenshire Council area, and a further 8% lies within the Dumfries & Galloway Council boundary. That means that, in total, one-third of Scotland's road network lies within the jurisdiction of these three authorities.

There were three million motor vehicles licensed in Scotland in 2018, which is 12% higher than in 2000 and up from a 0.9 million in 1964. Of

after the 'A' route it follows. The M9, therefore, follows broadly the route of the A9, as far north as the Keir Roundabout, south of Dunblane, and the M74 follows the route of the A74, although the section south of Abington is the A74(M). The A7 through the Scottish Borders does not have a motorway associated with it, so there is no M7. There are, however, several idiosyncrasies. The A92(M) is a spur off the M90, at Junction 2a in Fife, and the M85 was 'lost' when the Friarton Bridge was opened in 1978 and the road became

part of the M90, south-east of Perth. Similarly, the 6 miles of the A8(M), constructed as the Renfrew Bypass in 1968, became part of the M8.

Scotland also boasts the highest numbered motorway in the UK – the M898 in Renfrewshire – and it's also the shortest. At half a mile in length, it was constructed in 1975 as the spur route from the M8 towards the Erskine Bridge. It terminates at the A726 at the location of the former toll booths for the bridge, which were removed in 2006. Just as the A7 does not have a those with a car, 71% of households have at least one car available for private use, and 29% have two or more cars.

Another couple of statistics before we move on… Scotland has 10.4km of road per 1,000 of the population, compared with only 6.2km per 1,000 across the whole of Great Britain. And the roads are getting busier. In 2018 48.1 billion vehicle kilometres were travelled on Scottish roads, the highest recorded level and some 8% more than in 2008. The volume of car traffic on major roads has more than trebled, from an estimated 9,300 million vehicle kilometres in 1975 to between 28,000 and 30,000 million vehicle kilometres for the last ten years. More traffic chaos? Surprisingly not. Car and van users reported that 13% of journeys were delayed due to traffic congestion in 2018 – the same percentage as in 2008. So, the answer to the query 'Are we nearly there yet?' was the same in 2018 as it had been a decade earlier. Temperamentally, at any rate.

Our milestone heritage: Strathclyde, including Glasgow

Ayrshire

People collect the oddest things. Stamps, coins, football programmes – all these are commonplace. But milestones? Yet in 1922 the Glenfield Ramblers from Kilmarnock, visiting Montgreenan Estate – whether with the permission of the owner is unknown – came across clusters of milestones 'in twos and threes where the side-paths join the avenues'. Montgreenan is in Kilwinning parish in north Ayrshire, and the estate was owned by Sir James Bell, a Glasgow worthy. He was well-connected professionally, being the chairman of the Glasgow Life Insurance Company and the deputy chairman of both the Clydesdale Bank and the Glasgow & South Western Railway. He was well-connected physically, too, with his various offices in Glasgow, as the G&SWR had built a station at Montgreenan in 1878. Sir James purchased the estate, including the mansion house with its architectural features by Alexander 'Greek' Thompson, when he was created a baronet in 1895. I am somewhat at a loss to know the whys and wherefores behind his passion for collecting milestones to adorn the grounds of his property. 'Well, why not?' is probably the best response. Better milestones than garden gnomes, in my view, and certainly one way to secure their preservation, even if not in situ.

We're indebted to local historian David Courtney McClure for his researches on the Montgreenan milestones. David carried out a detailed survey in 2009, recording the 19 milestones found. Fourteen of them are red sandstone pillars, with the remainder being

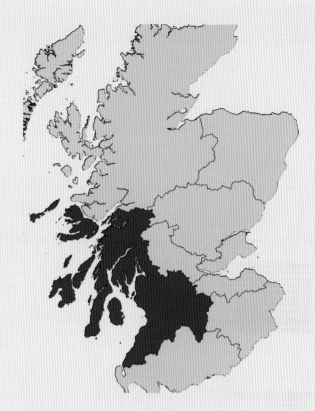

Strathclyde. *Wikimedia Commons*

granite. They are in varying conditions, the granite having weathered better, and they originate from various parts of Ayrshire. However, Bell had a field day on what is now the B730, as five of the stones originated on that road.

David has undertaken a significant body of research throughout Ayrshire and the website ayrshirehistory.org.uk contains much of the material in an 'Illustrated Catalogue of Ayrshire Milestones'. Well worth a look.

The various Roads Acts of 1767, 1774, 1805, 1809 and 1827 provided for a network of turnpike roads across Ayrshire, most notably, but not exclusively, in the north and east of

The Kilmarnock/Troon/Tarbolton guidepost at Mountgreenan. It would have originated from Bogend Toll, at the junction of the A77 and B730, prior to the construction of the flyover. *David Courtney McClure*

'Crosshouse (R) 1¼ miles 51 yards; Kilmaurs 3 miles 3 furlongs 66 yards.' *David Courtney McClure*

'Kilmarnock (R) 2½ miles 14 yards; Dundonald (L) 2 miles 7 furlongs 176 yards.' This milestone would have originated at the junction of the Crosshouse/ Kilmarnock roads (now the A759 and B751), near Gateshead. Although dating from circa 1860, it appears not to be the stone shown on the OS map of 1857. *David Courtney McClure*

the county. Early consideration of milestones seems to have been relegated in the order of priorities, however, and it's not until October 1778 that we see mention of them in a trustees' meeting held in Ayr. The Minutes record that the decision was taken to measure the roads and erect milestones. However, we await a further 30 years before evidence of action is forthcoming. Then, in February 1808, it is recorded that milestones are to be set up on the road from Irvine through

Stewarton and also on the coast road from Irvine through Saltcoats to Largs, as far as the county boundary at Kelly Bridge. As there is no mention of repair or replacement of existing milestones, it may safely be construed that these were new milestones 'to be set up'. These were two of the 25 principal and branch roads established by the Roads Act of 1767, so it had taken 41 years to get thus far.

The existence of milestones is confirmed

in June 1809, as representations were made by the Earl of Eglinton, through whose estate at Skelmorlie the coast road passed, that the inscriptions should be more conspicuous, so the stonemason had to set to work with his chisel. The Earl also proposed that

A milestone on the turnpike road from Kilmarnock to Stewarton via Kilmaurs (A735).
David Courtney McClure

A milestone at the junction of a minor road at Craigie on the Irvine to Dalmellington turnpike.
David Courtney McClure

'…handbills should be circulated offering a reward of two guineas for discovering the person or persons who have broken damaged or defaced or who shall hereafter break damage or deface any milestone erected on said road to be paid by the cashier (of the trust) on conviction of the offender, which was agreed to.'

However, the decision to erect milestones on the Irvine to Stewarton road may not have been acted upon, as in July 1832 a further decision was

made so to do. That's 65 years after the statutory provision, so in answer to the query 'Are we nearly there yet?', one might somewhat exasperatingly respond, 'Bide your time.'

Of course, route changes such as realignments due to road improvement schemes or boundary adjustments can result in the distances recorded on the milestones needing to be revised. We know, for example, that a re-routing had occurred on the Irvine to Largs road, described as 'a cut from the bottom of Chapelton Brae by West Kilbride, to the

junction of the main road at or near the south end of Kilrusken Wood'.

Administration of the turnpike trustees' committees was rationalised after the 1805 Act, with three distinct districts created for Ayr, Kilmarnock and Irvine. There was considerable activity in the Kilmarnock district in the 1830s. On 5 January 1832 the Kilmarnock trustees accepted an 'offer for erecting milestones and fingerposts':

Quote for milestones and fingerposts to Kilmarnock District Roads Committee (dated 5 January 1832):

Description   **Cost (£ s d)**
For repairing Mile Stones on the Irvine road:

37 Large Mile Stones	£20 7s 0d
24 Large Fingerposts	£15 0s 0d
54 less sized Mile Stones	£24 6s 0d
21 less sized Fingerposts	£11 0s 6d
Putting up one Fingerpost and repairing Mile Stones on Irvine Road	£2 2s 6d

Total	£72 16s 0d

A single large milestone was priced at 11 shillings, with a similarly sized fingerpost at 12s 6d.

By 1856 we have evidence of some degree of sophistication in the recording of road lengths, in the mapping and recording work by William Railton for the Kilmarnock District Trust, as described in Table 4, which is taken from 'Map of the Turnpike & Parish Roads in the District of Kilmarnock; prepared for the Trustees by William Railton, 1856'. In case you think you've heard the name William Railton in other connections, he was an English architect, best known for his design of Nelson's Column in Trafalgar Square in London.

Table 4: Kilmarnock District Roads, 1856

No	Description	Section		All	
		Miles	Furlongs	Miles	Furlongs
1	Kilmarnock to Flockbridge by Drumbowie	9	2		
	Including branch by Kingswell & thence	2	3½		
	To County March towards Eagle-sham	1	1	12	6½
2	Kilmarnock to Lochgate by Galston	11	0		
	Including Hurlford to Riccarton	1	6½	12	6½
3	Kilmarnock by Treeswoodhead			5	1
4	Kilmarnock by Craigie to Road No 16			3	6
5	Kilmarnock to Ayr by Monkton			8	2½
6	Kilmarnock to Dundonald			5	1
7	Dundonald to Troon			4	5½
8	Road No 6 at Damdyke to No 16 at Plowland			1	2
9	Kilmarnock to Irvine			7	0
10	Kilmarnock to Stewarton by Kilmaurs and	5	5½		
	Kilmarnock to Stewarton by Shaws Bridge	3	6	9	3½
11	Fenwick to Kilmaurs			3	4
12	Kilmaurs to Gatehead by Cross-house			3	3
13	Thornton to No 6 at Gatehead from No 6 at Fairlie Gate by Symington to No 5 at Bowbridgehill	5	2		
	Including from Fortyacres to No 5 at Backhill	1	0		
	And from Old Rome by Caprington to No 5 at Backhill	1	7	8	1
14	Braehead to Road No 15 at Grassyards	4	3		
	Including Branch by Silverwood to No 15 at Moscow	3	1	7	4
15	Galston to Road No 1 at Laighmuir			6	2
16	Irvine by Dundonald towards Little Mill			10	2
Total				**109**	**2½**

Left: This square-section stone is set in the wall of the graveyard of Riccarton Parish Church (at the junction of Old and New Streets). The left-hand face reads 'Hurlford 1¾/Galston 4¾', and the right-hand face 'Kilmarnock 1/Ayr 11'. There must be an arrow for Ayr below ground level.
Both David Courtney McClure

Ayrshire has a strong tradition of milestones, dating from the era of the turnpike roads. While some remain, many were removed, as in other parts of the country, during the Second World War, lest the Germans invaded and sought to find their way to Moscow. I have chosen Moscow, as it always seems odd to me for an Ayrshire village to have a Russian name. Legend has it that it's a corruption of Moss Hall, but the spelling was amended in 1812 to mark Napoleon's retreat from Moscow in Russia. Just to confuse the invading Germans further, the Volga Burn runs through the Ayrshire village.

Patna is another odd name for Ayrshire, but that village was created by William Fullarton in 1802 to house miners working down the coal mines on his estate. His father had worked with the British East India Company. Strange how names come about. Mind you, Major General Sir Thomas Macdougall Brisbane from Largs gave his name to the Australian city, and there's a California near Falkirk, a Denmark near Arbroath, a Joppa near Edinburgh, and a Jericho near Glamis…!

What became of all these milestones and fingerposts removed as part of the war effort? Some

Left and above: A refurbished milestone at The Cross, Mauchline, at the junction of the A76 and B743. *Both David Courtney McClure*

A milestone on the B7023 at Crosshills in Kirkmichael Parish, the distance to Newton Stewart concealed by paving. *The Milestone Society*

A milestone on the coast road between Girvan and Ballantrae (A77), 6 miles from Girvan, with a backdrop of 'Paddy's Milestone' (Ailsa Craig). This appeared on the front cover of Newsletter No 20 (January 2011 edition) of The Milestone Society. The drawing is by Terry Keegan from a photograph taken by his son, John. *David Viner, The Milestone Society*

were returned, others replaced, but undoubtedly many did not survive, at least not for their original purpose. You'll find a few in gardens, however, so perhaps we've much for which to thank Sir James

In Kilmarnock, the three 19th-century milestones all relate to the town's toll roads. The one on London Road is in a public garden, adjacent to No 18, past Deansburn, the inscriptions reading 'Kilmarnock [directional arrow to the right] 2 furlongs 63 yards' and 'Grassyards [directional arrow to the left] 4[?] miles 154 yards'. Grassyards was the name of a farm. On Portland Road the 1850s milestone is tall, squared sandstone with carved letters and numerics, with a later addition of a feather-edged capstone. The inscription reads 'Dundonald 5 Troon 9'; the inscription on the other side is eroded. The milestone is located within the grounds of the Holy Trinity Episcopalian Church. On Glasgow Road the milestone is a three-sided pillar of tooled ashlar with carved Baskerville lettering and numerics. The inscription reads, on the north elevation, 'Kilmarnock 1' and on the south elevation 'Glasgow 20'. This milestone is the only one of the three to remain in its original location.

Two miles west of Kilmarnock lies the settlement of Knockentiber, on the toll road between Kilmaurs and Crosshouse. On the 1860s OS map there's a milestone shown near Busbie Junction on the bridge over the Carmel Burn; it appears to read 'Glasgow 32 miles' and 'Gretna 84

miles'. The old railway from Kilmarnock to Irvine branches at Busbie Junction (Crosshill station) and is now a cycle path, maintained by Sustrans.

Ayrshire also has a tradition of fingerposts. Again we have to thank David McClure for his research here. He recorded 15 remaining fingerposts in the county in the 1990s, albeit that all but one was located in Carrick. Perhaps this is because they were, in general, on quieter roads or those that had not been subject to road-widening schemes over the years. These fingerposts were dated from about 1927, and the fingers were manufactured by the Royal Label Factory, at that time in Stratford-upon-Avon, for Ayr County Council. The company cast the fingers in spelter, the most common commercial form of zinc, which made them very heavy. The posts were bought in.

The spelling of Minnyshant (Minishant) is slightly incorrect, but this reflects an historical variant rather than an administrative error. Minnyshant was the home of John Loudon

Above left: Other stones, like this one on the B743 in Sorn, merely provide directions. *The Milestone Society*

Left: Straight-talking from this milestone on the A714, near Pinminnoch. *The Milestone Society*

An old fingerpost at the junction of the B742 and B7045 near Maybole. *Mary and Angus Hogg (Creative Commons Licence)*

Above: Compare and contrast: a milestone and fingerpost at the junction of the A77 with an unclassified road to Dailly. *The Milestone Society*

McAdam for several years following his return from America in 1783. (Don't confuse Minnyshant with Minnigaff, which is in Kirkcudbrightshire – both great names.) There was a substantial refurbishment programme carried out by South Ayrshire Council in 1999/2000, initiated by its Rural Affairs Committee, which also included old milestones. The local contractor for this specialist work was David Ogilvie Engineering Limited of Kilmarnock.

It's good to see that in some modern developments fingerposts are being incorporated as part of the street furniture, such as the example in North Ayrshire illustrated here.

A modern fingerpost in Stevenston, North Ayrshire. *Dr Adrian Sumner*

Arran

The largest island in the Firth of Clyde, Arran is often depicted as 'Scotland in miniature'. Brodick Castle was owned by successive generations of the Dukes of Hamilton until the National Trust for Scotland acquired it from Lady Jane Fforde in 1958, in lieu of death duties due by her mother, the Dowager Countess of Montrose. However, those of you of my vintage will find altogether more fascinating the tale relating to Lochranza Castle. It was used as the model castle in *The Black Island*, in Herge's *The Adventures of Tintin* Volume 7, if you want to re-read it.

The island is circumnavigated by a coastal road, declassified to 'C' for most of its 55-mile length, although the road (as the A841) rises to 660 feet through the Pass of Boguillie, between Sannox and Lochranza. The Arran Coastal Way provides the walker with a full 65 miles hugging the seashore. There are two roads across the island, both offering stunning views. The Brodick to Blackwaterfoot road is called 'The String' (the B880, a Telford road, named from the Norse word 'strengr', meaning 'cord' or 'bridle'), while the slightly shorter, termed 'The Ross', runs from Lamlash to Lagg/Sliddery via Glen Scorrodale. Lagg's claim to fame is its beach, known as Cleat's Shore, dubbed one of the 'quietest nudist facilities in the world'.

The builders of the coastal road in the 1850s erected milestones along its length, starting and ending at Brodick Old Quay, with its dramatic backdrop of Goat Fell. The String and The Ross also have milestones. On the 1910 Edition of the OS map the first two milestones from the west end of The String are numbered 26 and 27 (following on from 25), whereas they are actually 10 and 9 miles distant from Brodick. Perhaps this provides a clue to when the milestones were put in place, or is it a rare mistake by Ordnance Survey?

About 100 yards from milestone 52, at Corrie, between Sannox and Brodick, is the 'Doctor's Bath'. It measures 12 feet in length, 6 feet in width and 5 feet in depth, with steps down into it and a removable plug, hewn from the red sandstone rock above low-water mark. It therefore has a change of water with each tide. Whether Dr McCredy believed in hydropathic treatment or merely enjoyed bathing in seawater is unknown, but 170 years later people still enjoy using it.

There are 79 milestones recorded on Arran – 55 on the

Stone 2, overlooking Brodick Bay and beyond to Goat Fell on Arran. *Alan and Ruth Thompson*

A broken stone and its replacement on the A841, north of Bealach Gaothar in Kilmory Parish. *Christine Minto, The Milestone Society*

coastal road. For this, and indeed the fact that so many have been maintained, we have to thank Alan and Ruth Thompson. They retired to Lamlash and, picking up on earlier work in the 1970s by Anthony and Frances Campbell (*Courier – Milestones of Arran*), they published *Milestones of Arran* in 2000. Ruth and Alan even found nine of the stones previously recorded as 'missing'. They followed the Campbells' idea of using the milestones as a 'hook' to describe the island's scenery, geology and natural and local history. The Thompsons' dedicated conservation efforts are legendary. To celebrate her 75th birthday, Ruth walked all the 81 miles, passing all 79 milestones in three days. That's what I call a 'Milestone Birthday'.

Stone 11 on the Ross Road, Arran. *Alan and Ruth Thompson*

Lanarkshire

Lanarkshire county sign. *Ken Diamond collection, The Milestone Society*

One of only three milestones found in north Lanarkshire. *Christine Minto, The Milestone Society*

In South Lanarkshire is a milestone built into a stone wall. It's 8 miles from the centre of Glasgow and 1½ miles from Hamilton.

Also in South Lanarkshire, beside the B7078, which runs parallel with the M74, Alverie Weighill found a milestone 'resting' on the road verge. The B7078 and the B7076 to the south are actually the old carriageways of the A74, with the motorway constructed to its east. Imagine how long it took to drive from Glasgow to Carlisle in the 1960s and '70s? Much of the old road signage remains, including large white signs with a blue border for local destinations. Cycle route No 74 was also created out of one of the carriageways.

A South Lanarkshire milestone. *Christine Minto, The Milestone Society*

The M74 becomes the A74(M) at Abington, but the B7078 and B7076 are connected by a short section of the A720 between Junctions 13 and 14 on the A74(M).

The milestone, as found, on the B7078 to the north of Abington. *Alverie Weighill*

The main road from Ayr to Edinburgh is the A70, known to all Scots as the 'Lang Whang' – a 'whang' is a narrow strip of leather, usually a bootlace. Robert Burns was a frequent traveller – his Edinburgh Edition being the second publication of his works – and he stayed regularly at the then thatched Wee Bush Inn in Carnwath. All Burns could think of to engrave on the window (a habit for which he had a reputation), was 'Lang Whang, Lang Whang, Lang Bloody Whang'. This is undoubtedly Burns speak for 'Are we nearly there yet?' Burns first had his works published in the Kilmarnock Edition in 1785. Scottish historian Dr Ian Grimble claimed that 'the Kilmarnock Edition made Robert Burns Caledonia's Bard, but the Edinburgh Edition elevated him into a position amongst the world's greatest poets.'

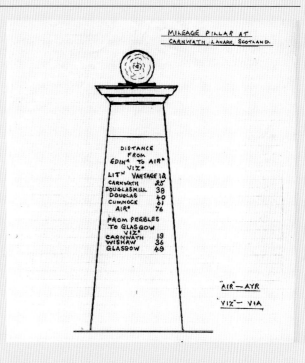

A drawing of an obelisk milestone in Carnwath. Note the misspelling of 'Ayr'. *Christine Minto*

Glasgow

The most populous city in Scotland, by some distance, but a paucity of milestones. Is that because Glaswegians are born with a built-in satnav, or were the vast bulk of milestones removed as the city was regenerated and the M8 motorway driven through its midst?

South of the Clyde we do find a milestone. It's set against the sandstone wall of a building on the south side of Paisley Road West, near its junction with Copland Road. The surface facing east is inscribed '2 miles to Glasgow' while the one facing west reads '5 miles to Paisley/21 miles to Greenock'.

Glasgow has a rich built heritage, magnificent structures and outstanding architecture. Without appearing rude, I don't think its milestone legacy matches that standard.

The Glasgow milestone. *Christine Minto, The Milestone Society*

Dunbartonshire

It's not all gloom, however. North-west of the city lie Bearsden and Milngavie, with a series of three mileposts dating from 1861, which are certainly worthy of note. Bearsden was the location of a Roman fort – indeed, Roman baths were unearthed in the 1970s – but the town grew substantially as a suburb when the railway arrived in 1863. In the centre of Milngavie there is a granite obelisk marking the southern end of the 96 miles of the West Highland Way. The milestones, all Listed Category C, are described as small, single-stage, rectangular, slightly bow-

fronted cast-iron posts with embossed pointing hands, names and miles. That in Milngavie Road (A81) in Bearsden is situated at the junction with Kilmardinny Avenue, at the entrance to Bearsden Golf Club, and shows 'Glasgow Royal Exchange 6/Balfron 13'. However, both of the other two mileposts, one at McFarlane Road, Bearsden, and the other at Glasgow Road, Milngavie, also show the distance to 'Aberfoil', which seems a schoolboy howler of a spelling mistake for Aberfoyle. Not so. 'Aberfoyle' is a 20th-century variant of previous spellings, to wit Abirfull, Aberfule, Aberfoill and Aberfoil.

Rather more splendid cast-iron mileposts can be found along the route from Glasgow to Aberfoyle, as that in Killearn Parish illustrated here.

The Bearsden milepost. *John S. Riddell*

Dunbarton county sign. *Ken Diamond collection, The Milestone Society*

The milestone near Killearn, showing 16 miles to the Royal Exchange in Glasgow and 10 miles to 'Aberfoil'. *The Milestone Society*

Argyll

Argyll county sign. *Ken Diamond collection, The Milestone Society*

The milestones on the road leading up to the Mull of Kintyre Lighthouse, described as the most tortuous in Scotland, are a legacy from the building of Scotland's second lighthouse. It was designed in 1788 by Thomas Smith. In case you thought all lighthouses are by the Stevenson family, then you are not wrong. Thomas was the first Chief Engineer appointed by the then Northern Lighthouse Trust and was the stepfather of Robert Stevenson. Young Robert keenly followed in his footsteps and the rest, as they say, is history. In fact, this lighthouse was rebuilt in 1820, by Robert, and the milestones may well date from then. To avoid you reaching for the excellent history of Scottish lighthouses, *At Scotland's Edge* by Keith Allardyce and Evelyn M. Hood (well worth a read), let me advise that the first Scottish lighthouse was completed in 1787 at Kinnaird Head in Fraserburgh.

The climb may be steep, but the views from the Mull of Kintyre are spectacular. On a clear day the coast of Antrim in Northern Ireland is visible, as is Ailsa Craig. You can almost hear the drone of the Campbeltown Pipe Band playing Paul McCartney's

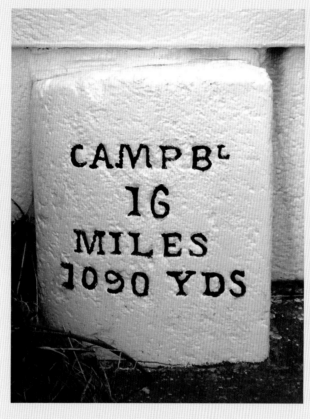

A 'Precision Milestone' at Kintyre Lighthouse. *Patrick Mackie, Geograph, Creative Commons Licence*

composition 'Mull of Kintyre' with which his band, Wings, had a Christmas No 1 in 1977.

The words are evocative, and personal too. Paul has long owned a farm on the peninsula and recorded the song in his studio there.

'Mull of Kintyre
Oh mist rolling in from the sea,
My desire is always to be here
Oh Mull of Kintyre'

And people bought it, making it the first single to sell more than two million copies.

Staying on the Kintyre peninsula, there are

good examples of milestone castings by the Bonnybridge Foundry on the minor road (B8024) between Tarbert and Kilberry.

Equally intriguing is a milestone on the B843, beyond Machrihanish, which is inscribed 'PANS/½ MILE'. There's no place named 'Pans', but close examination of the OS map from 1866 reveals the presence of 'saltpans'. Solved.

A Bonnybridge-style milepost. *Christine Minto, The Milestone Society*

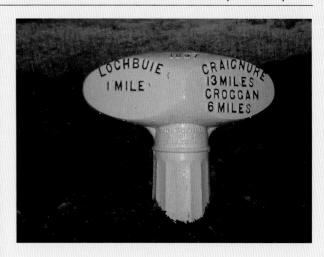

One of the Smith Patterson mileposts on Mull.
Christine Minto, The Milestone Society

Tarbert/Kilberry milepost. *Christine Minto,
The Milestone Society*

A milestone set into a stone wall on the B842, in the
parish of Saddell and Skipness. *The Milestone Society*

The Kintyre 'Pans' milepost. *Christine Minto,
The Milestone Society*

Mull

The island, not the peninsula, is best known for
the painted houses in Tobermory, immortalised
for children as 'Balamory', the magnificent beach
at Calgary and the splendour of Ben More. It also
hosts several appealing milestones on the road
from Salen to Ffionphort.

Cast by Smith Patterson & Co of the Pioneer
Foundry in Blaydon-on-Tyne, they are the only
ones on which that founder inserted the date –
1897 – which coincided with Queen Victoria's
Diamond Jubilee. It would make historical
research very much easier if the foundry or the
mason had inscribed the date on all their products,
but it's very much the exception.

On the road from Salen and Aros across to
Dervaig, the milestones are of a distinct pink
granite; the pink hue is due to the potassium
feldspar mineral in the stone, and the source is

A granite milestone, 2 miles from Dervaig.
Christine Minto, The Milestone Society

Tormore Quarry on the Ross of Mull. It produced high-quality stone for Iona Abbey, just a few miles away, for Dunrobin Castle near Golspie, Stevenson's Skerryvore lighthouse, 11 miles south-west of Tiree, for the High Commissioner's House in Wellington, New Zealand, and Eric Liddell's memorial in China, as well as many other structures around the globe.

Across the Sound of Mull lies the peninsula of **Morvern**, bounded to the south by Loch Linnhe and to the north by Loch Sunart. I spent a summer there as a student on Ardtornish Estate. The road from the Corran/Ardgour ferry to Lochaline (A861/A884 from Strontian) measures 32 miles; at least on all but one sign, where the total road mileage is shown as 32½ miles. Where that half-mile went is anyone's guess. The mileage posts continue past Lochaline, down the minor shore road (B849) past Clashfern, Fuinary and Dorlin, signposted originally to the road end at Bonnavoulin (10¼ miles), but this now appears as Drimnin, actually the same destination. The original road is shown on the OS map of 1880. The poor relief project that improved this road in the 1880s extended what is a track beyond Drimnin past Auliston Point leading to Loch Teacuis. These mileposts are similar to those encountered on Mull, being black and designed by Smith Patterson & Co. They do not have dates inscribed, however. There's also a minor road (B8043) leading from Lochuisge (which translates as 'loch water') towards the sea at Loch a Choire, before heading northwards to join the A861 at Inversanda. The mileposts here are described as 'small, slim, decoratively shaped post with two small flat plates just big enough to carry the information'.

As well as fingerposts, this road also has the remnants of old milestones, so all in all Morvern is well-endowed with old distance markers.

Right: One of the hazards of locating mileposts in the West Highlands! This Smith Patterson & Co post on the B849 indicates 'Drimnin ¾ mile' and 'Dorlin 6 miles'. *Ian Jolly, The Milestone Society*

Above: A fingerpost on the B8043 near Kilmalieu in Ardgour Parish. *Christine Minto, The Milestone Society*

Morvern has witnessed more than its share of population loss. There were 1,500 people living on the peninsula in the 1830s, when Lochaline was built. It was a measure by the British Fisheries Board to stimulate economic growth, and although this was sustained through the 1840s, when a new pier was constructed, within a few decades more than half the population had departed from the pier, emigrating to seek new lives in Canada, Australia and New Zealand. But Morvern still exports. Not people, but granite and sand. Aggregate Industries Ltd exports 6 million tons of granite annually from its super-quarry operation at Glensanda on Loch Linnhe. To minimise the visual impact, the granite is extracted from inside the Meall-na-h-Easaiche mountain by means of a 'glory hole' and conveyor belt, a pioneering development in alternative quarrying technology. It's estimated that the granite reserves at Glensanda will last for another 100 years. Silica sand, exceptionally white and of 99.8% purity, and the only source in Britain suitable for very high-grade domestic glass and optical lens manufacture, is mined by Lochaline Quartz Sand Company, the owners since 2012. These reserves may last another 40 years, thus ensuring Morvern's importance for its minerals.

Islay

On the road to Ardtalla there is a rock painted as a milestone. But that's only the start. The milestone at Keills (which changed from 'Keils' to 'Keills' in the 1890s) is painted with a map of the Isle of Islay on the top and two boats, the *Vital Spark* and *The Maggie* on each front face.

Also on Islay we encounter the use of Roman numerals in quoting distances. Mostly these are on conventional stone or concrete posts painted white. Occasionally, as seen in the photograph of the example on the road between Ardtalla and Port Ellen, a natural stone is used to very good effect.

The Ardtalla/Port Ellen stone. *Christine Minto, The Milestone Society*

It's not common to find a 'C' class road named on a direction sign. This example on Islay Christine has entitled 'ABC' – I wonder why? *Christine Minto, The Milestone Society*

Jura

Jura is renowned for its Paps (three steep-sided conical quartzite mountains), which dominate the landscape. The island is also well-known for its intermittent resident during the 1940s, George Orwell, who wrote *Nineteen Eighty-Four* while living at Barnhill. The farmhouse is at the northern end of Jura, and the Corryvreckan Whirlpool is the consequence of the fierce tides racing between Jura and its northern neighbour, Scarba, meeting the pyramid-shaped basalt pinnacle, reaching to just beneath the surface. It's the third largest whirlpool in the world. Well worth a visit, but get an experienced sailor to take you, and look out for the wonderful sight of white-tailed sea eagles. Orwell and his son lost their boat and nearly their lives on a fishing trip here.

The milestone on the A846 at Keills showing 'P(ort) Askaig 1/Bridgend 7' with decorative embellishments. Bridgend had originally read '6¾', so was rounded up when the paint job took place. *The Milestone Society*

A Jura 'triangular' milestone on the A846 near Feolin. *Christine Minto, The Milestone Society*

Although Jura is Scotland's eighth largest island, it's ranked 31st by population. It's remote. Orwell, who went by his real name Eric Blair while living on the island, called it 'extremely ungetatable'. There's only one road, a single track (A846), but there are 17 milestones, typically in the 'Jura style' of triangular section, ably demonstrated by the milestone between Craig House and Feolin illustrated here.

Easdale

Some 8 miles south of Oban, the Bridge over the Atlantic takes you to Seil and onward to Easdale and its former slate quarries. The post illustrated here is one of two complete examples remaining on the B844 from Kilninver, which are of the rarer Bonnybridge style with the ball on top. The milepost at Balvicar is included in Canmore's records, but it is part of a disappearing heritage.

At Knipoch (A816) on Loch Feochan stands a milestone inscribed 'AG 32½/MT 9½/ON 8'. 'AG' is Ardrishaig, south of Lochgilphead, 'MT' is Melfort, and 'ON' is Oban.

At the head of Loch Long, the junction of the A814 and B838, near Arrochar, hosts a milestone with fingers extended on directional hands, very ornate and well preserved, but the real pièce de

More welcoming than the rather bland Knipoch example is this simple stone advising the traveller in Argyll that there are 15 miles still to go to Inverary and 26 to Oban. *Christine Minto, The Milestone Society*

The Bonnybridge-style milepost on the A844. *Christine Minto, The Milestone Society*

The milestone on the A816 at Knipoch. *The Milestone Society*

résistance is where the milepost is mounted on its own decorative wall on the A814 at Colgrain, as illustrated overleaf.

More off the beaten track, on the south side of Loch Awe (B840), we come across the RAC village sign for Portsonachan, incorporating the distances to Ford and from Dalmally. Sadly

The ornate milestone on the A814. *Christine Minto, The Milestone Society*

somewhat rusted, it does strike a nostalgic note for those of us who remember this pedigree of signage.

At Duck Bay on Loch Lomond there is an example, one of many in the area, that records furlongs – 6 miles and 5 furlongs to Luss. That translates as 6 and five-eights of a mile, for those who need to reread the section on distance measurement.

At the Glencoe Visitor Centre, operated by the National Trust for Scotland, we find a granite

Portsonachan village sign. *Christine Minto, The Milestone Society*

Arriving at Dunoon Pier, you'll want to know both the direction and the mileage to your intended destination… *Christine Minto, The Milestone Society*

milestone. Glen Coe, a U-shaped glacial valley, is one of 40 National Scenic Areas in Scotland. In 2010 Scottish Natural Heritage described the area in terms of the 'soaring, dramatic splendour of Glen Coe' and 'the suddenness of its transition between high mountain pass and the lightly woodland strath in the lower glen.' The A82 is 'one of the classic Highland journeys'. The area also witnessed a bloody incident in Scottish history, the Massacre of Glencoe. On 13 February 1692 38 men of the Clan MacDonald were killed by Government forces who were billeted with them, on the grounds that they had not

…while across on the road to Tighnabruaich there can be little doubt you are nearly there… *Christine Minto, The Milestone Society*

been sufficiently prompt in pledging allegiance to the new monarchs, William and Mary. Very tough justice, if indeed it was justice at all. The episode, a clear breach of the Highland code of hospitality, has left a bitter taste in the Scottish gullet ever since, with the blame being levelled at the Campbells, who were Government supporters. There had been intense clan feuds between the Campbells and MacDonalds since the 13th century, prompted over land, and Kintyre in particular, down to Royal grants, confiscations and seizures, depending on allegiances.

The milestone in Glencoe, showing 9¼ miles to Kinlochleven. *Dr Adrian Sumner*

Bute

Bute straddles the Highland Boundary Fault in the Firth of Clyde. There's the eccentric Mount Stuart House, reflecting the third Marquis's passion for art, astrology, mysticism and religion, in what is often cited as the world's most impressive neo-Gothic mansion. From the popular 'doon the watter' destination of Rothesay, to the impressive land and seascapes, the island has an aura of its own. There's also the first waymarked long-distance route on a Scottish island, the 30 miles of the West Island Way.

The 1980 edition of the OS map shows 35 milestones. They are not all there to be found, and some still bear the marks of the grinder who ground out the inscriptions in 1940, lest the Germans invaded. The island hosted key naval activities during the Second World War. HMS *Cyclops*, the depot ship for the 7th Submarine Flotilla, was home-based in Rothesay Bay, while the Kyles Hydro Hotel was requisitioned by the Admiralty as the HQ for midget submarine operations. It was here that the top-secret and audacious attack on the German battleship *Tirpitz* was masterminded. That said, I do wonder whether, if the Germans had reached Bute, the absence of a direction and mileage inscription on the milestone at Kames Bay would have aborted the invasion plans in the event that they had inadvertently left their maps at home. The milestone at Kames Bay is painted with Scottish Bluebells nowadays.

Canmore records several of the Bute milestones. Barnauld on the B881 near Loch Fad is described as a 19th-century, round-headed sandstone block (0.36m in breadth, 0.3m thick and 0.61m in height). The inscription reads 'Rothesay 3', with an inscribed arrow beneath pointing north, and 'Kingarth Church 3½', with an inscribed arrow beneath pointing south. There is also an OS benchmark on top, and it is recorded on the 2nd Edition of the OS 6-inch map of 1897. The milestone located 1 mile closer to Rothesay may have been buried in the banking in the 1930s, so missed the grinder. Canmore also records the milestones at Sawmill Cottages (A886), Quogach (A884), and East St Colmac (B875).

The A844 extends round the southern end of the island, but there are two B roads cutting across to the west from Rothesay. So near Ettrick Bay, it is 4 and five-eights of a mile to Rothesay by 'Gn' (Greenan) Mill, but 5 miles by Bannatyne. Similarly, north of Scalpsie Bay it's either 6 by Birgadale or 5 and one-third miles by 'Gn Mill'.

Typical Bute milestones (plus Christine's bike). *Both Christine Minto, The Milestone Society*

6
A journey in time along Scotland's roads: the travellers' tales

Treading where the saints have trod

The adventures of the knights and the Crusades to the Holy Land in the early medieval period made for exciting learning in primary school, especially the tales of Black Douglas taking the heart of Robert the Bruce with him. That episode didn't end happily for Douglas, as he was diverted en route to fight the Saracens in southern Spain, where he found himself on the wrong end of a sword. Miraculously, for it was supposedly a Christian endeavour after all, Bruce's heart was returned safely to Scotland, to Melrose Abbey we're led to believe, or at least that's where it lies now.

But these grand exploits were not the only pilgrimages under way. Scotland is well-endowed with saints. Aside from the Apostle St Andrew, Scotland has a special place in its spiritual hierarchy for several others, most notably St Ninian, St Columba and St Kentigern (otherwise Mungo). Major shrines became associated with the 'reliquary' centres (churches where the relics of the saints are buried) at Tain, Iona, Kirkwall, Whithorn, Glasgow, Dunkeld, Dunfermline and, of course, St Andrews. Glasgow Cathedral is the most complete large medieval reliquary church remaining in Scotland – inspired by the burial place of the patron saint of Glasgow, St Mungo, who had died in 612. Even following the Reformation of 1559/60, which attempted to rid the country of the shrines, there remains a

remarkable legacy from earlier days. Leading to, or between, these shrines were established routes or ways, e.g. the Whithorn Way and the Three Saints Way at Abernethy.

Motivated by a perceived need to attain salvation for their immortal souls, people of all social and economic status embarked on long and often hostile journeys to these shrines. Those less pious probably joined the throng as an adventure, an opportunity to break the drudgery of everyday servile life and see new places. The Christian church was keen to promote this 'cult of saints' – an early form of 'Faith Tourism' – and the marketing exercise was extremely effective.

In those warlike times, safe passage was ensured to pilgrims travelling in foreign territories, a custom reciprocated to those visiting Scotland. In 1427 James I issued a general safe conduct for the benefit of those pilgrims visiting Whithorn: 'they are to come by sea or land [there were no flights in those days] and to return by the same route, to bear themselves as pilgrims, and to remain in Scotland for no more than 15 days; they are to wear only one [pilgrim's] badge as they came, and another [to be received from the prior of Whithorn] on their return journey'. It was an early form of visa.

This 'pilgrim industry' brought a complex network of ferries, roads, bridges, chapels, hospitals and inns, created along the pilgrims' way. Supporting this infrastructure was recognised as an act of piety. I wonder if they had milestones? Free ferries for bona fide pilgrims were provided across the Forth so that they could access St Andrews and Dunfermline. As early as the 11th century St

Margaret, Malcolm Canmore's wife, endowed the Queen's Ferry, the most westerly of the crossings. The other was to Pettycur.

It was no minor undertaking, but whether through fear, piety or adventure, many thousands of people made strenuous pilgrimages. James IV on his way to Whithorn in June 1504 met 'puir folk from Tain passend to Whithorn'. That's a return journey of at least 590 miles.

James IV was no stranger to these sojourns himself, being dubbed the 'Pilgrim King'. He succeeded to the throne in 1488 when his father was murdered after the Battle of Sauchieburn, and we know he made at least one pilgrimage each year from 1491 until he was killed, together with so many other Scots, at the Battle of Flodden in 1513. His most ambitious plan, which would have taken him to the Holy Land, did not materialise, but he went frequently to Tain. His objective was not only spiritually driven, but it was also an opportunity to assert his royal power in the area. The visits must have been something to witness and caused quite a stir in Tain because the King was invariably accompanied by a large entourage, on occasion including a party of Italian musicians and an African drummer.

So not all hardship. During his pilgrimage to Whithorn in 1503, James stopped over at Bothwell Castle to visit his mistress, Janet Kennedy. Her nickname was 'Janet bare ars', so leaving little to the imagination of their intent. She bore him three illegitimate children.

One pilgrimage to Whithorn had a more sombre ring, however. In 1507 James's first legitimate son, also James, and the infant's mother, Margaret Tudor, were both very ill and the King set off from Edinburgh on foot to seek the healing influence of St Ninian. It took him eight days to reach Whithorn, including two days of rest at Penpont where he paid a cobbler 16 pence to resole his shoes. Was the pilgrimage in vain? The Queen did recover, but his son didn't survive infancy. In fact, it was James's third child, also James, who succeeded him in 1513 as James V.

James IV's last pilgrimage to Tain was only months before the ill-fated Flodden. To rub salt in the wounds of defeat, the victorious English claimed that St Cuthbert had come to their aid at Flodden. In his book *Pilgrimage in Medieval Scotland*, Peter Yeoman observed that 'it is ironic that the death of the Scottish Pilgrim King was attributed to the intercession of another saint (as opposed to St Duthac) taking his enemies' part.' All too familiar is this claim that 'God is on our side'. James IV was the last monarch of a country in Great Britain to be killed in battle.

But hark! 'Faith tourism' has been revitalised in the 21st century and we'll encounter the modern concept of pilgrimage and how it's opened new doors on both our history and our countryside in Chapter 12.

While on the subject of saints, a puzzle in the July 2010 edition of The Milestone Society's Newsletter posed the question, 'Who is the Patron Saint of The Milestone Society?' Slightly tongue in cheek, I suspect, several candidates were nominated for consideration. St Peter is the patron saint of stone-carvers and also gatekeepers. St Clement is the patron saint of stone-cutters. The stonemasons have a choice from St Barbara, St Clement, St John and St Reinold. Tax (toll) collectors have their own patron saint in St Matthew. So, take your pick. What a shame those giants of Scottish sporting history, St Johnstone and St Mirren. were overlooked…

Troops: on the march

Throughout history, armies advancing to stage war on their enemies must have cut a swathe through the countryside.

Over on the east coast, an ancient drovers' road known as Causey Mounth provided a dry passage for travellers around the coastal fringe of the Grampian Mountains, between Stonehaven and Aberdeen, as early as the 12th century. Avoiding boggy ground at places such as Portlethen Moss, it endured until the mid-20th century when the A90 was constructed. The 9,000 men under William Keith, the 7th Earl Marischal, marched along the Causey Mounth on their way from Keith's stronghold at Dunnottar Castle to join the Marquis of Montrose in the Covenanters' first battle of the Civil War, against the Royalists, at the Brig o' Dee in 1639. This route was one of very few country roads on which tolls were imposed at this time to meet the cost of their upkeep. There were several Acts of Parliament between 1597 and 1669 that authorised tolls to be levied, although I haven't managed to source any evidence that William Keith was charged for the passage. In some areas, troops were permitted free passage.

A few miles inland, another ancient track, the Elsick Mounth, provided a route from Stonehaven, north past Netherley, through Durris Forest to Maryculter on Deeside. On first reading of this track I assumed, incorrectly, that this was probably the original route from 'Stonie' to Banchory, what is in more recent times referred to as the Slug Road – a road I know well from my days working in the area. But the Slug Road (A957) is altogether further westwards, through Fetteresso Forest to arrive at the River Dee at Crathes. Elsick Mounth may well have witnessed the Roman troops marching between their fortifications at Raedykes and Normandykes.

The thought has long fascinated me of clansmen gathering from their remote Highland glens to amass as armies in the struggle for independence, or some other just cause, on a battlefield many miles from their homes. The Picts, for example, in AD685, led by their wonderfully named King Bridei Mac Bili, to Nechtansmere (often spelled without the 'h'), near Dunnichen in Angus (or was it Dunachton in Badenoch, a recent historian has postulated?), to defeat the invading Northumbrians, who had sojourned northwards. Or the MacRaes from Dornie on Loch Alsh, who travelled the 160 miles to fight for the Jacobite cause under Lord Seaforth at the indecisive, but bloody, Battle of Sheriffmuir, near Dunblane, in November 1715. For those who survived, and many of them did not according to the Clan MacRae Memorial monument unveiled on the battlefield in 1922, it was a lengthy and miserable walk home in wintry conditions. Undeterred, the next generation would support the Young Pretender in his bid for the crown on his long march south, via Manchester, to Derby, only 125 miles from London, in November 1745, followed by the even longer trek back up north to the bloodbath at Culloden on 16 April 1746. If any of them had asked in whatever is the Gaelic translation of 'Are we nearly there yet?', the answer would have been a piteous 'No' – the cause was lost.

Seldom mentioned in the Jacobite military movements is the march to and siege of Preston, which was contemporaneous with the battle at Sheriffmuir. About 2,000 Jacobites from the Borders under Brigadier William Mackintosh joined forces with a group of English High Church Tories (who had just lost the General Election) and Catholic Lancastrians and marched from Kelso, down through Penrith and Kendal, arriving at Preston on 10 November. Travelling predominantly on foot between the main settlements en route was a distance of 181 miles. The Jacobites successfully held Preston for four days until they were overcome by Government troops under General Charles Wills. Although only 17 Jacobites were killed, some 1,468 of them were imprisoned, all of them subsequently

Bonnie Prince Charlie. *Wikimedia Commons*

pardoned under the Indemnity Act of 1717, with the exception of those in Clan Gregor.

Despite the fact that the Stuarts were the rightful Kings of Scotland and Ireland, and the legitimate senior heirs to the Sovereign Houses of Tudor, Plantagenet and Wessex – so dating back 1,000 years in English history – and that 57 people, all closer to the throne than George I, were 'discounted' because they were Catholics (the Act of Settlement of 1701 saw to that), the Hanoverians from what is now Germany became the monarchs of a United Kingdom. The Act of Settlement has never been repealed; it remains to a great extent extant – perhaps worthy of

reflection on another occasion.

To reflect on the great trek south to Derby, it's worthwhile recounting this sad adventure in Scotland's history. The headstrong Prince Charles Edward Stuart, the Young Pretender, arrived on Scottish soil on the island of Eriskay, between South Uist and Barra, on 23 July 1745. He spent the ensuing month canvassing support from Highland clan chiefs, who, truth be told, were largely indifferent to his cause that his father, the Old Pretender, should succeed to the throne of the UK – as James VIII and III. The chiefs were more concerned about the prevailing economic climate, which was at a low ebb. Undeterred, Bonnie Prince Charlie raised his banner at Glenfinnan on 19 August 1745. There were some highs, however. On 21 September, at 3.00am, his troops, under the command of Lord George Murray, the sixth son of the Duke of Atholl, routed the Hanoverians under General Johnny Cope at Prestonpans in about 8 minutes. By late October Charlie had mustered slightly over 5,000 men on what is now Portobello Sands, and with the promise that the French would support him, both numerically in terms of troops but also financially – which turned out to be somewhat economical with the truth – he set out to invade England.

In their paperback *Battles of the '45*, Katherine Tamasson and Francis Buist describe that journey as 'one of the most remarkable in British military history'.

In order to try and mislead General Wade, who was stationed with troops at Newcastle, it was decided to take two routes south from Edinburgh. Lord George Murray and the Prince took the easterly route via Lauder and Kelso, then headed west via Liddlesdale to converge with William Murray's men, who had marched down through Peebles and Moffat, at a site to the north of Carlisle. That's 110 miles via Kelso.

The 'western' flank camped overnight at Broughton, the village in Tweeddale some 12 miles from Peebles where Sir John Murray, 7th Baron Stanhope, was the local landowner. John was the

Secretary to the Prince, who described him as 'ane of the honestest, firmest men in the whole world', although in the aftermath of Culloden he was to be scorned and became an embittered exile. That night the army camped in Broughton Place Glen and the estate factor's house, known now as 'Beechgrove', was requisitioned as accommodation for officers. Many of the Highlanders visited the Broughton Inn and, returning to the camp in a merry or riotous mood, fired several shots at the front door of 'Beechgrove'.

The plaque at 'Beechgrove'. *Colin L. Shearer*

And the house is still there. It's been the family home of my great friend Colin Shearer for more than 60 years, where I've received a warm welcome and generous hospitality myself on many occasions.

The army arrived in England on 8 November. After a minor detour to Brampton (12 miles return) to head off Marshall Wade, who was allegedly en route from Newcastle, but didn't show up, the Jacobites accepted the capitulation of Carlisle on 14 November. All was going well so far.

On 20 November the army marched to Penrith (29 miles). Reaching Kendal on the 22/23 November (28 miles), they departed on the 24th to Lancaster (25 miles), continuing on the 25th to Preston (26 miles). There they managed to recruit only three more supporters, which must have been a disappointment. Undaunted, they marched on to Wigan (18 miles) on the 28th, then to Manchester (26 miles), where spirits were lifted by being joined by the Manchester Regiment of Jacobite supporters under the command of Francis Towneley. He was from an old Lancashire family and had seen service in the French army. His troops were somewhat less committed, however, being about 200 of 'the local unemployed who … explained that they intended to join whichever army first reached Manchester.'

Off again on 1 December to Macclesfield (21 miles), on the 2nd to Congleton (10 miles), on the 3rd to Ashbourne via Leek (26 miles), finally arriving in Derby on 4 December (26 miles) – a total distance from Edinburgh of 357 miles. With a more direct route nowadays it's still 280 miles. The Jacobites had reached Derby. It was only a further 120 miles to London. They were nearly there.

However, by this time the army was somewhat dejected. With the morning dawned reality, or what they perceived as reality – based on their poor intelligence of the enemy's situation. To be fair, the Government in London was getting somewhat agitated by this time and, with the prospect of a French invasion to counter too, they were on the point of even considering capitulating. The final decision to retreat was made, reluctantly, by Charles on the advice of a double-agent called Dudley Bradstreet, who told him that there were 9,000 Government troops in Northampton that would have blocked his route to London. In fact, that was a deceit and there were only between 1,000 and 2,000 troops between Derby and London, based at Finchley. How different history might have been had the Jacobites known this and mustered the resilience and ambition to succeed? As the historian and broadcaster Neil Oliver describes it, with just a nod to Churchill, 'The real miracle of "The 45" was that so much was accomplished by so few.'

But no. The Jacobites turned back. There is a cairn at Swarkestone, some 3 miles south of Derby, which marks the Jacobites' most southern advance. For my *Bridgescapes* readers, Swarkestone Bridge, with causeway, dates from medieval times and is the longest stone bridge in England.

The commemorative cairn at Swarkestone. The inscription reads 'This cairn marks the farthest point reached by the Jacobite Army of Prince Charles Edward Stuart on 4th December 1745.' *Craig Thornber*

The trek north from Derby retraced their steps, and the welcome for a retreating army from the towns it passed was not hospitable. Back they went – to Ashbourne on the 6th, Leek on the 7th, Macclesfield on the 8th, Manchester on the 9th, Wigan on the 10th, Preston on the 11th – where they rested for a day – then to Lancaster on the 13th, where they needed another day of rest, then Kendal on the 15th, Shap on the 16th (where there was a skirmish with the Government troops), crossing back into Scotland on 20 December and finally reaching Glasgow on Christmas Day.

By January 1746 the army was on the move again. 'The last hurrah', as Neil Oliver calls it, for the Jacobite forces was at Falkirk Muir on 17 January. There they encountered the Hanoverians, led by Lieutenant General Henry Hawley, and gave him a bloody nose. Heading northwards, with the Government troops retreating to Edinburgh, the Jacobites held a council of war in Crieff on 2 February. They then split into two divisions, the horse and low country regiments making for Inverness via Aberdeen and the coast, while the Prince and the Highland Clans headed to Dalnacardoch and up the Wade road to Inverness. Departing on 4 February they travelled through heavy snow and arrived in Inverness on the 20th. The 'east coasters' encountered Government troops at Keith in Banffshire, where a skirmish ensued, and there was a foiled attempt to capture Bonnie Prince Charlie at the rout of Moy.

The final encounter, the defeat at Culloden Moor on 16 April 1746, effectively ended the Jacobite cause. Lord George Murray, asked about the prospects ahead on the day before the battle, evidently commented, 'We are putting an end to a bad affair.' A sad affair, too, in Scotland's history, and not one we should forget.

I calculate that the total distance covered by a Jacobite foot soldier in the Jacobite army, between leaving Edinburgh in October, marching to Derby, then retreating and ending up, probably dead, on the battlefield at Culloden Moor, was approximately 967 miles. And it was the winter time too.

The 'what if?' question is always worth asking. What if the Jacobites had won? Professor Murray Pittock from Glasgow University postulated in his Gresham Lecture to celebrate the 300th anniversary of the Prince's birth in 2020, that a 'victory would have changed the whole narrative of European history.'

'If the Jacobites had won, one of the first things they would have done would be to dial down confrontation with France. That would have meant no Seven Years' War between Britain and France.'

France would have kept

'…chunks of India and Canada, and if the French had an army in Canada, the American colonists were going to think carefully about revolting, with a significant chance that the American War of Independence wouldn't happen. Without the Seven Years' War, France wouldn't become impoverished [and] there would be no French Revolution, which means no Napoleon.'

How different the milestones of history would have been … perhaps?

But the Jacobites didn't win, and there is some irony in the fact that the last stretch of their misadventure should be along roads created only a decade and a half earlier to quash their cause.

The travellers: on the trail of the early tourist

The world of the internet and social media has dealt us 'instant news'. When Queen Elizabeth I died at Richmond Palace in London on 24 March 1603, her first cousin, Sir Robert Carey, set off immediately to bring the news to Edinburgh. It was an epic ride of 60 hours. His aim was to ingratiate himself to Elizabeth's successor, James, when he arrived at Holyrood. Initially appointed as Gentleman of the Bedchamber, his haste was soon perceived as 'contrary to all decency, good manners and respect' and he was dismissed.

Thomas Telford's roads and bridges in the Highlands transformed communications, socially, culturally and economically. They were the internet of their day. By the 1820s seven stagecoaches journeyed to and from Inverness every day, and letters were sent three times per week from Dingwall to Skye. The London Sunday newspaper could be purchased in Portree the following Thursday.

In many ways the journey times involved in these travels are much more important than the mileages. The ratio of bridges constructed to miles of road tells you everything about the terrain being crossed. Anyone who has driven extensively in Canada or Australia, which I've enjoyed in years past, will know that the 'locals' talk in terms of 'hours travel time'. The distances may be much less, but so it is with Scotland. When I was a youngster in the 1960s we went to Prestwick Airport to meet my aunt and uncle arriving from Toronto. I was resplendent in my kilt, which my mother clearly thought was appropriate attire in which to greet my aunt, who had left Dundee a couple of decades earlier. Before they emerged through Arrivals, a large Canadian gentleman wearing a bright lumberjack shirt, not too distant a relative of my kilt tartan, came across and asked how many miles it was to Loch Ness. My father advised him that it was 200 miles to Inverness, journeying up the loch side through the Great Glen.

'That's great,' the Canadian responded. 'We'll do Loch Ness this morning and go onto Aberdeen after lunch.'

My father, clearly taken aback by the ambitious plans, went on to explain that having negotiated Glasgow, Inverness lay a good few hours driving beyond. He suggested a lunch break at Loch Lomond.

For our ancestors the idea of travel was at an altogether different pace. Prior to 1840 a Glaswegian wishing to travel to London embarked initially on a coach trip of 12 hours to Edinburgh before enduring another 13 days of travel southwards to his or her London destination. There were specific coaching inns in London for Scottish destinations. The White Horse in Fetter Lane saw departures for Aberdeen, Peterhead, Inverness, Edinburgh, Kirkcaldy, Kilmarnock and Selkirk. From the Saracen's Head in Snow Hill, mentioned in Charles Dickens's *Nicholas Nickleby*, you could catch a coach to Arbroath, Montrose, Forfar, Perth, Stirling and Paisley. For Glasgow and Stranraer, the coach left from The Bull & Mouth in St Martins Le Grand. By the mid-1800s Edinburgh was only 4½ hours from Glasgow. London was 72 hours from Glasgow, but the east coast journey time had been reduced to a very precise 42 hours and 33 minutes. The railways out-competed the coach travel hands-down by the mid-1840s, and the last coach from Newcastle to Edinburgh was in July 1847.

Travelling by coach had its dangers, however. There was always the possibility of an accident, or the coach might break down or collide with an obstacle or persons on the road. A gravestone in the Kirkton Kirkyard in Bathgate is inscribed:

'Here lieth the Mortal Part of Benjamin Shaw the affectionate, dutiful and only son of Benjamin and Sarah Shaw of St Paul's Church Yard, London, Who was suddenly kill'd by the breaking down of the Telegraph coach near West Craigs on Monday 16th February 1807 in the 18th year of his age.'

Perhaps young Ben was riding on the outside of the coach when it jolted to a halt? Or the accident might be due to a fault in the roadway or a missing bridge.

That was the fate of the mail coach near Lanark when it careered into the river after the bridge had collapsed. Clearly no warning signs or diversions were in place. It does not look a good outcome for the horses, passengers or the coach.

There were other perils too. There was the prospect of the traveller being subjected to robbery or his life endangered by highwaymen plying their trade. Perhaps more often there would be inclement weather with which to contend, especially in exposed or remote locations. There

This is a black and white lantern slide of a postal mail coach coming to grief near Lanark. *The Postal Museum*

are many tales of both encounters. Let me tell you of two such incidents, both from 1831.

The Glasgow to Edinburgh road became a main conduit for both commerce and civilian travel. George Gilchrist, owner of the 'Prince Regent' coach, based in stables in Engine Street in Bathgate, was commissioned by the Commercial Bank in Glasgow to convey funds to its office in Edinburgh. The date was agreed as 24 March 1831. The funds, comprising notes, gold and silver, amounted to £5,716 6s 0d. That's equivalent to about half a million pounds sterling in today's terms. Mr Gilchrist had fallen on hard times, and saw an opportunity to rob his own coach. He had ample time to hatch a nefarious plan, and devised a way to stage it as a highwayman robbery. We may think nowadays that the Bank was somewhat lax on security – after all, they'd given him so much information in advance, and on the day dispatched only one employee, James Smith, a porter, to accompany the money. The money box was placed

in the foreboot of the coach – easy pickings for Mr Gilchrist. His plan involved one James Brown, whom Gilchrist had recruited, George's brother William, and a young lad with a fair complexion, George Davidson. William and James joined the coach near Airdrie, followed by the two Georges some miles further on, towards Armadale. Both Georges, the young one dressed as a woman, sat inside while the other two were outside. As they travelled, the two external passengers engaged themselves in extricating the money box and removing the loot – wrapping it in handkerchiefs. At Armadale Toll the passengers alighted, tipping the driver a half-crown and leaving the coach to continue towards Edinburgh with James Smith. The robbers then hid the loot in a hole near West Craigs.

At Uphall Inn the coach was met by Robert Laurie, a porter from the Commercial Bank's Edinburgh office, who was due to take over from James Smith. It was then that reality struck. There was a box, but it was empty!

George Gilchrist would have got away with this highway robbery had he not been somewhat garrulous with his friend James Morrison, boasting about his ill-gotten gains. Sensing that a substantial reward might be on offer, Morrison informed the authorities and the four men were brought before the High Court of Justiciary. While William Gilchrist and James Brown were acquitted, George Gilchrist and George Davidson were sentenced to be hanged.

By a strange twist of circumstance, Davidson's mother Mary was a former lover of the sheriff, John McGregor, and the two conspired to overcome the guards and smuggle George out of the jail. He journeyed to Australia, then on to New York, where he died many years later with only his conscience to worry him. Gilchrist was not so fortunate. He went to the scaffold.

And the weather took its toll too.

At Annanhead, above the Devil's Beef Tub on the A701, stands a memorial cairn to two Royal Mail coach postmen, who lost their lives on 1

February 1831. They perished in a severe blizzard and freezing temperatures as they tried to get the mail through to Edinburgh. James MacGeorge and John Goodfellow, the guard and driver respectively, are buried in Moffat churchyard, a few miles to the south. Coincidentally, Moffat churchyard is also the resting place of John Loudon McAdam, who lived in the town in his final years.

'Stagecoach' is today a highly successful Perth-based FTSE 250 company, but its name has origins in early passenger transport, and, it may surprise you, in Scotland too. The first stagecoach route in the UK started in 1610 and operated between Edinburgh and the port at Leith. Sending your post by coach started in 1784, but within two years there was a regular mail service between London and Edinburgh, which endured until the railways came along in the 1840s. Pace was everything with this literal horsepower. Coaches could travel at speeds of 8mph in the summer, but in winter this was more likely to average 5mph. And, of course, every 10 to 15 miles there was a stop for fresh horses. Being a blacksmith was a smart career choice then.

The mail coaches ran to very specific timetables, and the toll keeper on turnpike roads would be fined for failure to have the gates open in advance of the coach's arrival. So although the coaches benefitted from free passage on turnpike roads, there was a strong financial incentive to provide the mail coach with a quality service.

We all take our IT world of instant communications for granted, but letter-writing really was an art 180 years ago. Composing your letter was one thing – delivering it was an adventure in itself. There's some controversy among philatelists as to whom to credit with the invention of the adhesive postage stamp. You may well have learned in your history class that it was Sir Rowland Hill, and that the stamp was the Penny Black in 1840. I can't refute the stamp, but there's a counter-claim on the adhesive nature of that stamp. A newspaper publisher from Dundee,

James Chalmers (1782-1853), campaigned long and hard for improvements to be made to the postal service, which met with some success as far as the London to Edinburgh service was concerned. His son claimed that old James had also invented the adhesive postage stamp in 1838. His idea was for a 'sticky stamp' to be used to seal the page of the letter, not being at all inclined to use an envelope, as extra sheets of paper incurred an additional charge. Seems good and prudent sense to me, so Mr Chalmers should get due credit.

Robert Burns had the uncanny knack of capturing in his poetry some unnervingly insightful commentary. One such example is his poem 'To a Louse' written in 1786, the last verse of which pleads, 'O wad some Power the giftie gie us, To see oursels as ithers see us'. What we'd learn!

In the late 18th and early 19th centuries, the era of the Scottish Enlightenment, we see the beginnings of the Scottish tourism industry. In part this was spawned by the tales related by early travellers exploring Scotland. Many of these were English authors and poets, and their reflections on their tours tell us much not only about the land of Scotland but also its people and customs. Such luminaries as Thomas Pennant, Dr Johnson, the Wordsworths, brother and sister, Samuel Taylor Coleridge, Robert Southey and William Daniell all left us insightful visions and strong opinions. We'll catch up with them later, but earlier than them – indeed, predating them by between nearly 50 and 90 years – Daniel Defoe, of *Robinson Crusoe* fame, had embarked on a series of journeys across Britain, writing descriptive letters about each of them. Defoe's character, Robinson Crusoe, was, of course, based on Alexander Selkirk from Lower Largo in Fife, who had spent more than four years as a castaway on an uninhabited island in the South Pacific. Defoe's book on Crusoe had been published in 1719, and between 1724 and 1727 he produced a collection of letters describing his travels, entitled *A Tour thro' the Whole Island of Great Britain – divided into circuits or journies.* Published in three volumes, Scotland appears as

three journeys in Letters 11 to 13, contained in Volume 3, published in 1726.

Remarkably, Defoe's journeys were undertaken at a time of great stress between the Jacobites and the Royalists. The Uprisings of 1715 and 1719 were within 10 years and, indeed, the final uprising, which concluded with Culloden in 1746, was nearly two decades distant.

His first journey was in south-eastern Scotland, starting just north of Berwick and proceeding round the coast by way of Eyemouth, Cockburnspath, Dunglass, Dunbar, Yester, Haddington and Musclebro to Leith, Edinburgh and beyond to Boristown Ness (Bo'ness – old spellings used). He quickly realised that Scotland was a different country…

'The first town we come to as perfectly Scots … nor is there the least appearance of any thing English, either in customs, habits, usages of the people, or in their way of living, eating, dress or behaviour; any more than if they had never heard of an English nation; nor was there an Englishman to be seen, or an English family among them.'

He found that from

'Dunbar to Edinburgh, the country may be reckoned not only as fruitful and rich in soil, but also as pleasant and agreeable a country as any in Scotland.'

Defoe wrote of

'…many open roads … from Edinburgh … towards England, as particular to Yester, and to Duns and Coldstream on the Tweed; another way to Kelso … to Tiviotdale, to Peebles and Jedburgh.'

Dunbar is described as 'a handsome, well-built town', but Haddington as 'an old half ruined, yet remaining town, which shews the sign of decayed beauty … 'tis easy to see it is not like what it has been.' We find references to the herring industry

at Dunbar, to woollen mills at Musclebro, and to Prestonpans, busy producing and exporting salt.

There's a detailed description of what we call the Royal Mile in Edinburgh, although his estimates of distance are somewhat wanting. From the gate at 'Haly-Rood House' he writes that

'…the street goes on in almost a straight line, and for near a mile and a half in length, some say full two measured miles, thro' the whole city to the castle, including the going up the castle to the inside; this is, perhaps, the largest, longest, and finest street for buildings and number of inhabitants, not in Britain only, but in the world.'

Defoe's second journey entered Scotland across the River Esk, north of Carlisle, turning westwards via Annan, which he found 'in a state of irrevocable decay', and hence to Dumfries, a thriving seaport on the River Nid (Nith). Kirkubright (Kirkcudbright), conversely, is described as 'a port without trade' and Port Patrick 'a mean, dirty place' – it's certainly far from that nowadays. From Stranrawer (Stranraer) Defoe heads northwards through Air (Ayr) and Irwin (Irvine), commenting unfavourably on the former ('At present like an old beauty, it shews the ruins of a good face'), but boasts of the latter's industry and especially its keen coal export trade with Ireland.

He visits Renfrew, Pasely (Paisley) and Greenock, and hails Glasgow as 'a very fine city … 'tis the cleanest and beautifullest and best built city in Britain, London excepted'. From Hamilton he travels to Kilsyth and Falkirk, before ending this journey in Sterling (Stirling). Towards the end of this epistle, Defoe concludes that what would benefit trade links in Scotland would be a canal linking the Forth and the Clyde. He was nearly a hundred years ahead of himself. From Stirling he journeyed to (Lin)Lithgow and thence to Lanerk (Lanark), 'thirty long miles, and some of the road over the wildest country we had yet seen'. Then eastwards to Peebles and Traquair (the oldest inhabited house in Scotland – to this day),

Mailross (Melrose), Kelso, and eventually back to Edinburgh via Soutra.

From Edinburgh, Defoe crossed the Forth at Queensferry, through Innerkeithen (Inverkeithing), Dumfermling (Dunfermline), Aberdour, Kinross, Lessly (Leslie), Kirkcaldy, Methuel (Methil), Criel (Crail) to St Andrew's (St Andrews), thence to Cowper (Cupar), Perth, Clackmanan (Clackmannan), Alloway (Alloa), Culross, then back to Perth and Scone.

All this was on horseback. In the mid-1720s. General Wade only arrived in Scotland in 1724. Undeterred, Defoe continued north to Dunkeld, then eastwards to Dundee (noting its brisk trade with the countries of Scandinavia and northern Europe), Montrose, Brechin and up the east coast to Aberdeen, and onwards to Inner-Ness (Inverness) via Pitsligo, Bamff (Banff) and Elgin. North of Inverness he called at Tain and Dunrobin, and up to Dingsby Head (Duncansby Head), along to Strathnaver and back via Inverness. He journeyed down the south side of the Great Glen to Fort William and as far south as the Mull of Cantyre (Kintyre). He also managed a trip to view Loch Lomond.

I've very roughly calculated the distance that Daniel Defoe travelled in Scotland. It's approximately 1,810 miles. He didn't manage the Northern or Western Isles.

The other English 'visitors' to Scotland who I believe merit a mention are from a period starting more than 40 years after Defoe.

In 1769 the Welsh naturalist and travel writer Thomas Pennant spent two months travelling from Berwickshire to Caithness, via Edinburgh, Fife, Perthshire, Deeside, Aberdeen, Inverness, the Black Isle and Sutherland, spending two weeks in the northern counties before returning south, via the Great Glen, Inverary and Edinburgh. He wrote his *A Tour of Scotland 1769* on his return to Wales. In fact, it is a much more detailed account than that furnished by our next two travellers seeking a 'taste of Scotland'.

Principal among these early 'tourists' were

two unlikely travelling companions, the English literary figure Dr Samuel Johnson (1709-84) and his Scottish friend and biographer, James Boswell, the 9th Laird of Auchinleck (1740-95). Setting out from Edinburgh on 18 August 1773, their journey across much of Scotland is captured in Johnson's *A Journey to the Western Isles of Scotland*, from which we can learn much of the lie of the land and the society, but also glean an insight into the roads as they existed, and indeed even occasional references to milestones.

The journey, initially in a chaise and latterly on horseback, crossed the Firth of Forth with a brief stop on the small island of Inch Keith, before continuing to St Andrews via Kinghorn, Kirkcaldy and Cupar, on 'roads, neither rough nor dirty;

James Boswell, engraved by S. Freeman from a painting by Sir Joshua Reynolds. *Wikimedia Commons*

and it affords a southern stranger a new kind of pleasure to travel as commodiously without the interruption of toll-gates'. However, the chaise was charged 4 shillings for the ferry across the Tay to Dundee, where Johnson could 'remember nothing remarkable'. Things improved considerably once they reached Aberbrothick (Arbroath), Johnson remarking, 'I should scarcely have regretted my journey, had it afforded nothing more than the sight of Aberbrothick.' The abbey, where the Declaration of Scottish Independence had been signed in 1320, left a lasting impression. Montrose was 'well built, airy and clean' and the roads 'by no means uncommodious'. Aberdeen comprised two towns – Old Aberdeen, 'a town in decay', and New Aberdeen, with the 'bustle of prosperous trade and all the "shew" of increasing opulence'. Both boasted universities, King's College in the old town and Marischal College in the new. 'The

Dr Samuel Johnson (1775), a portrait by Joshua Reynolds. *Wikimedia Commons*

road beyond Aberdeen grew more stony.' On to Slains Castle, near Cruden Bay, and by Banff and Elgin they journeyed, the ruinous condition of the cathedral in the latter being 'proof of the waste of reformation'. Onward by Forres, Cawdor and Nairn, via Fort George, to Inverness.

Inverness was where, according to Johnson, 'Hither the young nymphs of the mountain and valleys are sent for education, and as far as my observation has reached, are not sent in vain'. Clearly my own childhood 'flit' from Inverness to Edinburgh deprived me of this secondary education experience, but at least I left with the benefit of the 'three Rs' from Mrs MacQueen.

In Inverness our travellers exchanged the chaise for four horses (one for each of them, one for their guide and the fourth for provisions), before departing on the Wade road along the Great Glen via the Falls of Foyers to Fort Augustus. From there it was westwards along Glenelg and Glenshiel by way of Anoch. This is the only place name I've been unable to find on the itinerary, but as it consisted of 'three huts' there's probably good reason. By 2 September they had reached Broadford on Skye, where they found 'no roads, nor any marks by which a stranger may find his way'. Luckily Highland hospitality meant that they always had accommodation (there was allegedly only one inn on the large island, at Sconser), and normally a local laird willing to show them round.

Other sources are less generous to Johnson as a 'guest'. It seems he relied heavily on Boswell's good connections to scrounge invitations. They found their way to Raasay and across to the Chief of the Clan MacLeod's castle at Dunvegan. Local knowledge allowed them to travel along the ridges of hills or on the moss or peat bog where the ground was sufficiently hard to bear their weight. But 'journies made in this manner are rather tedious than long. A very few miles require several hours,' wrote Johnson of the travel in Skye, further commenting that 'the computation of miles is negligent and arbitrary' and 'that the nominal and real distance of places had very little relation to

each other'.

From Skye they boarded a boat and sailed to Mull, calling at Coll, where the laird had 'begun a road capable of a wheel-carriage'. It extended for about a mile and 'will continue by annual elongation from his house to the harbour'. Landing at 'Tobor Morar' (Tobermory) on 6 October, they found 'no roads on Mull', yet journeyed across the island to visit Iona and Ulva.

Arriving back on the mainland in Oban on 22 October, they made their way to Inverary and by the military road through Glen Kinglas and Glen Croe 'which rises from either end of the glen by an acclivity not dangerously steep, but sufficiently laborious.' They must have welcomed the seat at the top, at the appropriately named 'Rest and Be Thankful'. Onward down the other side to Arrochar and Tarbet on Loch Lomond, passing beneath the three summits of The Cobbler (Ben Arthur), towering 2,900 feet above them. 'Stones were placed to mark the distances, which the inhabitants have taken away, resolved, they said, "to have no new miles"'. Regrettably milestones are all too often the victims of theft.

After receiving hospitality from the local landowner, Sir James Colquhoun, the adventurers hired a post-chaise to convey them to Glasgow and onward to Auchinleck Estate, owned by Boswell's father, near Cumnock in East Ayrshire. Returning to Edinburgh, the pair had travelled, I calculate, approximately 775 miles, excluding boat trips, across Scotland's heartlands and the Inner Hebrides. Not inconsiderable for 1773.

I commented earlier about Johnson's lack of tact and diplomacy, or, more properly, plain good manners. It's amply evidenced in the oft-quoted commentary from James Boswell on the lexicographer:

'Dr Johnson proposed to define the word "oats" thus: "A grain which in England is generally given to horses, but in Scotland supports the people." And I replied: "Aye, and that's why England has such fine horses, and Scotland such fine people."'

In 1796 a London-based writer, Sarah Murray, spent five months touring Scotland by carriage, accompanied by a maid and a manservant. She was certainly confident that she'd 'done Scotland', writing in her guidebook, 'I think I have seen Scotland, and its natural beauties more completely than any other individual. I took great pains to see everything worth seeing'. Generally credited as being the first guidebook published in English, her account appeared in 1799, entitled *A Companion, and Useful Guide to the Beauties of Scotland, to the Lakes of Westmoreland, Cumberland and Lancashire.*

During August and September 1803 the poet William Wordsworth, accompanied by his sister Dorothy and friend and fellow-poet Samuel Taylor Coleridge, made a 663-mile journey over six weeks through the Scottish Highlands and Islands. Dorothy captured what was a literary pilgrimage, to places associated with William Wallace, Robert Burns, Ossian and their contemporary Sir Walter Scott, in *Recollections of a Tour Made in Scotland, A.D. 1803.* Not published until 1874, some 20 years after Dorothy's death, it became a classic of picturesque travel writing, being reprinted many times, most recently in 1997 by Yale University Press in an edition with hundreds of photographs of Scotland, maps, footnotes and scholarly commentary by Carol Kyros Walker.

Mr Coleridge had acquired a jaunting car, an Irish open-air two-wheeled cart drawn by a single horse, to undertake the journey, but the roads were of variable quality and often a local guide was necessary to ensure the party was headed in the intended direction. Dorothy described the roads along each section from 'most excellent' and 'roughish' to 'very bad' and to 'wretchedly bad'.

In 1813 William Daniell, an English landscape painter of considerable acclaim, decided to circumnavigate Great Britain, capturing the coastline in watercolours accompanied by a commentary describing the scenery and the conditions of the people. An ambitious project, but young Daniell had already completed a successful painting trip to India, sponsored by his uncle. On a series of trips between 1813 and 1823 he produced a magnificent set of 308 paintings in his six volumes of *A Voyage Round Great Britain*. He quickly discovered the impracticability of a coastal voyage, so most of his journeying was by road.

His first sojourn into Scotland was to Kirkcudbright in 1814, followed by a major tour in 1815. Arriving in Edinburgh in early May he met Sir Walter Scott, who advised him of places to visit and provided him with material for inclusion in the accompanying text and an introduction to 'friendly hosts' along his route. July and August found Daniell in the Western Isles, on Eigg, Rhum, Skye and Raasay, and seaward to Harris and Lewis. He then travelled up the west coast and along the north coast, reaching Orkney, before heading southwards to arrive in Dundee in October. During that leg of his journey he sketched Ackergill Tower, the Keiths' stronghold a few miles north of Wick, and Slains Castle, near Cruden Bay, from where Bram Stoker is thought to have been inspired for a similarly shaped room in *Dracula*, two of the 139 aquatint prints produced from that trip. The weather was exceptionally favourable that year, with good visibility and clear skies, providing perfect conditions for an artist, so Daniell extended his stay much longer than originally envisaged.

You have to make the most of what I call 'Scotsman calendar' days in Scotland – days when you can see every fissure in every rock and marvel at its beauty. Debbie and I experienced such a prolonged spell of weather in the summer of 2016 when we visited Orkney and Shetland and were inspired, not for the first time, by the majesty of Sutherland as we had the luxury of several days to spare on our route southwards.

Daniell's final visit to Scotland was in 1821, when he travelled south from St Andrews to Berwickshire. Publication of his prints in 1825 was heralded, but somehow they became 'lost' for 100 years before being rediscovered in 1962. Ronald Tooley, the expert on maps and cartography, has claimed that Daniell's work is 'the most important colour plate book on British topography', so let's hope that its home in the Tate Gallery provides a safe refuge.

In 1819 the poet laureate, Robert Southey, having befriended the great Scottish civil engineer Thomas Telford, accompanied him on an extensive tour of his projects in the Scottish Highlands, maintaining a diary of his observations. It was published 100 years later as *Journal of a Tour of Scotland in 1819*. Among the projects was Telford's bridge at Craigellachie, completed five years earlier; Southey commented that the bridge is 'of iron, beautifully light, in a situation where the utility of its lightness is instantly perceived'.

William Cobbett (1763-1835) visited Scotland three years before his death. In his *Cobbett's Tour In Scotland; and in the four Northern Counties of England: in the autumn of 1832* he relates his experience of travelling in and around Edinburgh:

'A friend took me round the environs of the city: he had a turnpike ticket, received at the first gate which cleared five or six gates. It was sufficient for him to tell the future gate-keepers that he had it. When I saw that, I said to myself, "Nota bene: gatekeepers take people's word in Scotland; a thing I have not seen before since I left Long Island."'

Cobbett was impressed by the turnpike roads too. About the road through Lord Roseberry's estate (Dalmeny) to Queen's Ferry, he wrote:

'Upon leaving Edinburgh along the finest turnpike-road that I ever saw, the cause-ways on the sides of which are edged with white stone, and the gutters paved as nicely as those of a street.'

In 1862 Hippolyte Taine, a Frenchman of letters, visited Scotland and explored using the canal and railway networks. Arriving in Glasgow, he boarded a steamer and headed westwards for the Crinan Canal and thence northwards to Inverness via Fort William on the Caledonian Canal. He returned to Edinburgh by train and carriage by way of Aberdeen. And he knew how to endear himself to Scotland and the Scots. The country he found 'more picturesque than England and her countryside less uniform and less manageable; [she] is not simply a meat and wool factory.' The Scots, he determined, were 'lively, and more mentally active here than in England'. I'll settle for that any day. No wonder the Auld Alliance is now the longest surviving extant treaty between two countries in the world, even post-Brexit.

These travels, nay adventures, undertaken and recorded by the learned, gifted and influential drew attention to the delights and wonders of Scotland, and made it fashionable, laying the foundations of the tourism business.

Little wonder then why Queen Victoria and Prince Albert became frequent visitors to Scotland after their first visit in 1842 and set upon finding a holiday home to purchase. Initial thoughts favoured Ardverikie Estate on the south side of Loch Laggan, but a particularly wet stay there convinced them to search further eastwards. In 1852 Prince Albert purchased Balmoral Estate for Queen Victoria and they built a splendid baronial castle in local granite, a short distance from the old hunting lodge that had originally been built by King Robert II of Scotland around 1390.

So that's why we now have Royal Deeside, but had the weather been better the year Queen Victoria visited, we might have had Royal Lagganside instead. Incidentally, or perhaps coincidentally, Ardverikie was where Sir Edwin Landseer painted 'Monarch of the Glen', where the television series of the same name was set, and where the Netflix series *The Crown* was filmed as a proxy for Balmoral. It's an equally magnificent setting to Balmoral, even in the rain.

Our milestone heritage: The Lothians, including Edinburgh

There's one mile in Scotland that merits its mention in despatches. Undoubtedly the most famous thoroughfare in Edinburgh's Old Town, the Royal Mile is in reality a succession of different streets. Leading from the Castle Esplanade down the 'tail' of this volcanic crag are Castlehill, Lawnmarket, High Street, Canongate and Abbey Strand at its foot, beside the entrance to Holyrood Palace and adjacent to the Scottish Parliament building. The structures on the Royal Mile, including John Knox's House, date from the 15th century, but the road only gained its sobriquet in 1901, in W. M. Gilbert's book *Edinburgh in the Nineteenth Century*.

Despite misconceptions that the Royal Mile measures one Scots mile, the equivalent of 1.11 modern miles, it is, as near as damn it, 1 mile in length.

You'd imagine that Scotland's capital has a wealth of milestones. Sadly, as we shall learn, only a very few survive in situ (42 as of 2020), but about these, thanks to the diligent research and recording by John Riddell, we have some considerable detail. I have to admit that before I became fascinated with this aspect of our country's heritage I never imagined either that there would be so many types of milestone or, indeed, so many variations on a theme. I thought there might be a few, perhaps several, but surely not an uncanny number of permutations. How wrong I was. I should have learned the lesson that 'it's all in the detail' from an earlier experience. Before we get too deeply into the milestones of Edinburgh, let me take you to a field near Roddinglaw, just west of the city.

It's the early 1980s and I'm working at the Department of Agriculture & Fisheries for Scotland, based in Edinburgh. Although I'm a

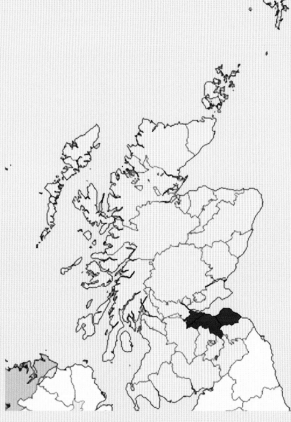

The Lothians. *Wikimedia Commons*

surveyor, clearly the advice on career development is to get as thorough an education and experience in as broad a range of topics as possible. That's where I was introduced to the humble tattie.

Scotland is renowned for its potatoes, grown for both seed and ware. The seed potatoes are particularly valued and there were, and are, strict certification schemes applicable to the crops. The Department's farm at Gogarbank hosts the potato inspection course to train would-be inspectors before sending them forth around farms to verify both the health and provenance of the crops. For

this purpose the field is planted with about 40 different varieties of potato, and the students spend a week, at least, being instructed in identifying the variety and the health of the plants.

My two colleagues, Maurice Archibald and Alan Mutch, the Department's gurus on potatoes, decided that what I needed was some training on their specialism, so they arranged for me to spend several days 'under instruction'. With the eager enthusiasm of someone who believes a new career path might open up, I listened intently as, in turn, they introduced me to the key characteristics to look for in identifying each variety. It started well. The first one was Pentland Hawk, developed as one of the many Pentland varieties at the Scottish Crop Research Institute at Pentlandfield, a mere few miles distant. The Pentland Hawk has a hook at the end of its leaf, just like the claw of a hawk. Easy! Then we moved on to Pentland Crown, Pentland Javelin (the Institute leaves a powerful legacy), Kerrs Pink and Maris Piper, each with its own distinguishing feature. However, I was bamboozled. Once we reached the eighth variety, I'd quite lost track of what the first looked like. That's when we started looking at the plant's health. Did it have blackleg, blight or a multitude of other dreadful-sounding viruses? I was lost. Hence why I remained a surveyor.

As for the tatties, so with milestones. Taking Edinburgh alone, John Riddell has sought out and recorded at least 13 different types of milestone. Each of the ten turnpike roads emanating from the city had a different style of milestone, all in sandstone, each with several design variations, some hybridisation, but all with their own distinct characterisation. Here's a summary of John's key findings. Bear with me, it's worth persevering… To mix my metaphors, like the potato, the proof of the pudding is in the eating.

Type A: Large 'Edinburgh cylinder' pillar with dome top; legend painted (designed visible height: 1.7m; diameter: 45cm). Used by the Cramond District Trust. It's easy to see the resemblance to

A Type A 'Edinburgh cylinder' at Hillhouse.
John S. Riddell

the Roman milestone Sibbald found at Ingliston, although without the degree of glorification the Romans afforded.

Barclay S. Fraser, who was a member of the Edinburgh University Turnpike Research Group (1969/71), writes about the turnpike road to

Cramond and Queensferry in a paper published by the Old Edinburgh Club in 1997. His research is from old Minute records of turnpike trusts, although these are by no means complete or comprehensive. There are several trusts involved – the Cramond & District Road Trust for the section in Midlothian, the Queensferry Road Trust for the section in West Lothian, then the Cramond Bridge Trust, established in 1821. He also relates the difficulties of negotiating the steep descent of Bell's Brae to the Water of Leith, before Thomas Telford's Dean Bridge was constructed.

It was a magnificent road. In 1845 it was observed that 'it cannot be exceeded in excellence'.

Fraser claims that the first installation of the Edinburgh to Queensferry milestones (1 mile to 7 miles from Edinburgh) was in 1766, but at different locations from the present milestones. The present milestones are from 1833, two years after the opening of the Dean Bridge, which shortened the route to Queensferry and reduced the number of milestones by one. He refers to milestones at Queensferry Terrace, Columba Road, Quality Street (off Hillhouse Road) and Drum Brae. The districts of Edinburgh along the Queensferry Road were all separate villages before the expansion westwards beyond the Dean Bridge, much of it speculative development at various times. They were swallowed up into the City of Edinburgh in the boundary changes in 1920. Blackhall was one, Davidson's Mains another. The latter only took on this name in 1776 from a wealthy owner, William Davidson. Prior to the 18th century the area was known as Muttonhole; I suspect the current residents might object to a reversal of names – it might impact the property prices.

Type B-N: Large quadrant-plan pillar with pointed pseudo-pyramid top; lower body rebated; legend inscribed on two radius faces towards road (designed visible height: 1.3m; overall width: 61cm; radius faces width: 45cm, including chamfers. When built into the wall, the arc-curved

A Type B milestone with a P-N plaque, set into the wall above a recess for the milestone below (both featured) on a commercial building in Corstorphine, Edinburgh (A8). *Both John S. Riddell, The Milestone Society*

back is concealed, and shows only the triangle plan. Used by the Corstorphine District Trust.

The milestone and mileplaque illustrated are located at 70 St John's Road, Corstorphine, on the north side of the road approximately 50 metres west of its junction with Clermiston Road. Although they are protected from the elements to some degree in the recess in the building, they were probably originally situated on the south side of this road. The milestone has had a chequered past, being used as a gatepost before being refurbished in 1985. The lettering is typical of the 1760s. The mileplaque is thought to date from a later period – the lettering is typical of the first quarter of the 1800s. Quite why there is a milestone and a mileplaque is unknown, but it raises the possibility that they may have been located in different parts of the village of Corstorphine at one time. The mileplaque bears holes that may have secured a cover plate, installed during the invasion preparations in 1940.

Type C: Medium quadrant-plan pillar (reversed) with asymmetric dome top; lower body rebated; legend painted. Similar to Type B, but installed reversed, with arc-curved face towards the road.

A Type C Edinburgh milestone at Camps, West Lothian. *John S. Riddell*

Height: 1.04m; overall width: 50cm; radius faces width: 38cm, including chamfer. Used by the Calder District Trust.

Type D-N: Small quadrant-plan pillar with pointed pseudo-pyramid top; lower body rebated; legend inscribed on two radius faces, each width

A Type D Edinburgh milestone at Pinkie Braes (Post Road District Trust). *John S. Riddell*

30cm. When built into the wall, shows only triangle plan. Used outwith Midlothian, especially East Lothian.

Type E: Square-plan 'diamond' pillar with pyramid top; legend on cast-iron plate or inscribed; designed for 'diamond' orientation to the road with legend on two faces towards the road. When

built into wall, shows only triangle plan; each face width approximately 36cm. Used by the Slateford District Trust, Dalkeith District Trust and the Post

A Type E Edinburgh milestone, built into a wall on Slateford Road. *Dr Adrian Sumner*

A Type E Edinburgh milestone at Inveresk. *John S. Riddell*

Road District Trust. An interesting example is built into the wall at the Caledonian Brewery on Slateford Road.

Type Hybrid C/E: Upper body is type C quadrant; lower body is type E, square-plan 'diamond' towards the road; legend painted; 'diamond' projects beyond quadrant arc-curved face, hence lower body has large upper-front bevel; deigned visible height: 1.37m. The hybrid was presumably associated with the merger of the Calder District Trust and the Slateford District Trust in or shortly after 1837.

John Riddell's excellent plan and isometric drawing of this sandstone block milestone provides detailed measurements of the hybrid C/E type found in Edinburgh. The upper body is Calder District Type C (head only), being a 90° quadrant plan with asymmetric dome top. The lower body is Slateford District Trust Type E – a square-plan 'diamond', without the usual pyramid top, with front bevel sweetening up to upper body. Other Slateford Trust milestones were fitted with a cast-iron directions plate, but on the illustrated example there are no fixing holes for the plate. This milestone is without inscriptions or paint traces, but it presumed that the painted legend once read 'Edinburgh 5/Glasgow 37' as per the OS 6-inch 1st Edition Edinburghshire sheet No 5, surveyed in 1852 and published in 1853.

All faces, including the dome, except the front of the quadrant, are vertical broached finish, with the buried base roughly hammer-dressed. All measurements are as per the actual milestone, except that for clarity the 3 cm edge chamfers are omitted, i.e. the dimensions are extended to 'sharp' edges. In 2020 the milestone was described as being in 'good condition, weathered. Lower part of front bevel is worn/ rounded. Minor delamination on right-hand side edge. Minor chips at both corners. Legend face has pit-marks. Lower body is stained black – reason unknown.'

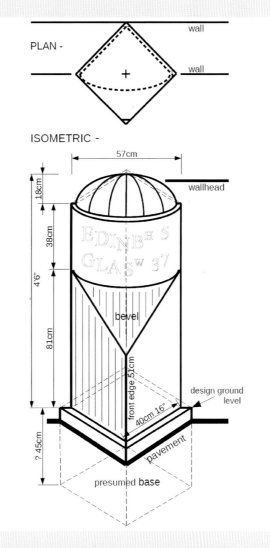

A Type C/E Edinburgh milestone at Hermiston. *John S. Riddell*

Above: An isometric drawing of the Type C/E Edinburgh milestone. *John S. Riddell*

A Type F Edinburgh milestone at Luffness. *Dr Adrian Sumner*

Type F: Slab with flat top; front top quarter is bevelled; upper front is bevel-tapered to thinner top; legend inscribed; width: 30cm; large variant is 53cm.

A large version of Type F, serving as a unique guide post, is found on Turnhouse Road at its junction with Craigs Road. Turnhouse Road was the route of the 'northern' turnpike from Edinburgh to Linlithgow, dissected by the runway of Edinburgh Airport in 1974 – when it was still referred to as Turnhouse.

Reassuringly, both this guidepost and the 5-mile stone on the Turnhouse Road, slightly nearer Edinburgh, are being removed to be stored and repaired while the land in their vicinity is being developed for housing in 2021. A win for our milestone heritage.

Type G: Slab/pillar with arched top; width 32-40cm; legend on cast-iron plate or inscribed. Many variants, including the Post Horse Duty stones described later, used by Wrightshouse District Trust and Lasswade (Straiton) District Trust.

Type H: Slab with convex bow front; front of base is rebated with three faceted faces; legend inscribed; width: 42cm; depth: 20cm. When built into the wall, the bow-front projects from the wall. Used by the Middle District Trust.

The Type F guidestone at 'Turnhouse'. The airport is visible to the west, on the horizon. *John S. Riddell*

Above: A stone milepost of Type G in Burdiehouse/Straiton on the A701, beneath the Edinburgh By-pass(A720). Note the bench mark. The small arched cast-iron plate is missing from the recess near the top. The inscription once read 'Edinburgh 4'. *Dr Adrian Sumner*

Inset above right: A Type G Edinburgh milestone at Liberton Brae. This is the only example with the original plate remaining. *Dr Adrian Sumner*

A Type H Edinburgh milestone on Dalkeith Road (A68), 1 mile from Edinburgh and 5 miles from Dalkeith; Lauder and Kelso are also featured. *John S. Riddell*

Type J: Pillar with convex bow front and partial dome top; legend inscribed. A variation has partial dome top. Used by the Middle District Trust.

A Type J Edinburgh milestone at Dalry. *John S. Riddell*

A Type L-N: Linlithgowshire Trust milestone at Cramond. *John S. Riddell*

Type K (Edinburgh): Pillar with bow front, arched top, lower body rebated; legend painted; design height: 1.1m; width: 45cm; depth: 33cm.

A Type K milestone at Beresford, Livingston, roughly hammer dressed. *John S. Riddell*

Type L-N: (Linlithgowshire) Square-plan pillar with convex bow front; flat top; legend inscribed; plan: 30cm square. When built into a field wall, the bow front projects from the wall. Legend on small 45-degree curved bevel on upper front; designed visible height: approximately 1.1m. A variation similar to Type J, except for the partial dome top.

John Riddell has unearthed an early photograph of a cast-iron milepost, adjacent to the Cramond example illustrated here. It is a product of the Grangemouth Iron Company (a two-band 'No 3 type' in the 'Bonnybridge' style, for the connoisseur). Distances are to Edinburgh, Queensferry, Bo'ness and Linlithgow. The milepost was removed in 1940 as part of the war effort, but the milestone remains in situ.

Type M: Horizontal 'pie-wedge'; legend inscribed on two faces; interesting design. The example illustrated is the junction of the A702 with the A703, just south of Hillend. As with other Edinburgh milestones, the measurement is taken to be from the west end of Princes Street.

Above: A Type M milestone, showing the inscriptions on both sides of the stone. *John S Riddell, The Milestone Society*

Type P: Mile plaque, wall-mounted; legend inscribed. An example is the plaque at the bank in St John's Road in Corstorphine above the Type B milestone.

Left: A cast-iron milepost at Cramond, from the Watts collection c1939. The Watts collection dates from the late 1930s and 1940s, and details are maintained by The Milestone Society. *John S. Riddell*

There are milestones in and around Edinburgh, along an arc measuring 5 miles from the General Post Office, bearing the date 1824, relating to Post Horse Duties payable by operators of hackney carriages under the Duties on Horses Act of 1823; John, with his characteristic pawky sense of humour, has described this series of markers as the 'largest standing stone circle in Europe'. One such marker stone is on Biggar Road, the A702, at Lothianburn.

The sandstone milestone is a variation of Type G, with the upper front bevel-tapered to a thinner top; it measures 0.97m in height, 0.37m in breadth and 0.27m in height. The stone edges are chamfered. The example illustrated has been moved previously, being used as part of the remodelled boundary wall of a former blacksmith's shop. This series of milestones was independent of the turnpike milestones.

The GPO was at 16-20 Waterloo Place at the east end of Princes Street, the mileage measured from a datum point marked by an iron bollard. It has been relocated since to the more recent GPO at the corner of North Bridge, opened in 1865.

Five surviving stones have been traced on the radial turnpike roads and a further three at crossroads. Interestingly, the 5-mile arc approximates to the route of the City Bypass (A720) constructed in the 1980s, so perhaps some stones were 'misplaced' during the construction of the junctions.

The stones were originally designed as

The GPO cab horse stone on the A702 at Lothianburn. The inscription is, in part, difficult to read, but is '5 miles from the General Post Office in Edinburgh. Erected to regulate the Post Horse Duties payable by Hackney coaches. 1824'. *John S. Riddell, The Milestone Society*

free-standing, as is the one at Dreghorn (CE-EDDH05P), with a visible height of 4 feet above the buried base – estimated at approximately 18 inches. The original legend inscription covered the entire upper half of the front face. The stones were probably produced by different masons, as evidenced by the variety of script styles and the use of upper-case and lower-case letters, line breaks and spacing variants.

This map shows the 5-mile radius from the GPO in Edinburgh, the location of the Post Horse Duty stones. *John S. Riddell, Phil Minto*

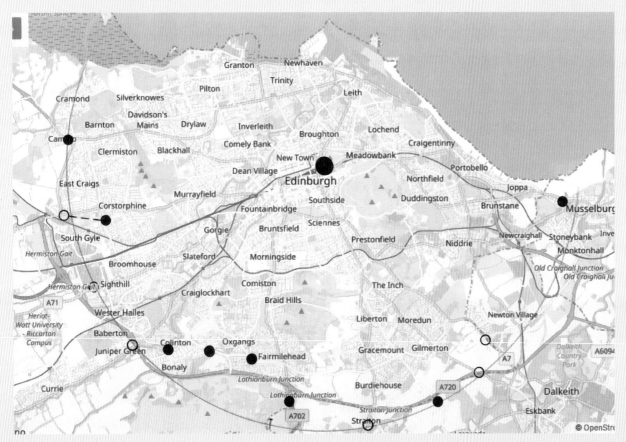

The other stones we know of – and the search for others is continued diligently by enthusiast John Riddell – are located as follows:

- CE-EDQF05P is built into the wall on the A9 Queensferry turnpike at Cammo, and states that it was restored in 1923.
- CE-EDGW05P, from the A8 Linlithgow/ Glasgow turnpike through Corstorphine, had been moved for use as a garden ornament at Dunsmuir House some time after 1850. When the house was demolished, the stone was displayed on a grassy area nearby.
- CE-EDLK05P at Colinton is on a non-turnpike road.
- CE-EDFH05P at Hunter's Tryst on Oxgangs Road is also at a crossroads, the B701. It has lost its top but was set into a garden wall, probably in the 1930s, and the top of the '5' has been inscribed into the wall above.

Apart from the Lothianburn stone (CE-EDBG05P) on the Biggar turnpike, there is another stone just outwith the bypass (ML-EDLW05P) on the Lasswade turnpike. It's now built into a garden wall after being damaged by a

The Oxgangs Post Horse Duty post. *John S. Riddell, The Milestone Society*

The Post Horse Duty stone at Cammo. *John S. Riddell*

vehicle at its original location some 60 feet distant. On the Great Post Road turnpike, the A199 at Fisherrow, near Musselburgh (EL-EDBE05P), is a milepost that has been restored, firstly in 1933, then again in 1998. The original inscription is lost forever. The date is shown as 1821, three years earlier than the remaining 'originals' testify, so probably an error.

Post Horse Duties were payable at set rates per mile upon coach horses and were charged as an addition to the turnpike tolls. They were not very popular, accentuated by the fact that the duties in Scotland were administered by the London Stamp Office. Only in 1787 did Scotland become the North Britain District, and the Post Horse Duties for each District were roup-auctioned (sold by public auction) by the Stamp Office for

The restored Post Horse Duty stone at Fisherrow. *Dr Adrian Sumner*

terms of three years to the highest bidder. The successful bidder would often rigorously enforce the collection of duties to maximise his profits. The system was open to abuse, especially when the longstanding Scottish 'owner' of the rights to the duties, John Mill, was also a magistrate who heard his own Post Horse Duty cases.

Court sanctions could be severe. One recorded sentence was six months' gaol for a threepenny offence. Tough justice. John Riddell has managed to unearth a 24-page private publication in the Edinburgh Central Library. Written by Charles Craigie, it dates from 1823, and is entitled 'Discovery of Great Abuses practised against the

Revenue and Public in General for a period of 43 years'. It's a wonder Craigie managed to capture all these abuses in a mere 24 pages. Craigie claims to have been persecuted by Scottish Post Horse Duty owners and government officials for eight years, leading to his eventual financial ruin. Mr Craigie, or so he claimed, was employed by the London Government to investigate and root out the offenders, in so doing discovering – or perhaps uncovering might better describe his finds – a loss or misappropriation of government funding through corruption to the extent of £10,000 per annum on stagecoaches and £1,800 on hackney coaches. Scandalous!

Whether it was a direct result of Mr Craigie's investigations or otherwise, the 1823 Act introduced to Edinburgh the Stamp Office licence system, which had operated in London for several years. This meant that standard Post Horse Duties were applicable to licensed hackney coaches only outwith the 5-mile perimeter. It was much easier to administer, too. However, within a few years the railways were on the ascendancy and the revenue from duties became fairly insignificant. In the 1830s the system transferred from the Stamp Office to the Excise Office, with the duties themselves being repealed in 1874. The legacy of this administration can, however, still be seen, evolving as it developed into the modern Council Taxi Licence system.

Mentioning Hunter's Tryst as the location of one of the Post Horse Duty 5-mile stones, brought to mind another piece of Scottish history with a measurement focus. The Hunter's Tryst has been a popular hostelry for many generations and hosted Edinburgh's Six Foot High Club after its walking expeditions to the Pentland Hills. Yes, there really was a Six Foot High Club. Indeed, the Edinburgh club, established in 1826, is recognised as the first such club in the world for those whose distance from head to toe measured at least 6 feet. It was a men-only fitness organisation created for the 'express encouragement, practice and promotion of all national and manly games'. The club met three

times a week and the criteria for membership were strictly enforced. Men had to attain at least 6 feet in stature in their 'stocking soles', and to ensure absolute accuracy an adjustable cross-bar set at a minimum of 6 feet from the ground was installed. If a sheet of writing paper could be placed between the head of the aspiring member and the cross-bar, he was declared 'wanting' and refused membership. There was a restriction on total membership of 135, itself somewhat of a tall order at a time when the average height for men in Scotland was approximately 5ft 3in.

There were 'rules' and there were 'rules', it seems, even in those days. Keen to attract notable literary figures, Sir Walter Scott, despite being vertically challenged at 5ft 4in in his stocking soles, was admitted to membership in no less a role than as Grand Umpire.

Another literary figure, Robert Louis Stevenson, who spent the summers between 1867 and 1880 at Swanston Cottage, a short distance from the Hunter's Tryst, joined the club later. The rules must have been invoked more strictly by that juncture, however, as he mentions the Six Foot High Club in his unfinished novel St Ives, commenting that the members 'all exceeded that measurement considerably'.

Before we depart from this slight diversion, or more a layby, on our journey, it's worth remarking that although Sir Walter Scott may have been diminutive by the club's standards on height, his monument in the city's Princes Street Gardens is the second highest monument in the world to a literary figure. At 200ft 6in, it is second only in height to the monument to Jose Marti in Havana, Cuba. Sir Walter was wont to use a descriptive phrase that is thought to have its origins in the 16th century, and meant that falling short of some goal by a small amount is as bad as falling short by a big margin. On 3 December 1825 he wrote in his Journal, 'He was very near being a poet, but a miss is as good as a mile, and he always fell short of the mark.' The original phrase was evidently 'an inch of a miss…', but the meaning is clear. Straight

talking.

Also, I mentioned Oxgangs Road as the location for the Hunter's Tryst. Yet more mensuration terminology…. An 'oxgang' was a measurement of land area, equivalent to the area an ox could plough in a year. It was anywhere between 13 and 20 acres, with the level of variation depending on soil type, gradient and field drainage. An 'ochdamh' was equal to four 'oxgangs', and two 'ochdamhs' (or eight 'oxgangs') equalled one 'ploughgate'. If you possessed four 'ploughgates' you owned or occupied one 'daugh' or 'dauch' or 'davoch'. Take your pick. Or was that a quiz show on television in the 1960s, hosted by 'your quiz inquisitor' Michael Miles? It's worth mentioning that Gunter's chain (of 66 feet) was also useful when it came to measuring land areas. An area measuring 10 chains in length by 10 chains in width would always contain 10 acres of land. 6,400 square chains, or 640 acres, is equal to 64 square furlongs or, more familiarly, 1 square mile. Turning to metric, a hectare is the equivalent of 2.471 acres. I've heard more than one person, and some who should know better, refer to a measured area of land as a 'hectacre', but now you've lost me. Once a surveyor, always a surveyor, so…

It would be easy, but slovenly, to claim that the area lying to the east of Oxgangs, known as Fairmilehead, related in some way to distance. However, the crossroads that was on the route of the Roman road and the site of a tollhouse when it was a turnpike road is more likely to have originated from the Gaelic 'Fair Meall Chuib', which translates as 'the hill in the cattle fold'.

But back to our tour of Edinburgh milestones…

Since 2014 Edinburgh has benefited from a 21st-century tram system. It was a long time in gestation and construction, but it has been a success and construction of an extension of 2.91 miles from York Place to Leith and Newhaven began in 2019. It's due to open in 2023. There was, of course, a much earlier incarnation of a tram system in Edinburgh, one that operated about 350 trams and was acknowledged as one of the most modern of its day in the UK. Trams first appeared in Leith in 1905 and became electrified throughout the city in the 1920s.

In 1952 Edinburgh Corporation took the decision to switch from trams to buses, and the last tram ran on 16 November 1956. Kenneth Williamson captured the history of *Old Edinburgh Trams* in his excellent 2019 book and he has kindly allowed me reprint one of his collection of photographs.

Although it's shaded, the milestone on the north side of the A8 at Roseburn is visible on the accompanying photograph, dated between 1952 and 1954, looking eastwards. It is sited on the other side of the railway bridge. John Riddell's photograph from the present day shows the

A tram and milestone in Roseburn, 1952-54. *Kenneth G. Williamson*

A Lothian Transport bus and the same milestone in Roseburn in 2020. *John S. Riddell*

And here's what it looks like, close up – the Roseburn milestone, with benchmark.
*John S. Riddell,
The Milestone Society*

milestone in the same location.

This milestone, together with one at Beechmount, a mile further west, has been celebrated by the Murrayfield Community Council. Plaques unveiled in 2021 provide the following information for both:

'Milestone by Corstorphine District Turnpike Trust on the "Middle Way" via Bathgate completed in 1798, the fastest of the three routes between Edinburgh and Glasgow. This is also the ancient route to Linlithgow, after 1751 the "Northern Route" turnpike to Glasgow.'

The plaques also advise that in the case of the Roseburn milestone, it is understood that the inscriptions were re-cut in about 1840, and, for the Beechmount milestone, that it was originally sited on the opposite side of the road.

The second half of the 1950s witnessed the demise of the tram systems operated in Dundee (October 1956) and Aberdeen (May 1958). Only the tracks in Murraygate remain in Dundee, but the Transport Museum hosts one of only two trams remaining from the Aberdeen fleet; the other, fittingly, is in the Grampian Transport Museum at Alford. Glasgow's tram system, which had been one of the largest urban tramways in Europe, with more than 1,000 municipally owned trams operating on more than 100 miles of route by 1922, finally closed in September 1962. Trams had been superseded by buses by the 1960s, and Glasgow's was the last traditional city tramway operated in Great Britain. It's a good step forward that trams have been reintroduced in Edinburgh, and perhaps other cities will follow suit.

A mile 'post' of a different style is recorded in Portobello. It is a Victorian pillar (post) box, in the High Street, near the former Burgh Chambers. As well as the traditional posting slot, the box incorporates the distance to Edinburgh as 3 miles and that to Haddington as 14 miles. Sadly, the pillar box is no longer in existence, but the late Ken Diamond took the accompanying photograph

The Portobello dual-function pillar box.
Ken Diamond collection, The Milestone Society

for posterity. It's a black and white photograph so not possible to tell whether the colour is red or the original green, which was the norm prior to 1879.

Ken started taking photographs of milestones, fingerposts, county boundary signs, AA boxes, and much else besides, in 1950, methodically recording information on milestones until his death, aged 92, in November 2000. He lived all his life in Lymington in Hampshire, but never tired of his travels throughout the UK, many times to

The Joppa milestone looking over the Firth of Forth.
Dr Adrian Sumner

Scotland. Ken had an eclectic range of cars over the years, which the photographs testify. I have not found any photographic evidence, however, of the claim in The Milestone Society's Newsletter in 2002 that, as an undertaker by profession, Ken often had to deliver corpses all over the country and that he never left home without his camera. There's not a hearse to be seen in any of the photographs. He left his 11 large albums, containing more than 2,000 photographs of milestones, and his many scrapbooks of cuttings about milestones and fingerposts to The Milestone Society. What a legacy!

And postboxes are something of a legacy too. In the UK there are estimated to be 800 different designs of postbox, 400 variations on the design of a pillar box, 160 types of wall box, and so it goes on. You'd think there must be a society for postbox enthusiasts. Indeed, there is – The Letter Box Study Group. I'll let you make your own enquiries (I'm confident the group responds to e-mails these days).

Heading east from Edinburgh on what was the old A1, there is a very well-weathered milestone at Joppa, marking 4 miles from the city centre. You'll no doubt recognise it from the photograph as another example of a Type E milestone.

A cast-iron milepost at West Barns, 2 miles west of Dunbar, signals 9 miles from Haddington and 26 miles from Edinburgh.

The West Barns milepost. *Christine Minto, The Milestone Society*

A modern milestone on the new section of the A1. Erected in 1999, by 2020 the plate had been stolen. *Dr Adrian Sumner*

Refuge for the Dunbar milepost at Riccarton Campus. *Christine Minto, The Milestone Society*

There is a relatively new section of dual carriageway bypassing Dunbar, the birthplace of John Muir, who emigrated to North America and founded the National Park movement. A new milestone has been erected in a layby on the new road, which marks a refreshing change from the modern practice of dispensing with physical milestones.

That said, milestones do turn up in surprising places, having been 'translocated'. Outside the School of the Built Environment on Heriot-Watt University's Riccarton campus stands a milepost that originated near Dunbar, presumably removed when the new road was under construction. At least it has found a safe home.

The old milestones on the A1 are of the 'lighthouse shaft' design with relatively bulbous heads (compared to those found further south in Berwickshire).

Midlothian

Midlothian county sign. *Ken Diamond collection, The Milestone Society*

The A702 leading south-west from Edinburgh to Biggar runs along the southern side of the Pentland Hills, established as a Regional Park in the 1980s and containing many of the reservoirs that provide Edinburgh's water supply. The burns that flow south-eastwards, mostly draining into the upper sources of the River North Esk, are, perhaps unsurprisingly, known by their distance from Edinburgh. Hence, illustrated here we have a milestone (unearthed from the roadside banking) at Eight Mile Burn. This road was the turnpike road from Edinburgh to Dumfries via Carlops and dates from 1753.

There is a private milestone at Penicuik Estate, the ancestral home of the Clerks, whose considerable wealth originated in the Loanhead coal mines. Clearly having one's own milestone was a status symbol, but it had the added benefit for visitors of forestalling disputes over hackney carriage distances/fares from Edinburgh. The milestone is of the Type F style, being a square pillar with an arched top, dating from 1770, as the inscription on the rear shows. During this period the numeral '1' script was similar to the modern 'J', possibly a deliberate archaic form.

Above: The Eight Mile Burn milestone, benchmark included, with the Pentland Hills beyond. *John S. Riddell, The Milestone Society*

Above right: The Penicuik House private milestone. *John S. Riddell*

Right: The date inscribed on the Penicuik House milestone. *John S. Riddell, The Milestone Society*

The Clerks made their contribution to our milestone heritage as trustees of local turnpike trusts, but more profoundly to our road network. The 3rd Baronet was said to be 'the first man in Scotland who appears to have conceived the idea of constructing roads through hilly and mountainous districts with a systematic attention to the most level direction'. That is, the most level route for wheeled traffic, replacing the most direct route for pedestrians and horses.

Providing something of a nameplate, the

milestone at Danderhall on the A68, marking 4 miles from Edinburgh, lies against the garden wall of a house named 'Fourmile'. A win-win for milestones, preserving our heritage while keeping the postie happy.

East Lothian

Fingerposts were common in East Lothian, but incorporating a subtle difference. Fractions of a mile were often shown down to fifths or eighths.

East Fortune houses the National Museum of Flight on what was a Second World War aerodrome. Well worth a visit, but don't be misled by one of the fingerposts in the vicinity, where the bottom section of the 'E' is missing, seemingly indicating the direction to 'Fast Fortune'.

These artefacts have a certain charm, and that was reflected, perhaps unconventionally for an official local authority document, in a Report by East Lothian Council in 1996. It described fingerposts as 'a distinctive and reassuringly familiar part of East Lothian's character and heritage'.

A fingerpost at West Garleton – note the use of eighths of a mile. *John S. Riddell*

A fingerpost at Kingston, East Lothian.
Dr Adrian Sumner

A traditional East Lothian fingerpost at Humbie House, near Upper Keith. *John S. Riddell*

West Lothian

On the other side of Edinburgh lies West Lothian. Very few milestones remain in this old county, with only a dozen or so found, at any rate. One rather anonymous example discovered by John

West Lothian county sign. *Ken Diamond collection, The Milestone Society*

Riddell on the A70 has been there since before 1893, as it appears on the Edinburghshire 6-inch OS map of that date. It's at East Haugh, 11 miles from Edinburgh and 21 from Lanark, along our old friend, the A70, the 'Lang Whang'.

John has also revitalised interest in the milestones around the new town of Livingston. At Alderstone a Type K milestone was found buried in a field in 2005 and sited on the Klondyke Garden Centre property. It is planned to relocate it closer to its original site on the turnpike road, which ran from Howden Bridge to Shotts, roughly the B7015. The milestone (the Edinburgh 14 miles post) is shown on the 6-inch 1st Edition OS map of 1853. The accompanying photograph shows it at an angle; it was hit by a lorry, but did not sustain other damage.

The milestone at East Haugh. *John S. Riddell*

The milestone at the Klondyke Garden Centre.
John S. Riddell

The Edinburgh Type K milestone appears to have been the favoured style in parts of what is now West Lothian. On the A71, which was one of the turnpike roads between Edinburgh and Glasgow, at Muirhall Mains near Mid Calder stands a reasonable example. Although weathered and with a broken top, it once had a cast-iron directions plate. We know from the OS 1st Edition Survey that the inscription read 'Edinburgh 18/ Ayr 53'. Mid Calder was a major crossroads, but missed out on the possibility of a railway station in the village as the local landowner in 1848, Lord Torphichen, declared that he did not want a railway station near his home. Hence the station that did bear the name 'Mid Calder' until 1982 was, paradoxically, at Kirknewton, some 3 miles distant.

This area saw the world's first commercial oil extraction and refinery, with 'Paraffin' James Young developing the oil industry from the 1870s. It transformed the world. Although it declined in the 1900s, with the American oil wells coming on stream, the Scottish industry lasted until 1962. Within a decade of that, of course, substantial oil and gas reserves had been discovered in the North Sea, and a new industrial age began. The legacy of the oilshale industry in West Lothian remains in the spoil heaps, locally called 'bings', the remnants of the 3 million tons of shale mined each year during the era of production. The grouping of bings near Addiewell is termed the 'Five Sisters' and is a Scheduled Monument. The bings are a not unattractive red in colouring, a sign of weathering of the initially blue-grey burnt oil shale.

Slightly further west, and probably following the route of the drovers' road, the B7008, leading southwards from the A71 at West Calder to the A70 (the 'Lang Whang'), has several milestones at East Torphin, Harburnhead and Powfasle Burn bridge. The network of unclassified roads in the vicinity has old milestones at Blackmyre, Muirhouse, Hartwood, West Harwood, Beresford, Skivo and Broadshaw. Many of these names are farms on which I recall digging holes during the

Land Capability for Agriculture classification exercise in the early 1980s. One day I must return to check that I filled the holes in again after the soil measurements were taken.

West Lothian's rich industrial heritage saw the creation of a turnpike road, known as Cleugh (or sometimes spelt Cleuch) Road, between Wilsontown (near Forth) running north via Bathgate, Torphichen and Linlithgow to the port at Bo'ness. It therefore followed approximately the route of the current A706. It was an entirely private venture, with milestones and tolls being charged, to provide a route to get the iron being manufactured at the Wilsontown ironworks to the port for export. This turnpike opened in 1781, two years after the opening of the ironworks, which at its capacity employed 2,000 workers and produced 40 long tons (41 tonnes) of manufactured iron per week. It was at this ironworks that James Beaumont Neilson developed the first hot blast form of blast furnace in 1828. The rail link between Wilsontown and Auchengray on the Caledonian Railway negated the need for road haulage and lasted a few years after the ironworks closed in 1842.

7
Promoting milestones

Salesmen have used all sorts of different campaigns to promote their products. We've had cigarette coupons with famous footballers, ships and trains. The oil companies brought us the tiger's tail with Esso's 'Put a tiger in your tank' campaign from the 1960s, and I've a shelf full of beer glasses and coffee mugs as 'free' marketing merchandise. Between the two World Wars, National Benzole issued a series of booklets on various topics to encourage interest from the motorist, including two editions of milestones in the UK.

National Benzole's *Famous Milestones. Ian Thompson*

The first edition, *Famous Milestones*, issued in 1925, included the stone at the top of the Rest and Be Thankful road (A83), indicating 15 miles to Inverary, 9 miles to Tarbet and 5 miles to Cairndow. It also featured the milestone near the junction of the A68 and the A6124, indicating

9 miles from Edinburgh. Sadly, neither milestone has survived significant roadworks, widenings and realignments over the intervening century. The second edition, *Passing the Milestones – Famous Milestones Second Series*, issued in the latter half of the 1930s, is silent on Scottish milestones. What a missed opportunity. It does, however, include the 'two centuries stone', the stone marker in Kirkstall, near Leeds, which records its distinction of lying 200 miles from both capital cities, London and Edinburgh. We also meet John Cobb again, the world speed record holder who lost his life on Loch Ness in 1952. He had become a national hero by July 1935, when he drove 3,325 miles in 24 hours at an average speed of 134.7mph, achieved in a Napier-Railton car on the Bonneville Salt Flats in Utah, USA. He broke many world speed records that day, including those over 1 hour, 12 hours and 24 hours. National Benzole was not slow either to miss a trick here. The Second Series booklet claims that Cobb achieved these records 'using standard grade National Benzole Mixture exactly the same as is obtainable from any "National" pump. A wonderful tribute to the reliability of this British Benzole motor fuel.'

Wonderful though it undoubtedly was, National Benzole has not survived intact, either. It started life as a petroleum brand in 1919 when a group of entrepreneurs saw the opportunity for utilising the 'benzole-lake' at the end of the First World War. It had been used to propel shells, so could equally well be used in motor cars. Concerns were raised, however, over the use of neat benzole. It was also an effective paint stripper and this, coupled with a coal strike in 1920, led to the product being marketed as a 50/50 blend of benzole and petrol, which, the motorist was assured, gave improved

fuel economy and efficiency. It was a marketing success story, and the Mr Mercury brand signage became a part of our motoring heritage.

The company became part of Shell-Mex & BP in 1957 and the 'National' brand name was phased out by BP in the 1990s. In Scotland the name made a brief reappearance from 2000 when Scottish Fuels branded its petrol as 'National', but that was relatively short-lived and by 2020 only a few outlets in Shetland remained so branded.

There's perhaps more to the name 'National' than meets the eye. Benzole is a mineral oil, one of a family of oils derived from oil shale, mined in West Lothian. The Bathgate Chemical Works, established by James 'Paraffin' Young in 1851, was the first site in the world where mineral oils were processed on an industrial scale, and by 1860 Young's company was producing oil from shale, rather than coal, in the world's first oil refinery. Try telling that to the Americans. The Museum of the Scottish Shale Oil Industry, based in Livingston, should be a must-do visit by everyone with an interest in Scotland's industrial heritage, and certainly every schoolchild too.

Marketing campaigners possess a special talent for inventing unique and often bizarre slogans. The 'knocking' sensation experienced in motor cars of bygone years, coupled with the associated loss of power, was reduced significantly by using benzole as a blend. Reference to knocking appears in a number of Shell posters, including one with a double-headed Loch Ness Monster, in one corner of which a fingerpost points to 'Knock-Less'. As someone who spent their very early childhood in a house overlooking Loch Ness, it's definitely time to move on…

That brings to mind another tale from the

world of yesteryear. As a child I was fascinated by die-cast cars and lorries manufactured by Dinky and Corgi. I had lots of them, including quite a number from the 1950s and early '60s that would be the envy of any collector nowadays. With the exception of a few that held sentimental value, in an uncharacteristic moment of spontaneous generosity when I was aged about 13 I gave most of them away to a younger lad who stayed across the street from us in Edinburgh. If he kept them, and their boxes, he's probably worth a bob or two now.

In 2002 Corgi produced, as part of its large model vehicles collection at 1:50 scale, an AEC Mk V flatbed, eight-wheel lorry and trailer set, in the livery of international haulier Smith of Maddiston. It was a beauty, but the feature that made it stand out was that the set came complete with what was described as 'an authentic non-scale milestone'.

The Corgi AEC lorry, trailer and milestone.

Maddiston, where the haulier's yard is located, is in Stirlingshire. The 'model' gave the distances to Linlithgow as 4 miles, Falkirk 6 miles and Polmont Station 2 miles. It's a fairly typical V-cast post with a rounded top. Therein lies the problem.

Milestone Society member Dr Adrian Sumner

from North Berwick explored the veracity of this milepost further, first by reference to maps, then by ground-truthing. At Laurieston, on the A803, Adrian located a cast-iron post indicating that it was 6 miles from Linlithgow, 1½ miles from Falkirk and half a mile from Polmont Station. A mile to the east he found a badly eroded milestone set into a wall, and a further mile on another cast-iron post indicating 4 miles to Linlithgow and 3½ miles to Falkirk, but no mention of Polmont Station.

At Maddiston, south-east of Polmont Station, Adrian found a reference to a milestone (MS) on the 1:50,000 map and to a milepost (MP) on older editions of the map. It was on the B825, and by careful measurement from the map Adrian calculated that it was about 4 miles from Linlithgow, 6 from Falkirk and 2 from Polmont Station. Could this be the Corgi milestone? A visit dispelled any notion of this. While it did indicate that it was 4 miles to Linlithgow, there was no reference to either Falkirk or Polmont Station. The other face of the milestone is inscribed 'Slamannan 7 miles'.

So the Corgi 'toy' milestone has been shown to be an imposter. In this geographically correct position, the Corgi model is authentic in neither design nor inscription.

Milestones become art! Ruth Slater has lived and worked on the Isle of Bute for many years, capturing local wildlife and artefacts in her artwork. From her *My Year in Small Drawings* sketchbook, Ruth produced the 'Milestones of Bute' card illustrated here. A great idea, playing on the concept that whatever the occasion – birthday, anniversary – here's the card to mark that milestone.

I couldn't resist enlightening the book with an image of Mr Happy and his success in raising Glasgow's image. It's 1980 and the perception of Glasgow, certainly among those who are not acquainted with the city's magnificent architecture and its rich cultural heritage, is far from outstanding. A foresighted and energised Lord Provost, Michael Kelly, hit on the idea of a

campaign that would promote Glasgow as a tourist destination and location for industry, engaging Struthers Advertising as the marketing agency. The slogan 'Glasgow's Miles Better' has passed

The Bute milestones card. *Courtesy of Ruth Slater,* https://www.ruthslaterartist.com/product-page/milestones-of-bute-1

into advertising history. Those of you interested in linguistics will already have spotted that the slogan is an excellent example of a 'null comparator'. It does not state what the starting point is for reaching this conclusion. Better than what? Thinking outside the box, Struthers approached Edinburgh City Council with the idea that the slogan be displayed along the side of Edinburgh buses during the Edinburgh International Festival. This was an anathema to the Edinburgh worthies, whose last wish was to promote its old rival

Glasgow. News of this rejection went viral, or whatever was the equivalent of viral 40 years ago, hitting the front page of the *Wall Street Journal* and thereby reaching a global audience. Own goal to Edinburgh! The award-winning slogan, indeed the

The 'Glasgow's Miles Better' banner, leaving no one in any doubt. *Wikimedia Commons*

whole campaign, is recognised as one of the world's earliest and most successful attempts to rebrand a city.

The slogan itself developed a life of its own, metamorphosing into 'Glasgow Smiles Better', which for anyone who knows the warm and genuine humour of the Glaswegian is certainly true, too.

Our milestone heritage: The Kingdom of Fife

Fife county sign. *Ken Diamond collection, The Milestone Society*

We're fortunate in Fife to have a very full record of the milestones, thanks to the East Fife Preservation Society, and the painstaking research of Alex Darwood and Paula Martin. An illustrated book, *The Milestones of Fife*, was published in 2005. Two other knowledgeable enthusiasts, Elizabeth and Michael Spencer, have published articles on the detailed researches they have undertaken in the Kingdom of Fife. We also have in Fife Council a local highways authority that has invested in securing the restoration of its legacy of milestones. Job done. But to give you a taster…

There are early records of road and bridge building in Fife from the start of the 18th century. The Commissioners of Supply, the local landowners appointed to oversee works, had a vested interest in improved communication as it facilitated the coal-mining and lime-burning activities on their estates. There were two very significant routes crossing Fife. The first was the 'Great Road', which ran between Kinghorn and

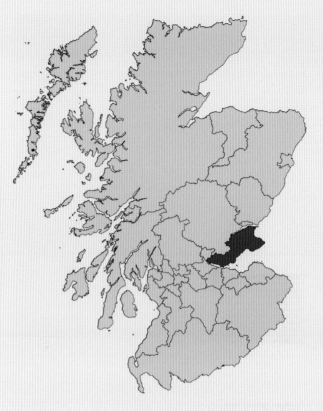

The Kingdom of Fife. *Wikimedia Commons*

Woodhaven, providing a means of transport from Edinburgh to Dundee and Aberdeen. The second was from Edinburgh to Inverness, via the Forth at Queensferry and heading north to Perth. In 1748 the Commissioners decided to concentrate the resources at their disposal on the Kinghorn to Woodhaven road (akin to the A92), via Cupar, and the road that branched off at the New Inn, towards Newburgh and Perth (akin to the A912). In 1753 the Edinburgh to Perth road became a turnpike, with an extension from North Queensferry to Kirkcaldy.

It didn't all happen overnight, however. The idea of a new road between Auchtermuchty and Newburgh was conceived in 1774, but the survey and getting agreement with all the landowners were protracted processes and the road was not

A distance marker at Town Pier, North Queensferry; the 11 miles to Edinburgh was via the ferry crossing. *Dr Adrian Sumner*

A Type A milestone with a metal cap on the A915, south of Lahill. *The Milestone Society*

The use of abbreviations helps when places such as Kilconquhar and Guard Bridge need to be featured on the milepost. Note the use of furlongs as a fraction of a mile to Elie. *The Milestone Society*

completed until the mid-1790s. By that time a Turnpike Act covered the whole of Fife, followed by a series of six further Acts, the last one, in 1829, providing for a few minor 'link' roads. By 1841 there were five bodies in Fife overseeing bridges, 14 turnpike trusts and four old statute labour organisations, responsible for the non-turnpike roads. All this cried out for local government reorganisation, but that did not arrive until the Road Boards were established in every county in 1878.

Other developments saw changes in ferry ports. Kinghorn was superseded by Pettycur (and later, in the late 1840s, by Burntisland, which had the first train ferry in the world), and Woodhaven was superseded by Newport.

The Fife Statute Labour Acts of 1797 and 1807 had permitted trustees to erect milestones, but it was the General Turnpike Act of 1831, amending the Act of 1773 of the same name, that made them compulsory.

For the first classification of milestones in Fife we have to acknowledge the work of Walter M. Stephen, who published findings in the 'Proceedings of the Society of Antiquaries of Scotland' in 1967/68 and wrote of Fife's tollhouses in the 'Industrial Archaeology' journal. Stephen compiled a table (unpublished in his papers) identifying nine variant types, six of which were

whinstone and the other three of cast iron. Type A was by far the most prevalent, accounting for more than 70% of the approximately 127 markers. These had a maximum height of 3 feet with a cross-section of 16 inches square, with the back corner rounded and with miles and fractions up to tenths shown, abbreviations used for place names, and a cursive script employed; each variant had more rounded sides and/or the use of upper-case lettering. All had cast-iron caps, except Type F, which is stone alone.

Type A was used on at least 13 roads across the county, with examples of the variants on the

A913, A91, A983, A90, B916 and A994. The three types made of cast iron are generally 3 feet high, with convex faces and curved tops. The predominant posts were produced by Alex Russell at the Kirkcaldy Foundry, are dated 1824, and are sited on the A91/92. Other cast-iron variants were produced by J. B. & Co (probably James Brown, Kirkcaldy) and are dated 1844 (when Burntisland replaced Pettycur as the ferry port). Bonnybridge Foundry produced cast-iron posts for the Dunfermline to Rumbling Bridge road (A823).

At Newport-on-Tay there are two excellent examples of cast-iron milestones from 1824, both made by the Alexander Russell Foundry in Kirkcaldy, and Listed Category C. The first is at Boat Road, described as 'Shouldered and slightly bowed cast iron milestone set into ground and attached to the stone wall at rear, adjacent to former ferry terminal building'. The milestone is approximately 3 feet high, 2 feet in breadth and 4 inches deep, and is inscribed 'Alexr Russell Kirkcaldy Foundry 1824' at the top, with the following script on the south side: 'To Pettycur 33, New Inn 20, Cupar 11, Newport 0'. It is painted white with raised black lettering and margins.

Its purpose was to advise passengers disembarking from the ferry at the adjacent pier at Newport, which had been improved by Thomas Telford in 1823. This was a very busy ferry service with Dundee across the River Tay. The first Tay Bridge, Sir Thomas Bouch's engineering feat but also his nemesis, was not opened until 1877. These impressive cast-iron posts mark the Great Road between the ferries, with 19 surviving between Newport and New Inn, a staging post. Mr Stephen relates the tale of finding the one missing stone in the 1960s, which would have stood in the centre of Cupar, 'in the garden of a house in Pollockshields, Glasgow', having been purchased 'many years ago' from a Cupar scrap merchant.

The inclusion of '0' miles on the signage is unusual practice; presumably the traveller arriving off the ferry would know where the ferry had landed.

The Newport Boat Road milestone – 'You've arrived at Newport!' *The Milestone Society*

'Yes, you're nearly there – providing you're going to Newport!' *The Milestone Society*

The second milestone is at Cupar Road. It's very similar but, just to assure the traveller travelling south that progress was being achieved, the sign reads 'Pettycur 32, New Inn 19, Cupar 10, Newport 1'.

Once Pettycur was reached, by way of the staging post at New Inn and the Great Road through Fife, it was another ferry, this time across the Forth to Leith, and thence to Edinburgh. The harbour at Pettycur dates from the 1760s, but there was a much earlier incarnation too, which the sands have covered. Nearby is Kinghorn, where King Alexander III of Scotland died when he fell from his horse in 1286, creating the succession crises that led to the Wars of Scottish Independence.

Intrigued by the zero milestone? They were not, in fact, too uncommon, but they do appear to have been a localised practice. Of the three known about in Scotland, all three are in Fife. The other two are in the East Neuk. One is at Kilconquhar, on the B941 between Peat Inn and Pitcorthie, and the other is at Kingsbarns on the A917 between St Andrews and Crail.

Another feature of Fife distance markers is the use of abbreviations for place names. 'L. Pr' is Largo Pier, 'Bt Id' Burntisland, 'Kil r' Kilconquhar, 'Osnabh' Osnaburgh, 'Ear.s Fy' Earlsferry, and 'Pitt m' Pittenweem.

Besides the routine '¼', '½' and '¾' fractions recorded on milestones, there are also examples of sevenths, eighths and tenths, the differences perhaps indicating a range of dates, although all, except Walter Stephen's Type H, are shown on the first edition of the OS map, surveyed in 1855. The foundry that produced Type H did not open until 1860, so that explains why.

There are also, within the St Andrews District of the Fife Turnpikes, what Stephen described as 'waymarkers', cast-iron signs, or panels, bearing the names of places, usually fastened to a stone mount. They are generally 3 feet in height, 1ft 11in wide, and 4 inches in depth, and bear Robert Douglas's hallmark. Stephen records five variations of the design. Some give no mileages, others rank the importance (or perhaps perceived importance?) of places by the size of letters, and the most charming, to my eye, are those that incorporate a distinctive cast-iron pointing hand.

Waymarkers were placed at selected road junctions, almost all at the junctions of turnpikes or of turnpikes with lesser roads. The names on the markers include not only principal towns and villages, but also farmsteads. The Spencers' research found 35 different population centres, 175 farmsteads, and four local roads to have been featured on the markers. Many of these include

the old spellings of places such as 'St Monance' for 'St Monans', 'Denino' for 'Dunino', 'Spinnistown' for 'Kingask' and 'Stravithie' for 'Wakefield'. 'Cowbackie' has not appeared as such on OS maps since about 1890; it's now the much more anglicised 'Vicarsford'. 'Ferry Port' is a shortened version of 'Ferryport-on-Craig', the old name for 'Tayport'.

Most of these waymarkers appear to date from the 1850s. Those with a banner heading, e.g. 'ST ANDREWS', were made by Robert Douglas, trading as Jackson & Douglas in Cupar, before he relocated to Kirkcaldy. St Andrews Foundry produced some of the markers with pointing hands. The one illustrated here is at the junction of the B9171 with an unclassified road at Newton of Balcormo, near Killie Castle, and shows 30

place names. It measures 3ft 6in in height, and the panels are 3ft 3in by 1ft 9in. The marker is fixed to a heavy masonry plinth standing proud of the wall bounding the road. At Upper Largo, the two panels of the marker are at right angles, fixed to the corner of a house at the junction of what was the A921 (now the A917) and the A915, both of which were turnpike roads.

Some of these waymarkers have been lost over time, including the unique version, raised on a cast-iron pillar, that used to grace the roadside at Arncroach, in the East Neuk of Fife, with ten places listed together with their distance in miles and fractions thereof. In the late 1990s it was reported as 'missing, presumed stolen'. However, due to the diligent efforts of Arthur Greene, a technician at Fife Council's

A typical cast-iron waymarker in Fife, with 'Left' and 'Right' directions only – not distances. *The Milestone Society*

An impressive list of places, with distances to each and a helping hand for directions. *The Milestone Society*

The waymarker at Newton of Balcormo in Carnbee Parish. *The Milestone Society*

TO	MILES		MILES
MOUNTURPIE		STRATHAIRLY	1
LAHILL MAINS	1	DRUMELDRIE	1
WESTER NEWBURN	1	DUMBARNIE	1
BALBAIRD	2	BALCHRYSTIE	2
GILSTON	2	LAHILL	1
LATHALLAN	3	COATES	2
LARGOWARD	3	CHARLETON	2
PEAT INN	5	COLINSBURGH	3
GREIGSTON	5	KELLIE	6
HIGHAM	5	KILCONQUHAR	4
LINGO	6	ELIE	5
LATHOCKAR	7	St MONANS	7
KINALDY	7	PITTENWEEM	8
FEDDINCH	8	ANSTRUTHER	9
St ANDREWS	10	CRAIL	13

The Upper Largo milepost, built into the corner of a house. *The Milestone Society*

Transportation Services department, and the skills of a Glenrothes engineering firm, Dawson, Downie & Lamont, working from an old photograph, a cast-iron copy has been produced. It was unveiled by Fife milestone expert Alex Darwood from Anstruther in September 2008. Acknowledging the cooperative approach to this project, including help from the East Neuk Preservation Society and Fife Council, Alex commented that such work was vital to maintaining and protecting these important elements of our heritage for future generations to enjoy. 'The interest of the national Milestone Society has been such that they regularly bring visitors to Fife to tour the East Neuk and so the guideposts are undoubtedly a great tourist attraction.'

Robert Douglas was an interesting character. A son of the manse from Kilbarchan in Renfrewshire, he was only 24 years old when he set up in business in Cupar in 1846. He began manufacturing munitions during the Crimean War but expanded to construct paper-mill machinery, and by the time he moved to the Dunnikier Foundry in Kirkcaldy he was working on steam engines. A visit to Calcutta led to the development of rice-milling machinery. He was quite an entrepreneur. In 1862 he shipped equipment to Port Adelaide, enabling southern Australia to construct its first ship-repairing facility. He formed a business partnership with Lewis Grant in 1873 and the firm flourished. It was awarded the Gold Medal at the Bangkok Exhibition in 1911, and Robert's son, Charles Edward Douglas, expanded the business further, opening branches in Rangoon, Saigon and Tanjore. Scotland has a very credible international legacy in engineering. I suppose producing waymarkers was a sideline, but a very useful artefact on which the young apprentice could learn his craft.

Another variation of the cast-iron waymarker was the guidepost, and there's an example, but with the arms removed, presumably during the last war, at Lundin Mill.

The other roadside 'asset' that accompanied the turnpike era was the tollhouse, where the tollkeeper lived and operated the gate. Some of these were of distinctive design, featuring a round or angular room with windows facing in both directions, allowing the tollkeeper to keep an eagle eye on approaching business. Walter Stephen did a lot of cataloguing. He recorded 119 tollhouses in Fife and adjacent counties, although very few survive today. Both Cupar East and Cupar South are worthy examples, and Edenside has been sensitively extended.

During the 1970s there was invaluable work carried out, voluntarily, by the Boy Scout groups across Fife in recording milestones. The surveys can be found in the Fife Folk Museum. Work undertaken by St Andrews University Student Conservation Society, led by Professor J. F. Allen, found and restored the caps on some 78 milestones in the East Neuk of Fife. Fife County Council was very supportive of these endeavours and this has continued through various iterations of local government to the present Fife Council.

The extensive promotion of the milestones and their history and preservation is in no small measure down to the enthusiasm and dedication of Alex Darwood – a very significant legacy of work. The booklet that Alex compiled with Paula Martin contains detailed gazetteers of 173 milestones and 28 wayside markers across Fife. It includes one milestone, on the B940 between Peat Inn and Crail, that it is claimed was hit by a German bomb. It's no longer there, sorry to say. Probably what the Monty Python crowd would term an 'ex-milestone'.

Over in the west of the 'Kingdom' the 3-mile post on the A823 between Dunfermline and Rumbling Bridge is a different, but rather soothing, shape from the others on this route. It's unusual because most of the markers on this 11½ miles of road are mileposts, of the Bonnybridge No 2 design by Smith & Wellstood. These were installed by Fife County Council in 1895. There must have been some confusion back at the foundry over the distances from Rumbling Bridge, as there is evidence that the numbers were ground off and the correct mileages painted on. The Listings Statements in 1998 notes the series of five mileposts on the A823 and comments that 'they are of particular interest for their survival and the continuous run on a short stretch of road'.

While the Frederick Schenck 'Plans of the Western District of Fife turnpike and statute labour roads, of the Outh & Nivingston District of turnpike roads, etc' from 1840 shows the route of the A823 near Rumbling Bridge, and shows the

The 3-mile stone on the A823. *Iain Davison, The Milestone Society*

A cast-iron milepost on the A823 – traditional on this road. *Iain Davison, The Milestone Society*

toll bars, it omits to indicate the milestones. The 6-inch OS map of 1894 (published in 1897) does not show the mileposts on what was to become the A823. These were first marked on the OS 6-inch revised map of 1913 (published in 1920). This shows the distances from Dunfermline to Rumbling Bridge as 10½ miles. Hence all the Rumbling Bridge distances are shown as 1 mile less than the milepost.

In Auchtermuchty, home town of the great Jimmy Shand of Scottish dance band fame extraordinaire, stands an old stone milestone sporting a somewhat newer cast-iron bonnet.

The Kinross-shire Roads Act of 1831 is referred to as the 'Four Counties Act', covering the counties of Fife, Kinross, Clackmannan and Perth. Despite its official title, according to the 1859 Report only 4 miles operated by the Outh & Nivingston Trust were in Kinross-shire, while 5 were in Perthshire, but 19 miles lay within Fife.

To cap it all – on Low Road in Auchtermuchty, the A91, 300 metres west of its junction with the B936. *The Milestone Society*

8
A short musical interlude

The inspiration for this book came from childhood journeys between Inverness and Dundee, but it won't have escaped the more mature reader's notice that *The Road and the Miles to Dundee* was a song popularised by the Scottish entertainer and impresario Andy Stewart in the 1960s. It tells the tale of chivalry and unrequited love when a young man meets a lassie who asks him 'to show her the road and the miles to Dundee'. All perfectly genuine and not a whisper of innuendo, even in his response 'If ye permit me tae gang a wee bittie'. Originally a bothy ballad from Buchan, composed in the early 20th century, the song has been sung by many over the years.

Calum Kennedy's recording of *The Road and the Miles to Dundee. Amazon*

The Corries do a particularly haunting version, as does the Gaelic Mod Medallist, Calum Kennedy.

'Cauld winter was howlin', o'er moor and o'er mountain
Wild was the surge on the dark rolling sea
When I met about daybreak a bonnie young lassie
Wha asked me the road and the miles to Dundee.'

Like so much of Scottish folk music, it travels well and appears in Ireland as *Sweet Carnlough Bay*. The tune didn't stop there, though. Bob Dylan used it for his song *Walls of Red Wing*.

Although Andy Stewart parodied Calum with

'I can sing like Calum Kennedy,
That's a thing I'll have to remedy'

it was Andy who was the expert mimic, and Calum who possessed the wonderful singing voice. Two years after winning the Gold Medal in Aberdeen in 1955, Lewisman Calum won the World Ballad Championship in Moscow.

The live entertainment business centres around touring. All these acts appeared in village halls the length and breadth of the country, covering many long miles on the road between gigs. No wonder that at least one band paid tribute to a milestone along the way. *The Silver Milestone* was an album recorded by Ian Hutson & His Scottish Dance Band in the Ballintuim Village Hall in Strathardle, north of Bridge of Cally. Actually the album dates from 2018 and it was compiled by Ian and the chair of the Village Hall Committee, Ann Martin, to celebrate the 25th anniversary of monthly dances being held in the hall. Together with the well-known traditional dances, Ann composed a

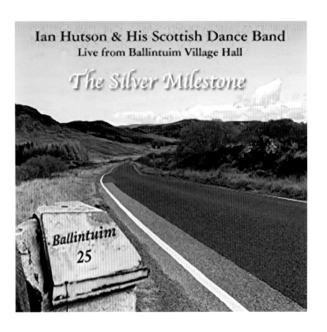

Twenty-five miles to go to hear Ian Hutson & His Scottish Dance Band in the village hall. *Amazon*

jig, *The Silver Milestone*, to include in the album.

Some of this touring became the stuff of legend. In the 1980s the BBC broadcast a programme called *Calum Kennedy's Commando Course*, documenting a chaotic tour around the Scottish Highlands in an old bus. It has become a piece of classic television. Perhaps disingenuous, it certainly is sad and more than unkind. The writer and presenter was Ian Wooldridge, an acknowledged southern English sports journalist. According to his biographical details, he left school with two certificates and I can't find any mention of him ever having been the World Ballad Champion.

The experience gained on tour provided an

excellent apprenticeship for young hopefuls. Perhaps the instant fame of modern television talent shows denies many young aspiring artists from learning their trade. My father seldom spent nights away from home on business during my early childhood, but on one occasion when the plans were being promoted for the original ski road into the Cairngorms, he spent a night in a hotel in Aviemore. It was the very early 1960s, before Aviemore became the centre of the tourist industry in Strathspey. He returned home, regaling us with a tale of a young comedian who entertained the hotel guests with joke after joke. He had quite a good singing voice as well. He obviously impressed my father, but not to the extent that he could remember his name. Several years later, watching Saturday evening television on the BBC, he suddenly announced that the entertainer on our screen was the same chap who'd had them laughing in Aviemore. It was Ken Dodd.

Keeping our entertainment musical for a moment, it's obvious that journeys to distant places, or even through life itself, are the very stuff of inspirational songs. You need look no further than the doyen of Scottish entertainers, Sir Harry Lauder, to see that in his song (*Keep right on to) the end of the road*. Nowadays it's not uncommon to hear his genre ridiculed, especially his penchant for appearing in full Highland regalia of kilt, sporran, tam o' shanter (bonnet) and cromach (twisted walking stick). But he was an entertainer from the music hall and vaudeville era. And a very successful one at that.

Sir Harry, who was born in Portobello but lived in Arbroath until he was 14, and worked in a local flax mill at the age of 12 to pay his school fees, became the highest paid entertainer in the world and the first to sell more than a million records. So perhaps he, and his derided caricature, did have the last laugh.

Sir Winston Churchill said Lauder was 'Scotland's greatest ambassador' for his enormous efforts to boost morale during the First World War, an atrocity in which he lost his only son,

John, in the aftermath of the Battle of the Somme. Harry was appearing at the Shaftesbury Theatre in London when he learned the tragic news in the closing days of 1916. Within three days he was back on stage singing 'Keep right on to the end of the road'.

One of Harry Lauder's most famous songs was *O'er the Hill to Ardentinny*, which features the lines

'O'er the hill to Ardentinny
Just to see my bonnie Jeannie.
Just to get one o' her smiles
I would walk a hunder' miles.'

As a youngster I thought Ardentinny must be a made-up name, contrived to sound Scottish. I then learned that it was, and is, real. Engaged on a project clearing rhododendrons and building a footpath with the Conservation Corps as a teenager, we worked on a Forestry Commission site at Puck's Glen in Argyll and I 'discovered' Ardentinny. And the evidence is illustrated here, in a milestone…

The quest for true love is nowhere better expressed than by the national bard, Robert Burns. In 'A Red, Red Rose', Burns gives his sweetheart the assurance in the final two lines of the song that:

'And I will come again, my luve,
Though it were ten thousand mile.'

A somewhat different genre, and much more recently, The Proclaimers, the twins Craig and Charlie Reid from Auchtermuchty, heralded *I'm Gonna be (500 miles)*, which was a major hit from the boys' album *Sunshine on Leith*. OK, so it's only a tenth of the effort that Burns was prepared to invest, but when it was released in 1988 the record reached the No 1 spot in Iceland, Australia and New Zealand. Re-recording it in 2007, as part of the UK's Comic Relief charity telethon, it reached No 1 in the UK and outsold the previous record sales.

The Ardentinny milepost near Whistlefield Inn, Strachur Parish. *Christine Minto, The Milestone Society*

'But I would walk five hundred miles
And I would walk five hundred more
Just to be the man who walked a thousand miles
To fall down at your door.'

The tradition of distance, journeys and perseverance lives on…

But that's not the end of this broadcast.

We'll be introduced properly to the Millennium Mileposts towards the end of our journey through this book. As a preview, come with me to Lanarkshire where a group of volunteers from LanActive have painted each of the 13 mileposts with a music theme, with sufficient clues to

'The Proclaimers' and 'Elvis Presley milepost', with Laura White. *Both Sustrans*

guess the identity of the artist or group, cycling the 58 miles of the National Cycle Network between each milepost, following Route 74 from Strathclyde to Elvanfoot.

Volunteers from Barnardo's North Lanarkshire Youth Housing Support Service were keen to capture something of The Proclaimers on their chosen milepost, and you can see Police Scotland Youth Volunteers' attempt to represent music genres through the decades among the collage of

photographs on the front cover. The inspiration for this project came from Laura White, the Artworks Officer at Sustrans. Laura was painting one of the mileposts only a few days after David Bowie died and paid tribute to the artist by including the legendary Aladdin Sane zig-zag make-up scar in the design. The 'Bowie Milepost' was born, and this certainly inspired other volunteers to get engaged in a colourful and eye-catching project.

Our milestone heritage: Central Region

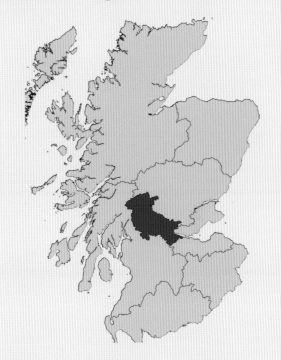

Central Region. *Wikimedia Commons*

This was without doubt the least imaginative nomenclature for a local government area upon regionalisation, and many breathed a sigh of relief when further reorganisation in 1996 restored the historic names of Stirling and Falkirk. But it's a land of rich contrasts, from the Carselands of the Forth to Ben Lomond in the west.

Stirling

Stirlingshire forms the eastern section of Loch Lomond & The Trossachs National Park, designated as Scotland's first National Park in 2002. The second and, as of 2021, only other, is The Cairngorms National Park, created in 2003.

Stirlingshire county sign. *Ken Diamond collection, The Milestone Society*

A cast-iron milepost on the A875. *Nigel Bishop*

the direction plates. Four of the original eight posts were found, one being completely overgrown by a rhododendron bush, and repainted to look as good as new. Others have been restored on the road to Port of Menteith (A81). Other rare surviving cast-iron mileposts on the A81 south of Aberfoyle are painted with a hand pointing towards Glasgow, with 'GLASGOW ROYAL EXCHANGE' in raised letters above, and 'ABERFOYLE' below. These mileposts appear on the 1865-66 OS 6-inch map, and an example of this style is illustrated here.

At Kingshouse there is also a well-preserved fingerpost, minus one arm, giving directions to Rob Roy MacGregor's grave at Balquidder. Rob Roy, a colourful character, was an outlaw or folk hero, depending on where you stand on the Jacobite Rising of 1689, led by Bonnie Dundee. Rob Roy

The area around Aberfoyle has a number of cast-iron mileposts, thought to date from 1859 when Queen Victoria came to open the Loch Katrine Reservoir, a major feat of engineering that gave Glasgow its public water supply. Those on the Aberfoyle to Stronachlachar road (B829), of which eight survive, were from the Grangemouth Foundry. Thanks to the sterling work of the Strathards Paths Group, ably supported by the National Park's Area Access Officer, Kenny Auld, and managed by the Countryside Ranger, Craig Walker, local volunteers magnificently restored these mileposts to their former glory in 2007. This work involved clearing vegetation around the posts and removing as much of the rust as possible by wire-brushing, before applying a coat of oxide and two coats of primer and one of white gloss. A steady hand was needed to paint in the lettering and numbers in black.

The volunteers then tackled the smaller cast-iron mileposts on the Loch Katrine to Callander road (A821). These were from the Bonnybridge Foundry of Smith & Wellstood. Research showed that they had originally cost 44 shillings each, plus 1 penny (that's an old, pre-decimalisation penny, for younger readers) for each letter and figure on

A milestone on the A821 near Trossachs Church, Brig o'Turk. *The Milestone Society*

A milestone on the A84, at Auchendoune, north of the bridge over the River Teith. *Nigel Bishop, The Milestone Society*

Two pieces of roadside furniture in one photograph. At Kingshouse on the old A84, at its junction with the unclassified road to Balquhidder, stands this milestone set in its own wall, with a red telephone kiosk behind. Has the mobile phone made such artefacts obsolete? There's no disputing the fact that it's at Kingshouse – the distance is zero miles. *Iain Davison, The Milestone Society*

The same plate on an old concrete milestone, before it was moved to its present status – a big improvement. *Ken Diamond collection, The Milestone Society*

Rob Roy's fingerpost. *Iain Davison, The Milestone Society*

and the whole of the Clan Gregor were excluded from the Indemnity Act of 1717, which pardoned others who had taken part in the 1715 Jacobite Rising. It seems that despite his efforts to be a trusted cattle dealer (somewhat of an oxymoron in those times) he was defrauded of his money and hence his lands. Much of his legacy is, of course, somewhat clouded by the romanticism of Sir Walter Scott in 1817, a Disney film in 1953 and his portrayal by Liam Neeson in the 1995 movie.

Falkirk

Heavy industry lies at the core of activity for centuries within what is now Falkirk Council. At the heart of that lay the raw resources of iron ore and coal. These fed the processing industries, such as the Carron Ironworks founded in 1759, which was at the forefront of the Industrial Revolution and became one of the largest ironworks in Europe in the 19th century. History repeated itself with the oil and gas resources of the North Sea giving birth to the petro-chemical works of the 20th century at Grangemouth.

So it's little wonder that many of the old milestones we encounter bear the mark of having originated from this area, most notably the 'Bonnybridge Foundry'. Actually Bonnybridge had little coal and no iron ore, but what it did have from the 1790s was the Forth & Clyde Canal, an ideal means of importing the raw materials and transporting the finished goods. Fortunately for Bonnybridge, the railway developments of the 1840s (the country's first inter-city railway) did not prejudice this locational advantage. So pig iron and coal arrived and the product of heat was poured into moulds to fashion any manner of items for industrial, commercial and domestic consumption. Some of these products were undoubtedly cast-iron milestones. What is less certain is to which foundry the trademark 'Bonnybridge Foundry' refers. For there were no fewer than 14 foundries operating in Bonnybridge at the time, including the most famous, Smith & Wellstood Ltd, which manufactured the American Esse stove, and milestones to boot.

Smith & Wellstood was founded in 1858 by James Smith and Stephen Wellstood. Edinburgh-born James had already made his fortune in America, where he had a factory in Mississippi making stoves. He returned to his homeland in the 1850s and was on a voyage back to the USA to sell his American business in 1854 when he was one of very few survivors of that century's most significant marine tragedies. It was Smith's thirteenth crossing of the Atlantic, which may be ominous. He was on board the SS *Arctic*, a very large paddle-steamer, between Liverpool and Boston, when the vessel collided with a smaller boat, the *Vesta*. Resourceful and resilient, he was also blessed with very good fortune. He managed to survive for three days in a steward's large wicker basket on a roughly made raft, 70 miles from land, until rescued by the *Cambria*, en route to Quebec. Of the 383 passengers and crew on board the *Arctic*, only 21 passengers and 54 crew survived.

Just as a brief aside, because the subject probably merits a book to itself (which hopefully my friendly

A 'Bonnybridge' milepost on the A803, east of Kilsyth.
Both Nigel Bishop

expert, John Riddell, will write), the production of cast-iron mileposts together with caps and plaques to masonry milestones and the posts and fingers/pointing hands/arrowhead arms and finials (both ball and cone variants) to fingerposts, all required the skills and facilities of the foundryman.

In the Industrial Revolution, cast-iron mileposts and mileplates developed as a substitute for the tradition stone milestone. Once the cast was made it was easy to mass-produce the product; even the lettering was much easier to produce than the skilled craftsmanship required to inscribe milestones. It was altogether a simpler process, which could be scaled, and hence a considerably cheaper option, especially when they were to be provided every mile along a route. It became even more cost advantageous when the mileposts were

redesigned from the complete 'all-round' mileposts to the front-half castings with an 'open back' – reduced material and lighter to instal.

The earliest example is accredited to Sir John Robison's design for the East Lothian Post Road Turnpike Trust in 1825. It was a 'complete all-round casting' model, in the form of a capital 'T', with horizontal oval heads upon shafts. This design was followed by the Edinburgh & Glasgow Railway Company in the 1840s. The Military and Parliamentary roads in the Highlands did not have cast-iron posts when constructed, but the arrival of county road boards in the 1880s, then county councils in the 1890s, saw their introduction on a widespread basis.

The Carron Ironworks near Falkirk was the 'godfather' of the iron industry and many young and aspiring foundrymen learned their trade there. It was established in 1769, but by the turn of the century and into the first quarter of the 19th century Scotland began to witness the rapid expansion of foundries.

We've already encountered the foundries in Bonnybridge, including Smith & Wellstood, but there were examples all over Scotland, most, if not all, capable of manufacturing the products for our mileposts. So we have the Grangemouth Iron Company (at Camelon), the Scottish Tube Company (Coatbridge), itself an amalgamation of eight pipe foundry companies in 1912, North Berwick Foundry, Douglas's Foundry at Cupar, Dunnikier Foundry at Kirkcaldy, St Andrews Foundry, James Abernethy & Co in Aberdeen, J. Affleck in Dumfries, and J. & A. Bridges, with its foundries in Haddington (Rosehall) and North Berwick.

Robert Bridges founded – if that's what one does with a foundry – his company in 1828, although the firm developed into J. & A. Bridges after his sons, James and Andrew. The foundry was in operation until 1896 making all manner of agricultural machinery and equipment. Mileposts may have been a relative side line, but the firm also manufactured a Ball Pattern Press for

moulding golf balls. Indeed, the legendary Ben Sayers, the professional golfer, golf club maker and golf course architect (including the East Course at North Berwick), was using such a press in the 1890s for his gutta-percha golf balls. It can be seen today in the British Golf Museum in St Andrews. You can still buy Ben Sayers golf equipment. There's a statute of Ben outside his company's former factory in North Berwick, but the golf clubs are now manufactured in China. Perhaps that's a consequence of globalisation, but even in the 19th century Scotland was importing some of its cast iron mileposts…

These were English 'imports', most notably from Smith, Patterson & Co in Blaydon, W. H. Smith & Co (Whitchurch, Shropshire), Stanton Ironworks Company (Ilkeston, Derbyshire), and the Royal Label Factory (Stratford-upon-Avon, Warwickshire).

If you look closely at the posts, you'll often observe the foundry name on the lower part, reading vertically. In some very early examples, e.g. Bonnybridge and Grangemouth, the foundry name reads horizontally around the bottom of the posts, just above ground level.

In many cases the catalogues of these companies have survived and they contain excellent illustrations of designs.

We also learn that the Scottish Tube Company exhibited at the first Irish Road Congress, held in Dublin in 1910, winning the First Prize medal from the organisers, the Irish Road Improvement Association, for a fingerpost design.

Sadly, almost all of the foundries have now closed. As of 2020, only the Royal Label Factory, now relocated to Buxton in Derbyshire, is still producing road signs in any great numbers. In Scotland, Ballantyne Castings of Bo'ness has manufactured three-fingerposts since the 1970s. Examples can be found in Fife, East Lothian and in Corstorphine in Edinburgh. But as the firm's director, Gavin Ballantyne, commented, 'Sadly, they're pretty much all made abroad now.' As for fingerposts, so goes the country.

9
Canal milestones

Before launching into canals, which helped forge the Industrial Revolution in Scotland, it's worth capturing that inland waterways have been around since the 9th century, and certainly played an important part in the sea-going and trading traditions of the Vikings.

Recent discoveries, yielded by aerial photographic surveys of the Isle of Skye, evidence a Viking boatyard, stone-built quay and canal linking the ancient harbour at Loch na h-Airde to the sea. The canal is approximately 380 feet long and it seems very possible that the now uninhabited peninsula of Rubha an Dunain was a bustling boat-building and repair yard from the 12th century right through the Middle Ages, when the Lord of the Isles commanded the area by sea.

Archaeological survey work by the Universities of the Highlands & Islands and St Andrews, including detailed research into the derivation of place names on Mainland Orkney, reveals a series of 'water highways' linking Harray through the Loch of Banks and the Loch of Boardhouse to Birsay. These canals would have carried both military and trade vessels, and have been dated from the 9th to the 12th centuries. The survey work reported in 2020, so what other features remain undiscovered is an open question. Enough has already been found to suggest that, as with so many aspects of Scottish life, the early inhabitants of Orkney were well ahead of the game.

That it was water, rather than roads, that drove the early Industrial Revolution can be seen in the writings of the 'Father of Economics', Kirkcaldy-born Adam Smith, in the late 18th century, in his treatise on the role of water transport:

'A broad-wheeled waggon, attended by two men, and drawn by eight horses, in about six weeks' time carries and brings back between London and Edinburgh near four-ton weight of goods. In about the same time a ship navigated by six or eight men, and sailing between the port of London and Leith, frequently carries and brings back two hundred [tons] weight of goods. Six or eight men, therefore, by the help of water carriage, can carry and bring back in the same time the same quantity of goods between London and Edinburgh, as fifty broad-wheeled waggons, attended by a hundred men and four hundred horses.'

So it was not only far more efficient but also considerably more cost-effective to use water carriage than land carriage.

Today, Scotland's five 18th- and 19th-century canals are managed by the appositely named Scottish Canals. The canals are publicly owned, not a charity as in England and Wales. The estate comprises five canals: Caledonian, Crinan, Forth & Clyde, Union, and Monkland. The canals extend to 137 miles of waterways, but the estate includes 17 reservoirs and the navigation rights over four lochs. The Caledonian Canal, through the Great Glen, links Loch Ness (itself 23 miles long), Loch Oich and Loch Lochy.

Canals provided the first real opportunity to transport heavy materials, such as coal, to the point of use in a steadily industrialising central belt of Scotland. The first canal was between Grangemouth and Dalmuir, built in 1768, followed 22 years later by the Forth & Clyde Canal. By the early 19th century nearly 300,000 tons of coal was reaching Glasgow every year from the Lanarkshire coalfields.

The construction of the **Forth & Clyde Canal**, together with feeder reservoirs, was the largest infrastructure project witnessed in Scotland since the building of the Antonine Wall by the Romans. You were probably wondering when they would turn up again. Ironically, the route of the canal follows, reasonably closely, that of the Wall. It is 35 miles long, with 39 locks, and linked the River Carron at Grangemouth and the River Clyde at Bowling. An important basin was added at Port Glasgow to satisfy the city's merchants that their interests would not be bypassed. John Smeaton, regarded as the Father of Civil Engineering, designed the canal, together with its many bridges and aqueducts, although he delegated the largest one, the Kelvin Aqueduct, actually the largest aqueduct in Europe at the time, to his chief engineer, Robert Whitworth.

By the 1960s the expenditure required on the canal's infrastructure was such that it was closed. Although trade and industry had declined substantially by this juncture, the closure did have some repercussions. Among these, it effectively stopped the east coast fishing fleets from crossing the country at its narrowest point in the Lowlands, to fish in the Irish Sea.

Of course, time marches on and we now recognise canals as an extremely valuable water asset and amenity, providing opportunities for the leisure and tourism sectors. So the Forth & Clyde Canal has been rejuvenated, having become semi-derelict with disuse. Although the Forth & Clyde Canal Society had engaged in a campaign to preserve, restore and develop the canal since the 1980s, it was the Millennium that provided the kick-start, and much of the funding, which the regeneration and re-servicing required. A magnificent boatlift was provided – the Falkirk

Wheel – thus re-establishing the link with the Union Canal. A short length of new canal links the Port Dundas Branch from the Stockingfield Junction to Pinkston Basin.

Among the many artefacts to be incorporated into the 'new-look' canal are a series of milestones. The sterling work under the Strathclyde European Partnership resulted in commemorative milestones being placed along the canal route, being cast-iron plaques giving distances, mostly in kilometres (I wonder if that was the European influence?), to local or more distant towns. At Kilbowie Road in Clydebank the distances are 6¼ kilometres to Bowling and 45¾ to Falkirk, and the one at Townhead at Kirkintilloch shows 11 kilometres to Glasgow and 25 to Falkirk. At Old Kilpatrick it's more localised, showing 2 kilometres to Bowling and 4½ to Clydebank. The Glasgow Road stone again shows relatively local places – Bishopbriggs 3¾km and Kirkintilloch 2½km – as does the one at Bonnybridge (Underwood Lock 2km and Falkirk 5½ km).

Rather curiously, but it may be because the European funding influence was not to the fore, two further distance markers record the miles rather than the kilometres. On the Main Line,

at the wonderfully named Cloberhill, Bowling is shown as 6 miles distant and Stockingfield Junction as 3¼ miles. However, on the Glasgow Branch, at Speirs Wharf at Port Dundas, Stockinfield Junction is shown as 2½ miles. No, that's not a typo – one spelling is with a 'g' and the other without. They can't both be correct. The influence of Mrs MacQueen has made me a pedant. Cloberhill has the correct spelling, in case you didn't know.

The completion of the **Edinburgh & Glasgow Union Canal**, to give it its Sunday name, in 1822, some 30 years after the Forth & Clyde Canal, realised the ambition to link the two cities by water transport. The 'link' to the Forth & Clyde Canal was at Port Downie at Camelon. Although primarily a commercial proposition to convey the coal mined and stone quarried in Lanarkshire across central Scotland, passengers benefitted too. It took 7 hours to travel the 32 miles from Port Hopetoun, in the centre of Edinburgh, along the Union Canal to Port Downie in a vessel called, perhaps appropriately at the time, a 'Swift', with a further 6 hours onwards for the 35 miles to Glasgow. It was popular – about 200,000 people made the journey in 1836. But things were about

Above: Forth & Clyde Canal milestones at Cloberhill and Port Dundas. *Both Dr Adrian Sumner*

Forth & Clyde Canal milestones, at Kilbowie and Bonnybridge. *Both Dr Adrian Sumner*

to get a lot swifter with the advent of the railway, which opened in 1842.

The **Union Canal** is what is called a contour canal. It follows the 240-foot contour for its entire length. This obviated the need for locks, except where it joined the Forth & Clyde Canal at Falkirk, where 11 locks were required to negotiate the 110-foot difference in height. But there was other infrastructure, most notably the three very substantial aqueducts that were required where the topography dictated – at Slateford, across the River Almond, and across the Avon Valley. Indeed, the Avon Aqueduct, the work of engineer

Hugh Baird and completed in 1820, is the longest and highest aqueduct in Scotland, and the second place in these rankings in the UK.

When I described this canal as one following the contours, you might not expect to find any tunnels along its length. However, one 696 yards long was excavated so that the owner of Callendar House, William Forbes, would not suffer the indignity of the sight of industrial cargoes passing his property. Water was provided from Cobbinshaw Reservoir in the Pentland Hills. In addition to cuttings and embankments, there were also 62 bridges across the canal, all at right angles to the canal so as to avoid skewed bridges, which would inevitably have led to cost increases. Even so, the total cost was £461,700, somewhat considerably in excess of the initial estimate of £240,468 17s 2d.

Milestones were encountered on canal journeys too. Those on the Union Canal were at one mile, and frequently half-mile, intervals along its 31½ miles. The canal was divided into four stages, each approximately 8 miles long, with the divisions marked by rectangular stones. The extent of the most easterly stage is marked at Ratho, with the other divisions marked at Winchburgh and at the Avon Aqueduct. To the west of the latter stands a dressed stone pillar, 2ft 9in high, mounted on an undressed base, square in section and measuring

10 inches on each side. Inscribed on different faces are the distances to Port Downie, to the west, at 7½ miles, and Port Hopetoun, 24 miles to the east. The Winchburgh pillar marks 15½ miles and 16 miles, and the Ratho pillar shows 23½ miles and 8 miles.

There is an original milestone in the tunnel. It is not engraved, as it would serve little purpose in an unlit tunnel.

At Polmont, and clearly marked on the 1st Edition of the OS 6-inch map of 1865, stands a milestone on the north side of the canal. It is inscribed 'Port Downie 4½ and Port Hopetoun 27'.

The canal closed to commercial traffic in 1933, then to all vessels in 1965. When the restoration of the canal began in the early 1990s, only about a third of the original milestones remained. To mark the reopening of the canal at the Millennium (well, 2001 to be precise), the missing stones were replaced, with the mileage on each face inscribed in a similar elegant style. These are at Harrison Park ('1/30½'), Sighthill East ('3½/28'), Sighthill ('4/27½'), Sighthill West ('4½/27'), and Hermitage Bridge ('6/25½'). Most of the remaining original milestones are in a worn condition, although the stage stones, dating from post-1822, have fared better. The milestones are plain sandstone posts (10 inches square in plan) with a shallow pyramid top. They are set at a 'diamond' orientation to the canal, on the towpath, visible above ground level to a maximum height of 24 inches. Of the originals, the best examples are at Clifton Hall (Ratho West) and at the west end of Lin's Mill Aqueduct. The original of the '21' milepost at Linlithgow is now in the Linlithgow Museum.

As part of the upgrade work, new milestones, 24 in total, were crafted by eight apprentice stonemasons based at the masonry training

Left: The Ratho division marker and stone on the Union Canal. *Dr Adrian Sumner*

Above right and right: The contrast between old and new milestones on the Union Canal. *Both Dr Adrian Sumner*

facility in Elgin, using sandstone donated by the contractor responsible for the restoration of the historic structures along the canal. The masonry work took 10 weeks to complete. It is projects such as this that provide opportunities for those seeking a career in stonemasonry to learn their craft. I recall as a schoolboy in Stirling in the 1970s a campaign to encourage school-leavers to train as masons, with the prospect of a lifetime's work at the likes of Stirling Castle. Surely a very satisfying life's work for anyone with the right skillset. Bodies such as the Scottish Stone Liaison Group are key to ensuring that these skills are not lost.

As we've seen for the Forth & Clyde Canal, developments over the ensuing century and a half, including major road-building in the 1960s, meant that the link by water between Glasgow and Edinburgh was lost. The ambitious Millennium Project to restore the link included the magnificent Falkirk Wheel, the only rotating boat lift in the world, completed in 2002, and transformed the waterway into a wonder of the 21st century. Immediately to the east of the Wheel the canal passes through a new tunnel, under the Antonine Wall dating from AD142. I wonder what the Romans would have made of that phenomenon?

As for the Fife milestones, we are spoilt, as a very well-illustrated booklet 'Milestones of the Union Canal' has been written by Jim Lonie, a former colleague of mine at the Department of Agriculture.

The rationale behind the **Crinan Canal** was to shorten the distance and travel time between Glasgow and Oban and the Western Isles beyond, and reduce the risks associated with the longer journey through the often stormy conditions encountered round the Mull of Kintyre. Stretching from Ardrishaig on Loch Gilp, an arm of Loch Fyne, across to Crinan, John Rennie designed the original canal, with works getting under way in 1794. The construction was fraught with difficulties due to terrain and flooding, but it finally opened in 1801. Substantial repair work was

required, however, by Thomas Telford in 1817.

In 2006, to mark the completion of the Dalriada Project, a milestone was erected at Bellanoch, from where the visitor can enjoy impressive views over the Moine Mhor National Nature Reserve. The Project, comprising ten initiatives to enhance the area's natural and cultural heritage across North Knapdale, Kilmichael Glassary, Kilmartin Glen and the Crinan Canal corridor, was a remarkable Landscape Partnership Scheme funded to the tune of £3.1 million by the Heritage Lottery Fund and many other charitable organisations. Public access was one of the key objectives and I can personally vouch for the network of paths and tracks that open up a substantial area of diverse habitats and landscape vistas, having walked many of them while holidaying in Argyll.

A canal almost lost in the mists of time nowadays is the **Aberdeenshire or Inverurie Canal**. It was designed by John Rennie and the 18¼ miles opened in 1805 to haul goods and passengers between Port Elphinstone, at Inverurie, and Aberdeen. Two boats per day plied passengers back and forth in summer, but the canal suffered from the vagaries of the winter weather and was closed between December and March. Its cargo

was most notably granite; approximately 700,000 cubic feet from the Kintore quarry was exported to Sheerness in Kent, where Rennie had designed the rebuilding of the naval dockyard in 1813. John Rennie Senior, who hailed from Phantassie in East Lothian, was indeed a busy man – always the type to ask if you really need something done.

The Aberdeenshire Canal is a great example of a canal being past its use-by date and infilled and overlain by a railway line. It's almost exactly the route that the Great North of Scotland Railway followed when it opened in 1854. But relics remain. About 190 metres west of the former Kinaldie station and built into the north face of a stone dyke, on what was most probably the towpath for the canal, is a granite column, 0.33 metres in diameter, with part of the rounded top bevelled to form a flat surface with the number '12' inscribed. Near Stoneywood House in Dyce can be found the 5½ milestone.

Another canal that is now a railway line is the **Glasgow, Paisley & Johnstone Canal**, located as the name implies west of Glasgow. Three milestones are recorded by Canmore. On the south side of the canal at Bankfoot Bridge there is a Listed Category C milestone, shown on the 1864 OS map and marked 'Glasgow 9/Johnstone

A new milestone on Crinan Canal. *Patrick Mackie, Geograph, Creative Commons Licence*

An old canal milestone at Dyce. *Bill Harrison, Geograph, Creative Commons Licence*

2'. At Castlehead Bridge is one with 'Glasgow 8/Johnstone 3', and at Blackhall 'Glasgow 7/Johnstone 4'. So, the direction of travel is towards the Second City of the Empire.

This canal, designed by Rennie and Telford and opened in 1810, has a chequered history. Intended originally to provide a link between Glasgow and all the booming industrial towns in Renfrewshire, down to the harbour at Ardrossan, it was never financially viable. It was a popular outing for Glaswegians, but on the Martinmas Fair in November 1810 passengers embarking on the *Countess of Eglinton* steamer at Paisley met those trying to disembark, with disastrous consequences. Many ended up in the cold water of a sheer-sided wharf, 84 of them perishing. The canal closed in 1881 and much of the route was developed by the Glasgow & South Western Railway as the Paisley Canal line. The line was reinvigorated in 1990 and uses the skewed River Cart Aqueduct, or Blackhall Bridge, for the railway track, making it the world's oldest railway bridge still in active use.

Our milestone heritage: Tayside

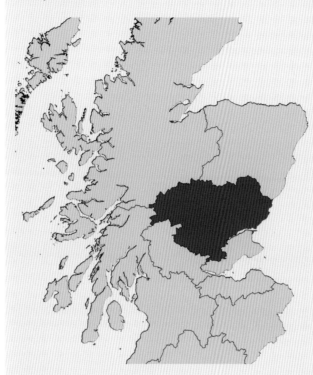

Tayside. *Wikimedia Commons*

Perth & Kinross

Perth & Kinross has a unity stretching back more than 90 years. Formerly Perthshire County Council and Kinross-shire County Council, the two counties merged in 1930 to form Perth & Kinross-shire County Council. Perth & Kinross Council was created in 1996 when Tayside Region was divided into three new unitary council areas, the other two being Angus and Dundee City.

The rich agricultural area between Perth and Forfar, in the Howe of Strathmore, has a wealth of traditional stone milestones, many remaining intact. Near Meigle, on the B954, for example, there is a particular attractive and well-preserved milestone showing Alyth 4, Dundee 13, Meigle ¼, and 'Co Angus' 5¼; the last-named is Coupar Angus, which, despite its name, is now in Angus.

Below: The milestone near Meigle. *The Milestone Society*

Left: Perthshire county sign. *Ken Diamond collection, The Milestone Society*

Perth & Kinross. In season, the snowdrops add an attractive backdrop on this country road verge.

Not many milestones specify thirds of a mile, but there's an example on the A984 near Spittalfield, not far from the Meikleour beech hedge. 'BRIDGEofISL' refers to Bridge of Isla, and there is another bridge nearby, Kinclaven Bridge over the River Tay, near its confluence with the River Isla.

Milestones can be adapted to be dual-purpose. While no one can be in any doubt that they've

arrived at Lechine Cottage, the traveller along the north side of Loch Earn is assured that he is 1 mile from Lochearnhead and 6 miles from St Fillans. Lechine Cottage once belonged to Milestone Society member Iain Davison's aunt and uncle. Iain spent his school holidays there between 1947 and 1956, which must have seemed like a world away from the west end of Edinburgh.

A mile along the road at Lochearnhead another milestone has been painted with the name 'Ben Ouhr', which Iain tells me was the

home of Ewen Cameron, the Highland Games champion who appeared alongside Bill Travers, Alastair Sim, Duncan Macrae and a young Stanley Baxter in the 1955 Scottish film *Geordie*. Several other stalwarts of Scottish television of the late 1950s and 1960s 'starred' in the film too. The actress Molly Urquhart played Geordie's mother and Jameson Clark, who went on to be a news reporter, appearing almost daily on television on the evening news, played his father. In real life, Ewen Cameron did much to promote both sports and tourism; he was the Scottish Heavyweight champion, hence the role in *Geordie* playing opposite Travers's character in the Olympic Games in Melbourne. He was the founder of the Lochearnhead Water Ski Club that same year with

The Meikleour and Bridge of Isla milestone. *Iain Davison, The Milestone Society*

The Lechine Cottage milestone on the A85, 1 mile from Lochearnhead and 6 miles from St Fillans. *Iain Davison, The Milestone Society*

The 'Ben Ouhr' milestone. *Iain Davison, The Milestone Society*

his wife Anne, improvising with the upturned bonnet of a Morris Minor as skis. His name lives on in 'Ewen', Kev Paxton's sculpture of a wee Westie in St Angus Churchyard at the start of the Sustrans cycle route.

Both the Lechine Cottage and 'Ben Ouhr' milestones had performed their primary function as distance markers for some time, however, as both appear on the 1867 and 1901 Editions of the OS maps. Ben Ourh, in case you're wondering, is the Corbett south-west of Loch Earn, on the hike up to Ben Vorlich.

Almost 5 miles due north, on the A827, a mile from Killin on the Crianlarich road, the former milestone has been relocated to the other side of the road to announce 'Breadalbane Killin Curling Club'.

Iain first became aware of the milestones in this area when, as a student civil engineer with Mitchell Construction working on the Breadalbane section of the North of Scotland Hydro Electric Scheme, he carried out a precise level survey of the 14 miles from Kenknock in Glen Lochay to Auchlyne in Glen Dochart. His measurements, and the accuracy thereof, provided a check on the levels of the tunnels being driven between the glens. Iain admits to using the milestones as 'change points' or as temporary benchmarks on the leg down to Killin.

What's in a name? We can't leave Perthshire without a visit to Dull, to the north of the River Tay, near Aberfeldy. Its name is derived from 'Dol', the Pictish word for a water meadow, or what the Scots term a 'haugh'. But it's the modern name that, although conjuring up an image of a lack of inspiration, has engendered a new lease of life for Dull and its 84 residents (as of 2012). Dull is now one of the 'Trinity of Tedium' settlements in the League of Extraordinary Communities – the other two are Boring in Oregon, USA, and Bland in New South Wales, Australia. What a great ploy to encourage tourism! Head for Dull in October if you want to participate in the annual festivities.

Not to be outdone, and getting slightly ahead of ourselves geographically, it's apposite to

include here the hamlet of Lost in Strathdon in Aberdeenshire. Situated close to the village of Bellabeg, at the confluence of the Water of Nochty and the River Don, Lost has a population of 'under 24' (sorry, can't be more precise).

'Lost is this way!' *Mike Lowson*

The 'Breadalbane Killin Curling Club' stone.
Iain Davison, The Milestone Society

'Dull by name…' *The Milestone Society*

'Lost' is the Gaelic for 'inn', although there isn't one. There have been more signpost thefts reported to Grampian Police for this settlement than for any other place name to any other police force, anywhere. At one stage in the early 2000s Aberdeenshire Council decided to stop replacing the sign after so many thefts. However, after a public outcry it was reinstated, presumably with stouter fixings.

Cast iron is the material of choice for the illustrated Perthshire distance marker post on the A923, better known as the Five Lochs Road, including the Loch of the Lowes, between Blairgowrie and Dunkeld. It is near Ardblair Castle, which lies to the east of Forneth Estate, where I cut my teeth as a young estate factor in the 1970s.

The Forneth mile plate. *Iain Davison*

A milestone on the A827 Aberfeldy to Ballinluig road. *The Milestone Society*

Angus

Angus county sign. Angus was known as Forfarshire until 1928. *Ken Diamond collection, The Milestone Society*

Three fingerposts in Angus, probably dating from the 1930s, have been Listed (Category C) by Historic Environment Scotland as of special architectural or historic importance. They are at Tigerton near Menmuir, at Bridgend of Lintrathen, and at Wellford Bridge, which crosses the Noran Water.

The Tigerton fingerpost. *Christopher Dingwall*

The technical description cited for the fingerpost at Tigerton is first class:

'…cross-plan post with ropework moulding at inner angles, formed to round at apex with ball-finialled columnar staff bearing arms… Each arm (of three) with black painted raised lettering giving distance, name and hand with pointing finger.'

The citation further notes:

'…rare survival, once ubiquitous on the roads of

There's a typical Angus glens backdrop for this milestone on the road to Glenisla. Dykends is at the junction of the road through Glen Isla, the B951, where it meets the B954 from the south. *Christine Minto, The Milestone Society*

Above left: The milestone at Inchture on the B953 (near the A90). *The Milestone Society*

Above right: A well-kept, though misspelled, milepost on the road home from Forfar. *Christine Minto, The Milestone Society*

Scotland and an important part of the history of road transport.'

Near Inchture, on the Carse of Gowrie between Perth and Dundee, stands a milestone advising travellers that they are 9 miles from Perth ('P') and 13 miles from Dundee ('D').

The road from Forfar to Arbroath, via Friockheim, is one I know well, having lived at Cotton of Guthrie in the early 1980s. The white-painted mileposts along the A932, passing Reswallie, Rescobie and Balgavies lochs, interlinked by the Lunan Water, signalled the end of another day working as a young surveyor in Forfar. The series of mileposts, manufactured by Anderson of Arbroath, are eye-catching, of a triangular plan 'V' design with top-front bevel, and each post bearing the maker's name in an oval on each face. But each of these mileposts bears a common error. Those eagle-eyed among you will notice from the photograph that the signwriter has misspelled the placename as 'Friockhiem', putting 'i' before 'e'. It's an unusual name, but there is no excuse for bad spelling, or so Mrs MacQueen believed. There are exceptions to the rule about 'i before e except after c', and with the surname of Keith I should not forget that one.

Friockheim translates as 'heather home', the 'Friock' from the Gaelic and the 'heim' from the German. Founded as a new village in 1814 by the local landowner Thomas Gardyne and John Andson from Arbroath, to house workers for their new flax spinning mill, Friock became Friockheim 10 years later, respecting the very large number of Flemish weavers who migrated to work in the mill.

There's a series of similar mileposts along the B9128 from Forfar to Carnoustie. That at Craichie, some 4 miles south of Forfar, does not carry the ovals, however. The manufacturer here is shown as 'SAE Coy/C-A'. Strangely, that's the same manufacturer shown on the milepost at Forneth, and the 'C-A' most probably stands for Coupar Angus.

Six of the first seven milestones on the Brechin to Arbroath road (A933) survive, but all were defaced during the Second World War. At least three of the stones bear the inscription '720Y', which appears in the style used in the mid-19th century. Why? I don't know, but if you do know about the inscription, please let me know.

The first three milestones on the Arbroath to Montrose road (A92) are still visible, but are all different. The milestone nearest Arbroath is a roughly squared block with a '1' inscribed on its west face. Milestone '2' is situated on the west side of the road at Marywell. It is a finely dressed sandstone block that has been painted white and has the letter 'D' inscribed on its west face. This milestone is shown on the OS 6-inch map from 1865, but the single letter inscribed may suggest that it started life as a boundary stone. Milestone '3' is at Wood Inn, which was built in 1805 but is now a private residence. It, too, is a finely dressed block in sandstone and more elaborate than the other two stones. It's inscription originally read 'To MON 9¾ M' and 'To ARB 3 M', but these have been chiselled off.

10
Railway miles

Scotland's first rail-way ran for 2½ miles, downhill, by gravity, from the coal mine at Tranent to the salt pans at Cockenzie. There the heat from the coal evaporated the seawater to produce salt, a valuable commodity. A horse then pulled the waggons back up the hill to the mine. The wheels and the rails were wooden. The year was 1722. Some 40 years later, with a similar system in operation, James Paterson, the son of the blacksmith at Cockenzie, was hit by one of the waggons and died from his injuries. James was the first person to be killed in a railway accident anywhere in the world.

By 1815 cast iron had replaced the wooden elements. In 2019 the 1722 Waggonway Heritage Group unearthed the original wooden rail tracks under what is now a public footpath.

The first passenger route, but also hauling coal, was the Kilmarnock & Troon Railway, opened in 1811 and financed by the local landowner, the Duke of Portland. Originally it was worked by horses, and the Laigh Milton Viaduct over the River Irvine is the oldest surviving public railway viaduct in the world.

However, thanks to Greenock-born James Watt (1736-1819) things were about to get a whole lot easier for the horses. Watt's development of Thomas Newcomen's earlier steam engine, from 1776 onwards, wrought fundamental changes to the Industrial Revolution. By 1847 the new locomotive engine, with much more substantial rolling stock, meant that the viaduct could no longer support the weights imposed, so it was bypassed. Not until the 1990s would it be restored as a legacy of railway history.

The first railway, as we might consider a railway, in Scotland was the Monkland & Kirkintilloch Railway, opening in 1826, again to haul coal.

But we get ahead of ourselves if we think that steam expedited only trains as a form of transport. First there were horseless carriages, and it's a Scot we've to credit with that development too.

John Scott Russell was born in Parkhead in Glasgow in 1808. He was a remarkable scientist and engineer – developing wave theory, building ships and a pioneer of steam vehicles. Russell developed a two-cylinder engine, each cylinder having 12 horsepower, for use in a 26-seater coach capable of travelling at between 15 and 20mph. He had six coaches built in Edinburgh in 1834, initially planned for the Glasgow-Edinburgh service, but the turnpike trustees objected. Instead the Steam Carriage Company of Scotland, the first of its kind in the world, operated coaches every hour between George Square in Glasgow and Tontine Hotel in Paisley, a distance of approximately 10 miles. These horseless carriages ran on the road surface, not rails, so there were complaints from the trustees, who placed obstructions of logs and stones in the roadway. These actually proved of more annoyance to horse-drawn carriages.

This episode in transport history had a sad and premature end. In July 1834 one of the coaches overturned, smashing the boiler, located below the axle, which exploded. Four passengers were killed and the venture failed. Russell managed to find a home for two of his horseless carriages in London, where they plied the route to and from Greenwich.

The day in 1834 when it all went wrong for horseless carriages in Glasgow. *Glasgow Libraries (Mitchell Library)*

By the 1840s the industrial Central Belt was well provided with a railway network, with connections to England. By 1874 the railway had reached Wick and Thurso, and by 1877 there was the first Tay Bridge. Although Thomas Bouch's nemesis was to be lost two years later, such was the resolve of the North British Railway Company that its replacement was opened in 1887. In 1890 the iconic Forth Bridge, the first major structure using steel and three times longer than any cantilever ever built before, was opened. By 1901, and thanks to 'Concrete Bob' McAlpine's use of mass concrete on his viaducts, the line to Mallaig was complete.

As the 20th century dawned, the railways in Scotland were run by five private companies – the North British, the Great North of Scotland, the Caledonian, the Glasgow & South Western and, finally, the Highland. The Railways Act of 1921 brought mergers into two companies, the London & North Eastern Railway (LNER) and the London Midland & Scottish Railway (LMS).

Nationalisation arrived with the 1947 Transport Act, the Scottish Region of British Railways becoming one of six 'regions'. The 'Beeching Cuts' – or amputations, rather, following The Reshaping of British Railways Report in 1963 – led to whole branch lines being closed and stations abandoned. The ScotRail brand saw the first light of day in the 1980s, then in 1997 came privatisation.

It's been a chequered history, for the transport enthusiast an interesting cacophony of success tainted by some major failures. Beneath the surface, another triumph worth trumpeting is the Glasgow Subway, opened in 1896, the third oldest underground network in the world, after the London Underground and the Budapest Metro.

It is not a track record without blemish, however, and some of the 'bad news stories' need to be rehearsed too. I've mentioned the Tay Bridge disaster of 28 December 1879, when a violent storm destroyed the bridge and the Burntisland to Dundee train careered into the river below,

with the loss of everyone on board. The structural failure was down to a fatal mixture of flawed design (no account taken of windloading), poor quality control of materials and construction, and a lack of proper maintenance. It was Sir Thomas Bouch's death knell and he died only six months after the disaster. It is a mark of true resilience and engineering prowess that the second Tay Rail Bridge was completed and open for business by 1887. It remains the longest railway bridge in Britain, carrying trains from Aberdeen, Stonehaven, Laurencekirk (reopened 2009), Montrose, Arbroath, Monifieth, Carnoustie, Broughty Ferry and Dundee to and from the south, as far as London and cross-country to Penzance. Opened on 6 October 1838 on the Dundee & Arbroath Railway, Broughty Ferry is the oldest railway station in Scotland still in operation. But there is another tragic rail accident to relate.

On 15 May 1915 a troop train carrying soldiers of the Royal Scots to Gallipoli crashed into a stationary local passenger train on the Caledonian Railway at Quintinshill Junction, near Gretna in Dumfriesshire. The initial collision was caused by signalman's error, and this was followed by a further collision when a northbound express train ploughed into the wreckage. The damage was accentuated by the light construction of the carriages. To compound the deaths and injuries further, the gas containers on the troop train caught fire. In total, 230 people were killed and 224 injured, making the Quintinshill accident the biggest railway disaster to occur in Britain.

The Board of Trade investigation and inquest started 10 days later, concluding that the signalmen, James Tinsley and George Meakin, were responsible for the manslaughter of those who died in the collisions. On 14 September 1915 Tinsley and Meakin were convicted of culpable homicide arising from gross neglect of their duties. Meakin was sentenced to 18 months' imprisonment, while Tinsley, who evidently suffered from epilepsy, was to be detained in Peterhead prison for three years, with hard labour.

The National Union of Railwaymen petitioned for reduced sentences, or even a Royal Pardon. In the event, both men were released on 15 December 1916.

Since we're thinking about distances in this book, you may be interested to note that, as of 2018, the total length of the rail network in Scotland was 1,724 miles (2,758km). Of that total, 558 miles (893km) are electrified. However, do note that these figures do not represent the total length of railway track, as a kilometre of single track and a kilometre of double track both count as 1 kilometre of route length. There were 97.8 million passengers on ScotRail trains in 2018, which is an increase of 31% over the statistic for 2007/08. The number of stations also increased, from 340 in 2003/04 to 359 in 2018.

If by chance you are a public transport advocate, you may be interested to note that there were 380 million passenger journeys on local bus services in Scotland in 2018, accounting for more than 73% of all public transport journeys. However, bus passenger journeys have been falling over the longer term, almost halving between 1960 and 1975, and roughly halving again since then. Air terminals handled 29.4 million passengers in 2018, with 5% being flights internal to Scotland, 39% within the UK, and 44% travelled between Scotland and mainland Europe. Oh, and not to forget the ferries, they carried 8.5 million passengers and 3 million vehicles on ferry routes within Scotland in 2018, increasing to 10.3 and 3.4 million respectively if the Northern Ireland service from Cairnryan is included.

I am an Honorary Railwayman, or so my friends with whom I have travelled and walked each May for nearly 40 years have dubbed me. They are all products of the British Rail Traffic Management Training Scheme in the late 1970s (you may recall the name British Rail – it's quite a quaint term). All went on to successful careers, and over the years we've visited almost every region of the UK, certainly all those with some vestige of railway heritage.

One thing sticks in my mind from their early days on British Rail. Regular formal testing on the railway rules and regulations from their line managers was an integral part of railway life. Failure was not an option.

So it was no surprise to me to learn that even in the provision of distance markers along railway lines there was a statutory requirement. If you feel compelled to check it out, it's in the Railways Clauses Consolidation (Scotland) Act of 1845. Section 87, to be precise, states:

'The company shall cause the length of the railway to be measured, and milestones, posts or other conspicuous objects to be set up and maintained along the whole line thereof, at the distance of one quarter of a mile from each other, with numbers or marks inscribed thereon denoting such distances.'

Primarily these milestones act as a reference point that can be used to specify a position on the infrastructure, for example engineering work or an accident. Railway mileages still use miles and chains, with each bridge or other structure bearing the distance, which cross-refers to the milestones along the route and the engineering drawings. In some cases these may be nearly 200 years old.

New engineering works are, of course, now measured in kilometres and metres and shown as such on the technical drawings. It must be a fascinating industry to work in, with the engineers working in metric while the operators rely on imperial references. There must have been a sigh of relief when satellite navigation technology came along.

The milestones also allowed travellers to verify that they had been charged an appropriate fare for the length of their journey, according to the tariff. While an obvious benefit to passengers, they also provided a means for the train guard to calculate the speed of the train. The engine was not equipped with a speedometer in these far-distant days. With stopwatch in hand, the guard would capture the time taken to travel between

two marker posts and hence work out the speed of travel.

Perhaps that's what gave my Dad the idea for exercising my brain during long car journeys. He had, after all, spent his secondary school days commuting to and from school in Arbroath and the family home in Carnoustie. Just as books were produced showing gradients of public roads, so the railway companies produced schematics showing railway gradients, another key factor affecting train speed and travel times.

Of course, rail enthusiasts in the days when trains went 'dickety-dum' as the wheels crossed the joints in the rails knew that those joints were 66 feet (20 metres) apart. Simple mathematics of counting the number of 'dickety-dums', or 66-foot lengths, in a given time interval using one's watch gave an easy method of calculating the train's speed. The use of continuously welded rail put an end to such simple pleasures, sadly.

Faithfully reproduced in *Britain's Scenic Railways* in *The Times* by Julian Holland and David Spaven is a cross-section of the route over the Galloway hills between Girvan and Stranraer (the Portpatrick Railway), including 'mileposts on down side from zero at Girvan No 1 to Challoch JC [Junction)]', to the east of Dunragit, and hence to Stranraer.

Although the requirement was to provide distance markers, the style to be adopted was left to the individual railway company. So there are some considerable variations on a common theme across the country.

Common to all was that the measurement was from a defined point of origin, in most cases a major station or junction. In some cases there might be a 'zero' post, or simply '0', but normally there was no marker used.

The pattern used did vary considerably. The milestone could either face the track with a single face or, alternatively, be angled, with two faces, so it could be read from an approaching train. Sometimes intermediate posts would record not only the fraction of a mile but also the full mileage,

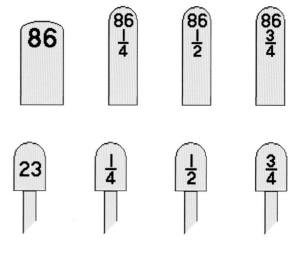

Types of railway mileposts.

An '85' milestone on the Highland Railway/Strathspey Railway, north of Aviemore.
The Railway Performance Society

A '77' milestone on the Glasgow & South Western Railway, north of Thornhill.
The Railway Performance Society

Different shapes distinguishing the quarter-mileposts.

Above left: A '63½' milepost on the Keith & Dufftown Railway, east of Dufftown.
The Railway Performance Society

Above right: A '¼' milepost on the North British Railway at Haymarket, Edinburgh.
The Railway Performance Society

When British Rail come along it introduced the use of triangular symbols and horizontal bars to indicate quarter-miles.

Above left: Metric mileposts.

Above right: A yellow-banded furlong post.

as in the Highland Railway, or in other cases not.

Another variation was to use different shapes for quarter-mileposts to make identification of the fractions easier, as adopted by the Caledonian Railway.

My appreciation goes to the Railway Performance Society for the use of the accompanying illustrations. Perhaps it's more than a nod to the importance of distance measurement along the tracks that the Society's quarterly journal is entitled 'Milepost'.

Unusually, the full mileposts on the Edinburgh & Glasgow Railway showed the mileage from both these cities.

Drawings are courtesy of *Railway Signs and Signals of Great Britain*

From 1983, mileposts were generally coloured yellow to coincide with the repainting of the permanent speed restriction indicators. The change from white to yellow also made them easier to see in the snow.

In some cases, kilometre posts are provided in addition to mileposts, often in association with electrification of the line, and two examples from Scotland are illustrated here.

Further detail was added in 1987 on some lines in the north of Glasgow. These were short posts with two yellow bands, provided midway between the quarter-mileposts as distance markers at 1 furlong intervals. As we know, 1 furlong equates to 10 chains and there are 8 furlongs in 1 mile.

When Scotland's first inter-city train service, the Edinburgh & Glasgow Railway, opened in 1842, the distances along the route were indicated by distinctive cast-iron mileposts, 45 in total, showing the miles to Haymarket station in Edinburgh in one direction and to Queen Street station in Glasgow in the other. The eastern terminus became Waverley station when it opened in 1846. The journey time was 2½ hours and two trains ran on a Sunday despite protestations from the Church of Scotland.

There is some evidence that the design of the mileposts, with polygonal heads supported on narrow stems, bore some pedigree to the style adopted on turnpike roads, as shown in the accompanying photograph of a restored milestone

The 'railway-style' cast-iron milestone near Kilsyth. *Christine Minto, The Milestone Society*

a mile east of Kilsyth, itself only about a mile from the line of the Edinburgh & Glasgow Railway.

Which foundry produced the mileposts on this line is uncertain, although McDowall & Robertson, based at the Milton Foundry in Port Dundas, seems most probable, as the Minute Books from 1841 evidence that it produced the cast-iron columns for Queen Street station in Glasgow. The foundry, established in 1828 by John McDowall, became McDowall Steven & Company in 1862 and won many contracts for ornamental works and Victorian post boxes.

Commenting in the 1960s, the railway historian Professor Jack Simmons from Leicester University considered the mileposts on the Edinburgh & Glasgow Railway to be the oldest railway mileposts then used anywhere in Britain. The guidebook published in 1992 to mark the 150th anniversary of the line noted that 15 of the 17 mileposts between Glasgow and Castlecary were still of the original pattern, although none survived at other locations. It is speculated, probably correctly, that the mileposts going eastwards from Castlecary were removed in 1940 under the invasion precautions. Several of the mileposts west of Castlecary, with its viaduct by John Miller, have found safe homes in museums. Milepost No 2 (originally '2/44', located at Ashgill Road near Cowlairs) is in the Scottish Railway Museum in Bo'ness, while No 6 (originally '6/40', located at Lenzie) is in the National Museum of Scotland in Edinburgh, and No 13 ('13/33') is housed in the collection of the Auld Kirk Museum in Kirkintilloch.

Two other mileposts are preserved and on display for the modern train traveller to admire. One was unveiled at Queen Street station in 2008, and has been reinstated there following the major modernisation of the station completed in 2020. It's even been repainted in its original white colour rather than the previous yellow travesty. The other, milepost No 5, has been on display in Haymarket station since 2017. Formerly sited at the Cadder Marshalling Yard, between

Bishopbriggs and Lenzie, it was Listed Category C in 1997 on the recommendation of Malcolm Reed, deputy chair of the Railway Heritage Committee, as the best surviving example of an Edinburgh & Glasgow Railway milepost. He also dubbed it 'Scotland's smallest national monument'. The largest, in case you wonder, is also an iconic piece of railway heritage, the Forth Bridge. The No 5 milepost features, unsurprisingly, in the *Edinburgh in 101 Objects* virtual tour.

The milepost displayed at Queen Street station in Glasgow. *John Yellowlees*

Of the others originating on the Edinburgh & Glasgow Railway, Nos 3 and 4 are bound for the National Railway Museum in York and the Glasgow Museum of Transport respectively. Milepost No 15 ('15/31') has turned up in a railway enthusiast's garden in Callander, alongside other railway memorabilia such as a signal, and a sign that reads 'Beware of the Trains'. Well, some people collect stamps.

On the electrified East Coast Main Line (ECML) linking Edinburgh to London King's Cross, we find another piece of railway heritage. On the section north of Berwick-upon-Tweed are two sets of stamped metal signs dating from the 1920s. One set, between Houndwood and Grantshouse, provides the distance to London (350 miles), while the other marker, near Ayton, shows the distance to Edinburgh (50 miles). These

The '5' milepost now on display at Haymarket, featuring Christine Minto to give scale and perspective. *John S. Riddell*

were showing their age in 2018 when Transform Scotland, the railway heritage advocate, raised its concern with John Yellowlees, one-time ScotRail guru and now Honorary Rail Ambassador. John quickly masterminded a collaborative project between Network Rail (Scotland) and the Railway Heritage Trust to refurbish the signs. Andy Savage of the Trust agreed to fund the materials while Russell Kimber's team at Network Rail (Scotland) carried out the work as volunteers – a splendid job, and meritorious of the Stagecoach Volunteers' Award at the National Railway Heritage Awards in 2018.

For those eagled-eyed commuters on the East Coast Main Line – and I was one myself for very many years – there are similar distance markers to Edinburgh further south on the route. In

Refurbishment under way on the East Coast Main Line metal railway signs. *John Yellowlees*

Nottinghamshire there's a 250-mile sign and, just north of York, a 200-mile sign.

The distance between Edinburgh Waverley (the middle of the station) and the border with England at Marshall Meadows is 54 miles and 50 chains, i.e. 54 and five-eighths miles. However, the locations of the series of stamped metal signs do not now completely reflect accurately the distance on the ground, for over the nearly 100 years since they were erected there have been several minor alterations to the ECML route.

Between Edinburgh and Berwick there have been alterations at Prestonpans and Penmanshiel. The roof of the tunnel at Penmanshiel, just north of Grantshouse, collapsed in 1979, with two operatives losing their lives. Hauntingly, two of my close railway friends, Colin Shearer and Mike Lowson, were travelling north together to Edinburgh from London that evening on one of the last trains to pass through the tunnel shortly before disaster struck.

The collapse resulted in the permanent closure of the 267-yard-long tunnel and a realignment of the tracks through a cutting. There have also been diversions created south of Alnmouth and at Newton Hall curve, to the north of Durham, and,

more significantly in 1984, around the Selby area in Yorkshire. So when you spot these signs on your train journey, don't take the distances as gospel.

The introduction of the high-speed Inter-City 125 trains in 1977/78, including on the 'Flying Scotsman' service, reduced the travel times between Edinburgh and London by as much as 1 hour; obviously the margin depended on the number of stations called at en route. It's traditionally been the ambition of most schoolboys to be a train driver. It certainly was in the glorious days of steam rail travel. But travelling continuously at 125mph for mile after mile isn't exactly the most exciting experience for a train driver, so the alternating speed limits in force between Berwick and Edinburgh make for an altogether more challenging but satisfying job.

In those 54 miles, the maximum speed limit varies between 95, 80 and 90 from Marshall Meadows to the curves at Grantshouse and north to Penmanshiel. The top speed of 125mph is experienced around Innerwick, before slowing to 95 through Dunbar and accelerating again to 115 to 125mph past Wallyford and Prestonpans. Approaching the rail depot at Craigentinny, the train slows to 90, then to 40 travelling through the Calton Tunnels and into the platform (frequently No 11) at Waverley.

I've arrived and departed from Perth station many times, especially during my career with SSE plc, whose head office is in the Fair City. It's a very fine station, designed by architect Sir William Tite, whose other commissions included the Royal Exchange in London. Perth General, as it was known when it opened in 1848 as the terminus of the Scottish Central Railway from Glasgow, quickly became a railway hub of considerable importance. It was the junction where four main lines converged, the other three being the Dundee & Perth Railway from Dundee, the Edinburgh & Northern Railway from Ladybank in Fife, and the Scottish Midland Junction Railway from Forfar. By 1856 the last-named became the through route to Aberdeen.

Subsequently, the Perth & Dunkeld Railway, which became the Highland main line to Inverness, and the Perth, Almond Valley & Methven Railway were added. A very busy station, and one to and from which measurements were made. Records show that Perth station is 20 miles 64 chains from Dundee. From Platforms 5 -7 it is 151 miles 25 chains to Carlisle, measured via the former Ravenscraig No 1, and from Platforms 5 and 6, the two disused platforms at the northern end of the station, it is 151 miles 36 chains from Carlisle. This is the 'zero point' for the Highland main line, although the mileposts do not change until Stanley Junction (158 miles 38 chains from Carlisle – and, yes, you've worked it out, 7 miles 2 chains from Perth). Why Stanley Junction? Because that's where the Highland Railway and the Caledonian Railway officially met.

It's always been a tradition, perhaps a rather strange one, to include mileages in railway timetables, shown as a separate column. That veritable old worthy, *Bradshaw's Guide*, on which Michael Portillo has themed his wonderful railway journey television programmes, contains detailed mileages. Likewise, the Thomas Cook Guide. The Great Britain Time Table, the go-to reference for railway enthusiasts, if not the ordinary traveller, who may prefer simpler travel information, published in printed format all railway journey times in the UK, including distances, down to quarter-miles. When the last published – that is, printed – timetable expired at 23.59 on Saturday 8 December 2008, one might have expected that the rationalisation of data content arising from a massive computerisation exercise might have been the death knell for the mileage information. Not so. The electronic timetable has retained mileages – just have a look online if you don't believe me.

Lest you think this is bizarre, in Australia the railway timetables included not only mileages, but also the altitude above sea level. Perhaps this data may come into its own with concerns about the impact of climate change and consequential sea level rise?

Our milestone heritage: Grampian

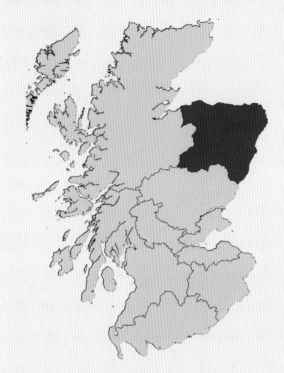

Grampian. *Wikimedia Commons*

Aberdeenshire county sign. *Ken Diamond collection, The Milestone Society*

The Aberdonians certainly call a spade a spade, if not a bloody shovel. The Lang Stracht, one of the Granite City's principal thoroughfares, is aptly named. And it seems even longer if you have to walk this built-up section of the A944, in the snow, as I did one winter's evening when my car refused to start.

Talking of snow, invariably the first road to get blocked with snow each year is the A939 Cock Bridge to Tomintoul road north of Strathdon. The milestones along Strathdon have recently been refurbished and repainted. It was a summer's day near Corgarff when the accompanying photograph was taken.

A milestone on the A939, west of its junction with the A944 (inscribed '51', it is, in practice, equidistant between Aberdeen and Banff, travelling on A roads). *The Milestone Society*

There's no point in being too effusive. On the Royal Deeside road (A93), in the parish of Aboyne and Glen Tanar, stands a granite milestone that simply reads '28'. It's miles from Aberdeen, if there's any doubt.

Milestones around Haddo House, a property now in the care of the National Trust for Scotland, state the distance, one up to 5 miles from the house, 'HH'. The 2-mile stone, for example, is opposite the church in Methlick.

An early milestone in Deveron Road, Huntly, on the A920 to Dufftown. *The Milestone Society*

The milestone on the A93 at Drumgesk, stating miles from Aberdeen. *The Milestone Society*

The 5 miles from Haddo House stone, duly 'floodlit'. *Christine Minto, The Milestone Society*

Kincardineshire

Kincardineshire county sign. *Ken Diamond collection, The Milestone Society*

The milestone set into the wall of a furniture workshop in Stonehaven, next to the bridge over the Carron Water, is Listed Category C, but also of interest is the former toll house. When it was built in 1806 it was occupied by Alexander Reith and his wife and 15 children. His descendent, born in Stonehaven, was Lord Reith, the first Director General of the BBC.

Above and below: Milestones in Auchenblae Parish. The 'L' is for Laurencekirk and the 'S' for Stonehaven. *Both The Milestone Society*

On to the rich farmland of The Mearns to the lands of Lewis Grassic Gibbon's *Sunset Song* (voted Scotland's most popular cultural novel in 2016), the network of country roads linking farmsteads and villages has now been bypassed by the A90. Here we find old milestones, like the two illustrated here on the B966 near Auchenblae.

When I was travelling the A90 between Forfar and Aberdeen regularly in the late 1970s/early '80s, the main road still went through the towns of Laurencekirk and Stonehaven. And it had been the main road to Aberdeen, the oil capital of Europe, for more than a decade by that time. I often wondered what the Americans made of it.

Stones, of course, come in all shapes and sizes and are put to multiple uses. As well as milestones, there are gravestones, tombstones, quernstones and, if you are really unlucky, kidney stones. They have also been used for many centuries as boundary stones, to mark out or delineate the extent of a town or city or a private estate. It's cheaper to use a stone at each corner or change of direction than use a whole heap of stones to build a wall. Surveying these boundaries has become a tradition, no more so than in the Borders, where Riding the Common Marches is part of the town's calendar of celebratory activities. Towns such as Hawick, Lauder and Selkirk have held the ridings for more than 800 years, but the relatively 'younger' events in Jedburgh, Melrose, Kelso and Peebles date from more than 100 years ago. Elsewhere, there are festive events in Annan, Langholm, Musselburgh, Lanark and Biggar – as far north as Kirkwall, all have such days, often also associated with a local historic anniversary.

Boundary stones can be found in most towns, most of them hidden away or used as a garden ornamentation these days. Averill Weighill has researched the boundary stones in Dumfries, which include not only ancient boundaries, but also those used by the War Department in the First World War, and marked 'WD', used to delineate land acquired for military purposes.

Indeed, there are 26 property boundary stones.

each marked 'WD', round Edinburgh Castle – on the Esplanade, in Princes Street Gardens and on surrounding streets. These date from between the early 1850s and 1877, and are of igneous rock, possibly from the volcanic Castle Rock itself, and inscribed with 'WD', the upward-pointing arrow symbol and the number in Roman numerals. The example shown here is on the north side of the entrance to the Esplanade, at the corner of the former Castlehill Reservoir building, which was built in 1851.

The reason for including this reference on boundary stones in the Grampian section is that Aberdeen City Council has promoted the boundary stones around the Granite City in not one but two trails, captured in its booklet *Boundary Stones Trail*. The inner march stones mark the boundary of the crofts that ringed the medieval Royal Burgh of Aberdeen. The outer march stones define a much greater area, known as the Freedom Lands, which were brought within the city's jurisdiction at a later date. The booklet provides maps and routes and a brief history of the numbered stones. For a detailed history you therefore need look no further than James Cruickshank's book *Freedom Lands and Marches of Aberdeen, 1319-1929*.

Boundary stones are not always where they were originally placed, or may not be what they first appear to be. In many cases their siting can be traced back several centuries. An example of this is found in the booklet 'The Historylinks Trail' for Dornoch. A massive stone marked 'St Michael's Well' in Embo Road was placed there by one George Gunn, the chief of the Clan Gunn and estate factor to the Duke of Sutherland in the first half of the 19th century. Mr Gunn had the stone hewn, inscribed and erected here – near enough to his home in Rhives, just south of Golspie, so he could retain his vote in local elections.

'WD' boundary stone No IX at Edinburgh Castle. The Witches' Well memorial drinking fountain on the other side of the doorway was erected in 1894, as a monument to witches burned at the stake in medieval times.
John S. Riddell

11
Going the distance – fastest and farthest: the top 50 Scots

Wyndham Halswelle in the final of the 400 metres race. *10C Archives*

Having established the distance from point A to point B, the competitive nature in us all triggers the urge to determine how quickly we can reach point B. The mile has become the imperial benchmark here, too, hence miles per hour (mph) for calibrating speed.

We've already encountered Cobb's albeit ultimately disastrous attempt at the world water speed record on Loch Ness, but when it comes to records for both speed and endurance over long distances, native Scots are no slouches. Whether the mode of travel be running, cycling or driving over land, or swimming, rowing or sailing on water, the Scots have set some impressive records – and produced some real characters as well. In 2002 the Scottish Sports Hall of Fame was established. All worthy of their place, this chapter pays homage to 50 Scots (and a few others) who have gone that extra mile demanded in achieving success in breaking records for speed and endurance by being the fastest or travelling the farthest.

The first official list of Scottish records was produced in November 1886, when one D. S. Duncan ran 1 mile in 4 minutes 32.2 seconds. The record for the 1-mile walk was set by J. Harvie in 7 minutes 2.4 seconds. For comparison purposes, the current Scottish record for the 1-mile distance is held by Graham Williamson, who ran it in 3 minutes 50.64 seconds on 13 July 1982 in a race in Cork.

Mr Duncan may well have won the 1-mile race in 1886, but the Scot who dominated the record

books that year was A. P. Findlay (initials were the style in those days), who performed the fastest times for races over 3, 5, 6, 7, 8, 9 and 10 miles. He ran the longest distance in 55 minutes 16.8 seconds.

Today's Scottish long-distance runners set a cracking pace too. Callum Hawkins, born in Elderslie in 1992, has, by the age of 18, achieved the records for each of the 10, 15, 20, 25 and 30-kilometre road runs, he's the course record holder for the Great Scottish Run, and completed the London Marathon in 2019 in 2 hours 8 minutes 14 seconds. That's fast. The girls are not far behind. Laura Muir holds the Scottish female record for the mile at 4 minutes 18.43 seconds. In the Frankfurt Marathon in 2019, Stephanie Twell completed the 26 miles 385 yards in 2 hours 26 minutes 40 seconds.

The Olympics are the truly international testing ground, however. When the modern Olympics started, held appropriately in Athens in Greece, a Scottish weightlifting champion, Launceston Elliot, carried off the gold and silver medals. By the 1908 Olympics, staged in London, the Scots had got off the starting blocks on the track, with Arthur Robertson winning gold in the team steeplechase event and Wyndham Halswelle securing gold in the 400 metres.

Not that Halswelle's win was without controversy. He qualified for the final in 48.4 seconds (an Olympic record). The 100 metres was not run in lanes at that time and, on entering

the last straight, John Carpenter ran wide, forcing Halswelle to within 18 inches of the outside of the track, using his right elbow to prevent Halswelle from overtaking. The umpire, Roscoe Badger, observed Carpenter's actions and declared the race void, with Carpenter disqualified. The rerun was to be staged two days later, but two American athletes refused to participate, so Halswelle ran the 400 metres alone, in a time of 50.2 seconds. It is the only occasion in Olympic history where the final was a walkover. Lesson learned, however, and at the 1912 Olympic Games separate lanes were introduced. Two years previously Halswelle had won the 100, 220, 440 and 880 yards titles one afternoon at Powderhall in Edinburgh, a feat never since equalled. Tragically, Halswelle was killed by a sniper's bullet at the Battle of Neuve Chapelle in France in March 1915.

The Royal Clyde Yacht Club won the sailing competition in the 12 metres class in 1908, but at the 1912 Olympics in Stockholm Philip Fleming

Eric Liddell, the principled athlete. *Wikimedia Commons*

Sir Chris Hoy. *Wikimedia Commons*

and Angus Gillan won gold in the rowing eights and Wally Kinnear likewise in the single sculls. In, rather than on, the water, Isabella Moore was Scotland's first female swimming gold medallist in the 100 metres freestyle.

Antwerp in 1920 saw Robert Lindsay win gold in the 400 metres relay, then in 1924 one of this country's great sporting legends, Eric Liddell, a missionary in China, won gold in the 400 metres and a bronze in the 200 metres. The poignancy of this should not be lost. Liddell refused to compete in the race scheduled to be run on a Sunday, due to his religious beliefs of observing the Sabbath. The drama unfolds in the 1981 film *Chariots of Fire*, with Scottish actor Ian Charleson portraying Liddell's anguish, but then the bitter-sweet irony as he wins gold in the 400 metres, which had not been hitherto his strength. Liddell was to return to China as a missionary and tragically his life ended prematurely in a Japanese internment camp in 1945.

James McNabb won gold in the coxless fours in 1924. Then there is a conspicuous gap of 44 years while the country was 'resting', in the sense that an actor rests, before again achieving gold in Mexico in 1968 and Munich in 1972. The honours on both occasions were due to Rodney Pattison, born in Campbeltown in 1943, for his prowess in yachting.

Another justly celebrated Scot, David Wilkie from Edinburgh, won gold in the 200 metres breaststroke in 1976. When Edinburgh athlete Allan Wells won the 100 metres sprint at the 1980 Moscow Olympics, he was asked if had run the race for Harold Abrahams, the last 100 metres Olympic runner from Britain, who had died two years previously. 'No,' replied Wells, 'I would prefer to dedicate this to Eric Liddell.'

In both 1984 (Los Angeles) and 1988 (Seoul), water was the medium for gold success, for Richard Budgett (rowing) and Michael (Mike) McIntyre (sailing – Star class) respectively. There then followed another prolonged period of fallow for Scotland – well we've learnt to live with it in both football and on the rugby field too – until 2000 in Sydney, when Andrew Lindsay and Shirley Robertson delivered golds for rowing and sailing respectively. Stephanie Cook also rose to the challenge to walk away with gold, and probably a few tender muscles, after winning the modern pentathlon.

And now we encounter a true giant of Scottish – nay world – sport, Chris Hoy, the Edinburgh cyclist with more than a spring in his step, or pedal. In Beijing in 2008, Chris took the world by storm, winning not one, not two, but three gold medals, in keirin, sprint and team sprint races. He followed that with two further golds in the London Olympics in 2012. He is the greatest Olympian Scotland (and well beyond) has ever produced, a fantastic ambassador for sport and a thoroughly good egg, too. *Sir* Chris now, of course – and there could not be a more deserving knight.

While we're in London, let's not

forget that Scotland's proud heritage of water-based golds was also being complemented, with golds for Heather Stanning and Glasgow-born and Aberdeenshire-raised Katherine Grainger for rowing, and Ian Baillie in the canoe slalom.

Heather, who was head girl at Gordonstoun and ranked the No 1 female rower in the world, delivered gold again in 2016 in Rio, joined by another two champion cyclists, Callum Skinner and Katie Archibald.

The 2020 Olympics might have been somewhat of a damp squib – postponed, due to Covid 19, until 2021. But they were well worth the wait in anticipation. The Scottish star was undoubtedly Duncan Scott, the 24-year-old swimmer from Alloa, who made history after winning four medals. That's more than any other British athlete at a single Olympic Games. Duncan achieved one Gold and three Silvers in Tokyo. Katie Archibald continued her cycling successes with one Gold and one Silver medal, and fellow Scottish cyclist Jack Carlin achieved one Silver and one Bronze in the sprint events at his Olympic debut.

Since 1908 the Scots have won a total of 175 Olympic medals: 59 Gold, 73 Silver and 43 Bronze. Of these, 153 were won in the Summer Olympics and the other 22 in the Winter Olympics. The most gold medals at any Games is seven, and that was achieved exactly 100 years apart, in Stockholm in 1912 and in London in 2012. The Scots also won five medals in London in 1908. In the Winter Olympics, the country's best performance, to date at any rate, is five golds at Salt Lake City in 2002, where our lady curlers, skipped by Rhona

Martin, triumphed. All in all, not a bad record for a small country with a population of around five million.

Yet it is not just at the Olympics where the Scottish stars of sports win glory. Dundee-born Liz McColgan (now McColgan-Nuttall) won a silver at the 1988 Olympics, but a gold at the 1991 World Championships for the 10,000 metres and two golds at the Commonwealth Games. Barely stopping to regain her breath, she won the 1991 New York City Marathon, the 1992 World Half Marathon Championships, the 1992 Tokyo Marathon and the 1996 London Marathon. She is only the third woman in history to run 10,000 metres in less than 31 minutes.

Yvonne Murray, born in Musselburgh in 1964, was, as of 2020, Scotland's most decorated individual athlete in Olympic, World, European and Commonwealth competitions, with 11 winning medals. Yvonne has held the 2,000 metres record since 1986, breaking her own record in 1994 with a time of 5 minutes 26.93 seconds.

Being fleet of foot is an attribute if you are a professional footballer, but it also impresses on the racetrack. George McNeill, born in Tranent in 1947, played for Hibernian ('Hibs'), Greenock Morton and Stirling Albion before switching to become a sprinter in the fast lane. McNeill is the only man to have won both of the most famous footraces in the world, the New Year Sprint in Scotland in 1970 and the Australian equivalent, the Stalwell Gift, in 1981.

Behind the wheel the Scots have also impressed on the world stage. Like many of my generation, my boyhood hero was Jim Clark, twice Formula 1 World Champion (1963 and 1965), with 25 Grand Prix wins under his belt when he met an untimely death in a Formula 2 race in Hockenheim in Germany in April 1968. At that time he had more Grand Prix wins and had achieved more pole positions (33) than any other driver. No wonder that in 2009 *The Times* newspaper placed Clark top in the world league of Formula 1 drivers. The newly expanded museum to Jim Clark in

Katherine Grainger. *Wikimedia Commons*

Duns, opened in 2019, is a fitting tribute to his contribution to the sport. Although Jim was a Fifer by birth, from Kilmany, he farmed in Berwickshire and had long associations with Duns.

Just three years younger than Clark, Jackie Stewart was quick to take the reins (it that's at all an appropriate metaphor for a racing car…). Sir Jackie, the 'Flying Scot', won three Drivers' World Championships and secured his position as an ambassador for sport with his endless efforts to improve safety on the race track. This is an impressive legacy, if one compares the current safety record with the appalling roll call of tragic deaths of young motor-racing drivers in the 1960s and '70s. And not at all bad for a youngster from Dumbarton who was branded 'stupid' at school due to his dyslexia.

On the Formula 1 race track, Scotland has also

been well represented by David Coulthard, born in Twynholm in Kirkcudbrightshire. Coming from solid family stock – his grandfather competed in the Monte Carlo Rally and his father was Scottish National Champion in karting – David was the first winner of the McLaren/Autosport Young Driver of the Year Award. His success culminated as runner-up in the 2001 F1 Championship, driving for McLaren, but he nevertheless took the chequered flag for 13 Grand Prix wins and had 62 podium finishes.

Sport is a great leveller – it's open to all, even the aristocracy. John Crichton-Stuart, 7th Marquess of Bute (born 1958), sounds an unlikely character to find in the pits. His ancestral pile includes Mount Stuart House on the Isle of Bute, and, until 2007, Dumfries House in Ayrshire, which his family sold to the state, aided and abetted, it should be added, by another member of the aristocracy, the Duke of Rothesay, aka Prince Charles, for £45 million. Motor sport is an expensive business. Around the pits he's simply Johnny Dumfries, and an impressive racing driver at that. With two team mates, he won the 24 Hours Le Mans Race in 1988, driving a Jaguar XJR-9. Sadly, Johnny died prematurely in 2021, just as I was writing this part of the book.

Jim Clark at the 1967 US Grand Prix in Watkins Glen, New York. *Wikimedia Commons*

Not that Dumfries is our only Le Mans champion. In two consecutive years, 1956 and '57, Edinburgh-born Ron Flockhart was part of Scotland's Ecurie Ecosse Team to win Le Mans. In the 1957 race the team set a distance record of 2,732.8 miles. Allan McNish, born in Dumfries, won the 24-hour race on three occasions, in 1998, 2008 and most recently in 2013. I witnessed Allan's win in 1998, on the first of my seven visits to Le Mans with my late friend Keith Little. Allan also triumphed in the USA, winning the American Le Mans Series three times. Another Scot, Dario Franchitti, from Bathgate, also flew the Saltire in the USA, winning the Indy Car Series four times, the Indianapolis 500 three times and, for good measure, the 24-hour Daytona race.

Scotland can boast a further Le Mans champion, Paul Di Resta, born in Uphall and raised in Bathgate, who has won the Le Mans Prototype (LMP)2 Class race three times to date, in 2018, 2019 and 2020. The distance his car covered was 3,134 miles, at an average speed of 130mph. Comparing that to the record Flockhart set in 1957 makes me realise how much life has speeded up within my lifetime.

Also in motorsport, Colin McRae from Lanark was the World Rally Champion in 1995, being the first Scot (indeed, British driver), and the youngest at 27, ever to win the title. Colin was tragically killed, together with one of his young sons and two friends, in a helicopter crash in 2007. The McRaes are sporting legends in Scotland. Colin's father Jimmy was five times British Rally Champion and his younger brother, Alister, has also had success on the rally course, being the British Rally Champion in 1995. Oh, and the boys' uncle, Hugh 'Shug' Steele is also a former rally driver.

Returning to cycling, for sheer stamina and endurance on a bike you can't surpass another Scot, Blairgowrie-born Mark Beaumont. He holds the record for cycling round the world. The 18,297 miles took less than 79 days, knocking Jules Verne's 'Around the World in Eighty Days' into a cocked hat. Somewhat saddle-sore, I imagine, he

dismounted from his bike on 18 September 2017.

He should have been used to the discomfort, however, having been previously part of a team that rowed from Resolute Bay in Canada to the Magnetic North Pole, and having ridden his bike from Cairo to Cape Town (10,000km) to break the world record for the fastest solo ride for the length of Africa. It took him 42 days 8 hours. But that's not all. He first entered the *Guinness Book of Records* in 2008 for his first circumnavigational bike tour of the world. It took him 194 days. Then Vin Cox came along in 2010 and beat Beaumont's record. What do you do in such a situation? You jolly well get back on your bike and sock it to him. Small wonder that trophies closer to home count for something too. In November 2015, Beaumont established the world record by completing the North Coast 500 (NC500) by bicycle in 37 hours 56 minutes 44 seconds, although James McCallum bettered this in 2016 with a completion time of 31 hours 23 minutes.

But records are there to be broken, and the Scots are always up for the challenge. In September 2020 Josh Quigley from Livingston beat McCallum's record by 6 minutes. What is so amazing and inspiring about Quigley's achievement is that on 21 December 2019, while attempting to beat the round-the-world cycling record, he was hit by a car at 70mph in Texas, USA, and sustained heel, ankle and neck injuries.

And the NC500 is no mean feat. It has total ascents of 34,423 feet, some 5,394 feet higher than Mount Everest, and Quigley was required to cycle 12 hours in darkness through some of the remotest landscapes in the UK.

The long-distance walks and cycle tracks attract competitive record-seekers too, few more so than the 96 miles of the West Highland Way between Milngavie and Fort William. Gary McDonald from Fort William set a new record in August 2020 in an impressive time of 9 hours 28 minutes, only to be upstaged the following month by Rab Wardell from Glasgow. Rab's time was 9 hours 14 minutes 32 seconds. These are

no weekend cyclist enthusiasts, however. Rab is a seasoned British and Scottish Championship medallist and a winner of the Race The World USA championship.

Another Scot, Jenny Graham from Inverness, proved endurance races are not the sole preserve of males. In 2018 she became the fastest person to cycle round the world unsupported. In preparation for this feat she cycled the 750-mile Arizona Trail Race and, with the Adventure Syndicate (a collective of female endurance cyclists), she cycled from Land's End to John o' Groats in four days, spending 20 hours on the bike each day and, as it was done over the New Year period, mostly in the dark. Jenny was honest enough to admit that the attempt was both 'brutal' and 'absolutely disgusting'.

Mark Beaumont – Transworld cyclist.
Wikimedia Commons

Not dissuaded by this experience, she set out in June 2018 to attempt the 18,000-mile journey round the globe, carrying all her own kit. Arriving back in Berlin in October 2018, having crossed four continents and encountered bears in the Yukon Territory, she completed her feat in 124 days 10 hours 50 minutes, her achievement confirmed by the *Guinness Book of Records*. An inspirational speaker, Jenny claims to have been born with FOMO – the Fear of Missing Out!

I couldn't leave the *Guinness Book of Records* without including a tribute to Thomas Chambers from Glasgow. Tommy cycled for more than 51 years, accumulating a world record of a staggering 799,405 miles. Relaxing after yet another day in the saddle, he wrote down all his journeys in his diaries, detailing the number of punctures he'd endured, and repaired, and the expenses incurred in keeping his bike roadworthy. Now that's what I call a record.

Another character worthy of mention is Graeme Obree. Although he was born in Nuneaton, he's a Scot by residence and adoption. His life and exploits have been dramatised in the 2006 film *The Flying Scotsman* and in the documentary film *Battle Mountain: Graeme Obree's Story*, which tells of his journey to Nevada to compete in the 2013 World Human Powered Speed Championships. He's unconventional and non-conformist in almost every sense. His bike is called 'Old Faithful' and comprises the bearings from a washing machine, and the straight, rather than dropped, handlebars force him to adopt a riding posture akin to a downhill skier. Having said that, in July 1993 at the Vikingskipet Velodrome in Norway he did set a new record of 51.596 kilometres for the world hour velodrome record, beating the previous record by 445 metres. That record stood one whole week, but, undeterred, Obree tried again, regaining the record in April 1994 in Bordeaux, only to lose it five months later. However this may sound, Obree was a serious if somewhat idiosyncratic competitor. He was the individual pursuit world champion in both 1993

and 1995 and, among other achievements, won the RTTC 50-mile championship in 1993 and the 25-mile championship in 1996. Although 'Old Faithful' was eventually banned from competitions, the original is on display in the National Museum of Scotland in Edinburgh and two replicas, used during filming, are in the Riverside Transport Museum in Glasgow.

Jenny Graham – another transworld cyclist.
Jenny Graham

For endurance, sailing single-handed non-stop around the globe takes some beating. But another Scot, Hawick-born Chay (Sir Charles) Blyth, did exactly that in 1971, the first to achieve success in a westwards circumnavigation, in a 59-foot boat called *British Steel*.

Ever since Sir Hugh Munro devised his Munro Tables in 1891, people, young and old, have risen to the challenge of reaching the summit of all 282 mountains in Scotland that are higher than 3,000 feet. As at 2020, some 6,700 folk have succeeded, although it's taken most of them about two decades to 'bag' all of them. In the 'lockdown' summer of 2020, Donnie Campbell from Inverness wore out seven pairs of trainers breaking the time record – ascending all 282 summits in 31 days 23 hours 2 minutes. The challenge saw him not only power-walk up and down the equivalent of

14 Mount Everests, but then cycle 896 miles, run and walk 883 miles and kayak between Munros, stopping overnight in a campervan driven by his wife. He started on 1 August with Ben More – the one on Mull – and finished with Ben Hope, the most northerly. He even had the good grace to be human. On Day 29 he missed reaching the last summit due to 'cloud and lack of concentration'

Graeme Obree on the way to winning the 1991 Scottish 25 Miles Time Trial Championship. He's in the colours of the Glasgow Wheelers Cycling Club, near Inchture on the A90. Despite heavy rain he was the first cyclist to break the 30mph barrier at that distance in Scotland.
Thomas Nugent, Wikimedia Commons

at what he thought was the top, so re-climbed it. 'It was annoying… It was my own fault,' he said, showing us all the true metal of this guy. Donnie's record was exceptional on many counts, breaking the previous record by one week.

Donald Sandeman, the ultramarathon runner from Edinburgh, described Donnie's feat as the 'toughest challenge in the UK – physically, mentally and logistically'. He didn't pass comment on the state of Donnie's feet.

14 August 2021 witnessed a remarkable achievement. Just as I was finishing writing this book, news came through that members of Carnethy Hill Running Club in Edinburgh had

'bagged' all 282 Scottish Munros in a single day! They were about 120 members involved in this feat, and the exercise – and it sounds a bit of an understatement to call it that – was completed in 16 hours and 48 minutes.

And Jenny Graham, our endurance cyclist, has not let the heather grow beneath her feet during the pandemic. Together with her friend, Calum Maclean, a broadcaster and filmmaker from Aberfeldy, in August 2021 they set a new record for walking in a straight line! Not any old straight line, of course. In 2018 staff at Ordnance Survey worked out the longest walk in Britain that went in a straight line without hitting a road. It's 44 miles long and follows a bearing of 67 degrees east-northeast from 460 metres high on the A9 at Drumochter Pass to the A939, just south of Corgarff in Aberdeenshire. It may be straight, but the route is far from straightforward, crossing thick heather moors, soggy bogs, mature forests and mountain tops in the Cairngorms National Park. The walk included reaching the summit of Beinn a' Bhuird, at 1,196 metres the 11th highest mountain in the UK. The total ascent in the walk is 5,706 metres. Jenny explains:

'Walking in a straight line sounds like the simplest of all adventures but it turned out to be the most complex navigation of any trip I've been on… You think you know what a straight line is, but then you look at the GPS and realise you don't.'

It took Jenny and Calum 11 hours to cover the first 10 miles of the gruelling terrain, and four days to be the first ever to complete this challenge.

All the champions I've paid tribute to here are from the world of speed and/or endurance. The 'Top 50' would be a fitting title. However, don't forget that Scotland has also produced sporting champions in tennis, football, golf, curling, snooker, boxing and darts, among other 'firsts'.

Whether the record attempt be a short sprint, a marathon or a long haul round the globe, these athletes will have set themselves targets –

milestones, physical and mental – to be achieved along the route, against which they can pace their progress. Many of them will have passed the traditional milestones, many hundreds of them, which form the subject matter of this book. Few, I doubt, will have taken the time to stop and record them.

However, my last record-breaker has done just that over the last 50 years, as she and her late husband Frank toured the length and breadth of Scotland on their bikes. Christine Minto was introduced to me as I started my research for this book. Although living in Yorkshire, she's maintained close links with Scotland and is the country's representative on The Milestone Society, maintaining records of milestones and fingerposts across the land, from Shetland to Coldstream and Lewis & Harris to Aberdeenshire. Christine's passion and commitment to the cause of milestones has been my good fortune, for she has shared her knowledge and enthusiasm and the Society's extensive photograph archive with me in developing this book. I am forever grateful.

But that is only part of the story. Christine and Frank also cycled competitively, and Christine holds seven women's national 'time trials' cycling records, including from 10 miles to 24 hours (426 miles). Christine started cycling in 1958 and her trophies include competitions on tandem and solo tricycles. The couple contributed hugely to promoting cycling as both a sport and a pro-active social community, being the C. A. Rhodes Memorial Award winners in 1999. Christine has been a lifelong member of the Birdwell Wheelers, near Barnsley, and was President when the Club celebrated its 70th Anniversary in 2019.

To all these record-breakers I can only salute you and utter two words: 'Amazing' and 'Awesome'.

Our milestone heritage: Highland

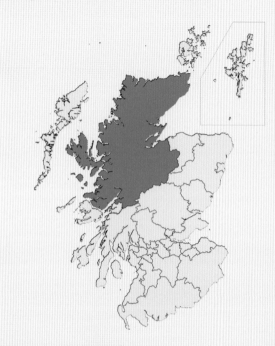

Highland. *Wikimedia Commons*

Caithness

Caithness county sign. *Ken Diamond collection, The Milestone Society*

Let's start at the very north, at John o'Groats. It's not really the northernmost point on the Scottish mainland, of course – that's a few miles further west on the windswept headland that is Dunnet Head. But John o'Groats is where the famous signpost stands.

The fingerpost illustrated here is relatively recent. The property changed ownership a few years ago and the sellers relocated the original post to a nearby field. There's been criticism of the labels that visitors have plastered along the new pole, suggesting that it's unwanted and unsightly graffiti. I'm not so sure. Art is art, after all, and free expression is a value worth protecting. The most surprising fact, to me at least, and one that was reinforced when I last visited John o'Groats, is that Shetland really is a lot further north than the Scottish mainland. Lerwick is on the same latitude as Helsinki in Finland and Anchorage in Alaska.

Sutherland

Sutherland county sign. *Ken Diamond collection, The Milestone Society*

John o'Groats landmark, with Orkney in the distance. *Deborah M. Keith*

The most northerly milestone on the British mainland (with benchmark) – on the B855, 1 mile from Dunnet Head (date circa 1831). *Dr Adrian Sumner*

Heading westwards along the north coast (it's the northern section of the now famous 'North Coast 500' route), at the extreme north-west corner of the Scottish mainland, some 11 miles from Durness, stands Cape Wrath lighthouse. It's another legacy of the Stevenson family, Robert in this case. The lighthouse dates from 1828 and was only automated in 1998. The light is visible up to 22 nautical miles offshore (a nautical mile is equivalent to approximately 1.15 miles, since we've mentioned distances a few times). The access road from the Kyle of Durness was built to facilitate the construction of the lighthouse and includes milestones dating from the same period. They are mostly flat slabs with large numbering, although those at 1, 10 and 11 miles are more substantial, with numbering on the bevel. There is a new addition, however, at 8 miles, installed when the Cape Wrath Marathon was inaugurated a few years ago, with a splendid image of a puffin celebrating the rich conservation value of the area.

Aside from international nature and landscape designations, this remote wilderness, known as the Parph, has an altogether more hostile

Milestone No 7 on the road to Cape Wrath.
The Milestone Society

A touch of local interest on milestone No 8 on the road to Cape Wrath. *Christine Minto, The Milestone Society*

environment. A large area is owned by the MOD and is operated as a military training zone and live firing range. But it was different less than a hundred years ago. Sheep farming supported a population of between 30 and 40, with the village school at Achiemore having 10 pupils in the 1930s. It closed in 1947.

The lighthouse has saved many lives since 1828, but the seas around it have witnessed many wrecks over the centuries since the Vikings. On 27 September 1915 the RMS *Dunottar Castle* (a misspelling, surely, of the Keith Family stronghold south of Stonehaven?), en route to Scapa Flow, floundered off Cape Wrath in bad weather, with the loss of 15 lives. The wreckage was only discovered in 2004, some 35 miles off the headland at a depth of 315 feet of water. That ship had taken Winston Churchill, then a young journalist, to the Boer War in 1899.

The road south from Tongue, heading towards Strathnaver, which witnessed some of the most severe ravages of the Highland Clearances in the 18th century, has a rugged beauty of mountains and moorlands. It's apposite that the milestones echo that, with even the Highland granite worn bare of its inscription.

A Highland granite milestone on the A836, north of Loch Craggie – the inscription once read 'Lairg 34/ Tongue 3'. *The Milestone Society*

Sutherland has its share of old fingerposts too. There's a Royal Scottish Automobile Club fingerpost at Ledmore Junction, where the A837 through Strath Oykel and onward to Lochinver meets the A835 from Ullapool.

Coldbackie village sign. *Ken Diamond collection, The Milestone Society*

Ledmore Junction. *Ken Diamond collection, The Milestone Society*

Ullapool Museum houses a fascinating relic, previously lost to development. It's a marker stone that originally stood on the old road between Ullapool and Garve and was buried for concealment at the outbreak of the Second World War. However, the coming of the hydro-electric scheme in the late 1940s meant that the glen, along which the old road ran, was flooded to create Loch Glascarnoch, by building a damn at Aultguish. Local man Dorrie Urquhart remembered the marker stones being concealed and, in 2010, when the water level in the loch was at its lowest since the construction of the dam, Dorrie and a group of friends located the stone, unearthed it and presented it to the museum for display.

Over on the east coast, the Sutherland Arms Hotel in Golspie has enjoyed an enviable reputation, hosting guests from around the globe since its opening in 1808. It's a fitting place to site a milestone, giving distances to both local and far-flung places, including Land's End at 777 miles distant. For those with a keen eye for 1960s motoring, the backdrop to the Golspie photograph includes two classics – the somewhat rare Austin Cambridge estate car and the stylish elegance of a fine example of the Jaguar Mark 2 series.

The old milestone in the Ullapool Museum. *Christine Minto, The Milestone Society*

Golspie hospitality. *Ken Diamond collection, The Milestone Society*

Ross & Cromarty

1066 is a landmark year in English history, but it's also important to the history of Easter Ross. Tain was granted its first royal charter in that year by King Malcolm III, making it Scotland's oldest royal burgh. Lying to the east of the town is the Tarbat Peninsula and another first, the site of the first confirmed Pictish monastery. Although that was destroyed by the Vikings in AD800, the area has been a thriving centre of activity throughout history, with the village of Portmahomack and its Telford-designed harbour being the centre of

Ross & Cromarty county sign. the *Ken Diamond collection, The Milestone Society*

the white fish industry up until the early part of the 20th century. This attractively named village shares something in common with a popular tourist destination in Norfolk – Hunstanton. Both settlements are on the east coast, but face westwards. The network of unclassified roads on the peninsula will also attract the interest of the milestone enthusiast. They are cylindrical white stones, with the lettering painted green – unusual, and eye-catching. There are two or three of these remaining. The one to the south of Portmahomack is inscribed 'PORT/1/MILE'. There's another at Bindal Farm and another 2 miles further on, just before the road end at the Stevenson lighthouse at Tarbat Ness.

At the top of the staircase in the Cromarty Courthouse Museum there's an example of a late-Victorian mile marker that was recovered from Jemimaville, on the road between Dingwall and Cromarty (B9163). The Cromarty/Nigg Ferry has provided a key link across the Firth from the days of the pilgrims journeying to the Chapel of St Duthac at Tain.

The original positions of markers such as this one are shown on the 25-inch OS map of 1913. The road followed the south shore of the Cromarty

Old mile marker at Cromarty. *Paul Monk, Cromarty Courthouse Museum*

Firth, as, of course, this pre-dated the Cromarty Bridge. Interestingly, the mileages are given in decimals (4.31 miles to Cromarty) and not as miles and furlongs or fractions of a mile. The courthouse has one other example, but it is in a broken condition. It also originated in Jemimaville and shows the distance to Fortrose as 6 miles and to Invergordon Ferry as 3.19 miles.

I am hugely impressed by the efforts made by archaeologists to, literally, unearth structures and artefacts that reveal the lives of our ancestors in many centuries past. Modern technology, such as X-ray and infra-red photography, especially used in aerial observations, and improved interpretation of landforms, have identified settlement patterns and agricultural activity that had hitherto gone

undetected. These new technologies have spawned a new golden age of archaeology. The new finds in Scotland in the last 20 years have been outstanding and unsurpassed for many decades.

One example of such painstaking work is reported in the North of Scotland Archaeological Society's (NOSAC) account of its surveys in 2007/09 on the Strathconnon Estate in Ross-shire. Part of the Scotland's Rural Past Project, among many 'finds' were four old milestones. At Carnoch Farmhouse, near Contin, the team found an upright slab of dressed stone with a curving upper edge, measuring 700cm in height, 500cm in width and 100cm thick. Other milestones at Clach Loundrain, Creag Lucharaidh and Drumandarch, in the same vicinity, in various states of repair, or more accurately disrepair, all add to the sense that the area enjoyed a more vibrant past. That's the echo of many a glen and strath in the northern Highlands.

Inverness-shire

Inverness-shire county sign. *Ken Diamond collection, The Milestone Society*

Skye

The opening of the Skye Bridge in 1995 gave a physical link to mainland Scotland, but this island is 50 miles long and maintains the majesty and aura of days past. That's despite the very significant numbers of tourists, some 650,000 each year, who make their way there, to 'get away from it all'. Hence the sign in Broadford showing a relocated milestone beneath, with a typical West Highland kirk behind (from 1839, so post-dating Thomas Telford's Parliamentary churches by more than a decade). Christine described this milestone prosaically, but accurately, as 'a ubiquitous lump of anonymous granite'.

My early childhood memories of trips to Skye from our home near Inverness include single-lane

The Broadford milestone. *Christine Minto, The Milestone Society*

roads with passing places and, I'm sure I recall this correctly, an abundance of milestones. Changed days now, and besides the very significant road upgrades the number of milestones remaining are sadly depleted. Some are still visible on old roads, now bypassed through realignment schemes. I'm reminded of one, however, that may have resulted from an error rather than any sense of mischief toward the traveller. It's a polished granite milestone, set in concrete, which records the distance of 7 miles to Dunvegan and 3 miles to Struan. On the top face it reads '7/OSE'. As it is situated barely 1 mile from Ose, is this a case of the stone mason misreading his instructions and mistaking '1' for '7'?

If your travels take you to Uig to catch the ferry to Lochmaddy or Tarbert, then journey a distance further to Kilmuir towards the northern end of Skye to visit the Museum of Island Life. On display is an old photograph of a milestone that reads 'MARBLE ARCH/684 7/8th'. The caption advises that the milestone was located near Broadford and had been removed when the road was widened. Where it is now is anyone's guess. The route to London would then have been by ferry, either at Kyleakin (the bridge was opened in 1995) or at Armadale for Mallaig. The question to ask is not why the sign was there in the first place, but rather how they could have been so specific about the distance? Perhaps there was life before the satnav.

And it's not unique on Skye… Pictured is a milestone showing the distance to Coventry. And a 'do it yourself' milepost can also be found on the scenic route over the Quiraing. If the Council don't oblige, then paint your own direction sign!

While we are at Kilmuir, it's worth reflecting that this vicinity and the Outer Hebrides across The Minch is home to the highest concentration

Being 'sent to Coventry' from Skye involves quite a journey! *Christine Minto, The Milestone Society*

The Ose milestone. *Christine Minto, The Milestone Society*

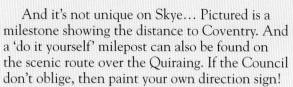

From Skye to Marble Arch. *Ken Diamond collection, The Milestone Society*

'Do it yourself' on the road to Uig. *Christine Minto, The Milestone Society*

of native Gaelic speakers anywhere on earth. Which linguistic discussion brings us neatly to the use of bilingual road signage, a contentious issue.

The debate has a long gestation period, with many educated Gaels resentful of the Anglicisation of place names in the 18th and 19th centuries. Matters were brought to a head in 1973 when Aird District Council proposed to build a new road south from Portree. To facilitate the line of the road, the council required to purchase a strip of land from the local landowner and entrepreneur, Iain Noble. Being a magnanimous, yet shrewd, benefactor, Noble offered to donate the land on the condition that the three signs that were to be erected on the section of road be bilingual. The council fiercely resisted the proposal, mustered and cajoled by Lord Burton, the chairman of the Roads Committee. Indeed, so opposed to the Gaelic language was this character that later that year he attempted unsuccessfully to introduce legislation in the House of Lords limiting the use of Gaelic by Scottish local authorities. A public outcry resulted. There are few things more certain to rile any true Scot than being imposed upon by a London-based unelected second chamber. In an effort to negotiate a compromise and avoid the costly and time-consuming compulsory purchase option, the council agreed that Portree (Port Righ) and Broadford (An t-Ath Leathann) would each receive a bilingual signpost on an 'experimental basis'.

As Noble no doubt hoped, and the council feared, this set a precedent, and the practice became widespread in the 1980s and through the '90s. In 1996 Highland Council even decided to make use of Gaelic-only signposts in some areas, and from 2001 the Scottish Government has been erecting bilingual signage along many of the trunk roads in the Highlands.

Based on research into road safety, bilingual signs in Scotland typically use white letters for English and yellow for Gaelic. ScotRail has also adopted the practice of bilingual signs at its stations.

The 'experimental' bilingual road sign.
English Wikipedia Commons

It's worth noting that just as bilingual signage gathered pace, the number of Gaelic speakers declined yet further. Somewhere between the national census of 1971 and that of 1981, a milestone was reached. There are no longer any monolingual Gaelic speakers. The last died, or perhaps left Scotland because there was no one else with whom to have a blether. The 2011 census records 57,375 people as being able to speak Gaelic; that's 1.1% of the Scottish population over three years old. A comprehensive survey of Gaelic communities conducted in 2020 by the University of the Highlands & Islands found that only 11,000 people used Gaelic as an everyday language, and the majority of those were over 50 years old. My primary teacher, Mrs MacQueen, was a native Gaelic speaker. She taught me many things that have stood me in good stead for life, but, before you ask, Gaelic wasn't one of them.

Our chronicler, Dr Samuel Johnson, had some terse and inflammatory words on Gaelic when he visited Skye in 1773. Writing in *A Journey to the Western Isles of Scotland*, he commented: 'Of the Earse language [i.e. Scottish Gaelic], as I understand nothing, I cannot say more than I have been told. It is the rude speech of a barbarous people, who had few thoughts to express, and were content, as they conceived grossly, to be grossly understood.' To add insult to injury, he then wrote that, 'The Welsh and the Irish are cultivated tongues.'

It's a particularly venomous remark, coming as it does from a man acknowledged (by others) as one of the greatest literary figures of the 18th century and the compiler of *A Dictionary of the English Language*. Let's move on…

Raasay

Lying to the east of Portree, between Skye and the mainland at Applecross, and a short ferry crossing from Sconser, we find the island of Raasay, extending to 24 square miles. Its fame lies, in part, to its being the birthplace of Gaelic poet Sorley MacLean, one of several modern Scottish poets I studied for my Higher English, if that doesn't sound odd. It's not really. MacLean was Head of English at Plockton High School as well as being revered as a cult figure when his poem *Hallaig* was translated into English in the 1970s.

But our interest in Raasay is in 'Calum's Road', built about 40 years ago by Calum MacLeod at the north end of the island. Over ten years Calum, armed with a pick, a shovel and a wheelbarrow, single-handedly constructed a road, widening a former footpath, between Brochel and Arnish, a distance of 1¾ miles across rugged, untamed terrain. He'd exhausted the usual channels for help, including the Department of Agriculture, the major crofting landowner on Raasay, and Inverness County Council, so took it upon himself to undertake the construction.

Roger Hutchinson, a journalist with the *West Highland Free Press*, wrote about Calum's endeavours in a book of the same name. Well worth a read. Perhaps the most deft book review was by Tavish Scott in *The Shetland Times*, who wrote:

'A tremendous read. Not just of construction, determination and a desire to better a community that had shrunk through the clearances. But an attitude. If no council, organisation or body will help us, we must do something ourselves.'

If the name Tavish Scott rings a bell, it's because he went into politics and became Scotland's Transport Minister.

Perhaps you wouldn't expect to find milestones on an island offshore of another island, where there's basically one road, albeit with a few spurs, and almost everyone lives in or around Clachan. That's what surprised Ian Thompson, who was visiting on his motorbike in 2010. Ian is The Milestone Society's heritage and conservation advisor who wrote the definitive history of Cornish milestones. He claims not to have been on a 'busman's holiday', but he found a 2-mile milestone just along the road from the Creachan Cottage youth hostel, where he was staying, then, with only a tenth of a mile between them, two 3-mile milestones. Ever curious, Ian consulted the OS 6-inch map of 1901 to find that there had been no fewer than nine milestones at the start of that century (of which eight remain), stating the distance to Raasay House, as far north as Brochel Castle.

The A9 south of Inverness is the road, much realigned, on which I made the childhood journeys from my home. Several of the old milestones have been restored, but they are few and far between. Pleasing, therefore, to come across the illustrated example of an original from Ken Diamond during his many Scottish travels. I used to think that Tomatin was a strange name – as a child I called it 'tomato'.

Raasay, looking north from Creachan. *Ian Thompson*

Another road I remember well was the 'Road to the Isles', from the Great Glen to the Kyle of Lochalsh. In the late 1950s our home was in Dores, a village on Wade's road between Inverness and Fort Augustus, on the south side of Loch Ness. To get to the 'Road to the Isles' there were two options, one via Inverness and the A82 south to Invermoriston, the other along Wade's road to Fort Augustus, then southwards to Invergarry and westwards along the A87. The late Terry Keegan, a founding member and honorary secretary of The Milestone Society, recalled travelling the road from Invergarry in the 1950s in his Ford Prefect. In those days the road was single track with passing places. Instead of heading northwards through Glen Loyne to meet the Invermoriston road (A887) to the east of Loch Cluanie, as it

A milestone on the A9 north of Carrbridge. *Ken Diamond collection, The Milestone Society*

does now, the old road continued a further 7 miles along the north shore of Loch Garry to a hostelry at Tomdoun. Thereafter it rose steeply to cross Glenquoich Forest and the head of Glen Loyne, to descend again to Cluanie Lodge. Revisiting the area in 2002, Terry was delighted to find that most of the granite milestones as far as and beyond Tomdoun were still in situ, although the track is now a walker's paradise.

Strathspey

Moray county sign. *Ken Diamond collection, The Milestone Society*

The drive along the A95 through Strathspey from Grantown-on-Spey to Telford's iconic bridge at Craigellachie can only be bettered by using the old road, the B9102 along the north bank of the river.

A milestone near Davoch of Grange (A95/B9108), opposite Auchinhove tollhouse. *The Milestone Society*

On Advie Bridge, some fuller mileages are provided on this fingerpost. *Ken Diamond collection, The Milestone Society*

Left: A milepost at the Advie Bridge junction on the B9102, in the heart of the Whisky Trail. *Christine Minto, The Milestone Society*

Below: A milestone on the A8007 near Mingary. *The Milestone Society*

Ardnamurchan

The most westerly point on the Scottish (and, for that matter, UK) mainland is on the Ardnamurchan peninsula. The journey in from Strontian, along Loch Sunart and past Glenborrodale, is well worth the effort. The 23 miles from Salen were constructed in 1900; until then the only access was by sea. Milestones mark the route to Kilchoan, the most westerly village on the A8007, from where you have another few miles to travel to reach Ardnamurchan Point, jutting into the Atlantic Ocean.

One milestone, however, marks the distance to Mingary Pier, where, aside from viewing Mingary Castle on its rocky outcrop, you can recharge your electric car. Amazing where sustainable travel takes you. The ferry crossing to Tobermory takes 35 minutes. The mileposts on the Kilchoan road were all made by the Royal Label Company.

12
Millennium milestones: putting milestones back on the map

It's enshrined in human nature to want to mark milestone dates. Changing from one century to the next is cause enough for some festivities, but when it's the millennium that is changing too, from a 1 to a 2, you'd expect some special effort. For my generation, we had a double whammy. And for many it was a chance both to cast an eye back and make some resolutions for the future.

That's more than 20 years ago now. I wonder how many of these well-intentioned aspirations, fresh and hopeful as the final strains of 'Auld Lang Syne' faded, came true? I'd a huge amount for which to be thankful as the new millennium dawned, but that's for another reminisce.

'A healthy mind and a healthy body' is a great adage, and the 1990s saw a burgeoning interest in both exercise and adventure. Put the two together and cycling offered a low-cost solution and an almost limitless opportunity to explore your country. What better way to mark the Millennium than to build on a project that had its genesis about 15 years earlier, and formally create a National Cycle Network? Sustrans, which I had first encountered during my time on the Scottish Youth Hostelling Association's Council in the mid-1990s, led on this bold endeavour to develop the cycling routes across the UK into a National Cycling Network. There are now more than 16,575 miles of signed cycle routes, 70% of them on roads, mostly secondary and minor roads, but also putting to good use disused railways and canal towpaths, providing open access to the cyclist. As well as nine primary routes there are a wealth of more local routes already created, about 50, with more in progress.

The bicycle has a very special connection with Scotland. Yes, you've guessed it, a Scot invented it. The question is – which Scot?

Kirkpatrick MacMillan (1812-78), a blacksmith from Dumfries-shire, is credited with building the first mechanically propelled two-wheel vehicle. It was a rear-wheel-drive design, claimed a nephew some years later, using mid-mounted treadles, connected by rods to a rear crank. MacMillan is also associated, perhaps mistakenly it has to be admitted, with the first recorded instance of a bicycle traffic offence. A Glasgow newspaper reported in 1842 that an anonymous 'gentleman from Dumfries-shire … bestride a velocipede … of ingenious design' knocked over a pedestrian in the Gorbals (an area of Glasgow, and not an anatomical appendage). Whether or not this was MacMillan cannot be confirmed, but the said gentleman was fined 5 British shillings. Stories grow arms and legs (which *are* anatomical appendages, so to speak), and it was also claimed that MacMillan's niece, Mary Marchbank, had an illicit ride on her uncle's machine, thereby becoming the world's first female cyclist.

What of the other contenders as inventors? In about 1845 Gavin Dalzell, who lived in Lesmahagow, built a machine that was similar in design to MacMillan's 'bike' and used it to make deliveries from his drapery business to the rural community. Dalzell never claimed the honour of having invented the machine, but a replica is held in the Glasgow Museum of Transport and it is claimed to be the oldest bike in existence today. The first documented producer of rod-driven two-wheelers was Thomas McCall (1834-1904), who was born in Penpont in Dumfries-shire, but lived and worked as a cartwright in Kilmarnock. This was a treadle bicycle and was based on a design of a velocipede by the French.

That's sorted for the bike then. When it comes to rubber tyres, there's another misunderstanding.

Every schoolchild, in my days anyway, believed

'Thomas McCall and his Bicycle', from a photograph by Bruce and Howie of Kilmarnock, from *Bicycling News* of 2 June 1892. *Wikimedia Commons*

that the rubber tyre was invented by a Scot, John Boyd Dunlop (1840-1921), born in Dreghorn. We'd all heard of Dunlop tyres. Dunlop was a veterinary surgeon by profession and ran a very successful practice in Northern Ireland. He developed a pneumatic tyre for his son's tricycle, saw its potential and sold it commercially in his native Scotland. Willie Hume, in Ireland, began winning all his cycle races on Dunlop's tyres, so the president of the Irish Cyclists' Association, Harvey Du Cros, went into partnership with Dunlop, under the name of the Pneumatic Tyre & Booth's Cycle Agency. They discovered, however, that the original idea had been patented by another Scot, Robert William Thomson, in 1847. Oops! However, the Dunlop name stuck, and although John Boyd Dunlop withdrew from the business, his name lives on as Dunlop Rubber, which became a multi-million public company in the early 20th century.

What of Robert William Thomson (1822-73)? He may not have made a fortune or achieved the acclamations from his tyres, but he did very well from other inventions, including the fountain pen in 1849. Robert was born in Stonehaven and, like John Loudon McAdam, went to North America at the age of 14 to work for an uncle. Returning at 16, his inquisitive mind began to invent a myriad of different devices. In his early twenties he developed a tyre consisting of a hollow belt of India rubber, inflated with air so that the wheels presented a 'cushion of air to the ground, rail or track on which it runs'. The elastic belt of rubberised canvas was enclosed with a strong outer casing of leather, which was bolted to the wheel. It was a great success. One set of Thomson's 'Aerial Wheels' ran for 1,200 miles without sign of deterioration. Hence Thomson patented the pneumatic tyre in France and the USA, and was thereafter forgotten, at least by Dunlop.

If, like me, you are fascinated by trivial facts, here's one that might just win you a quiz. Mr Thomson's daughter, Elspeth, was the wife of Edinburgh-born Kenneth Grahame, whose book

The Wind in the Willows became a classic.

Today's revival in cycling is welcome. It's an essential part of the health, exercise and well-being agenda. But since its early days in the 19th century it's spawned its fair share of eccentric characters who've added more than a splash of colour to history. Few can surpass the Hon Ian Keith-Falconer, a Scottish missionary and Arabic scholar, and the third son of the 8th Earl of Kintore. There's a family connection here, albeit at a distance, which can probably be measured in miles in the family tree. The 8th Earl was the hereditary Chief of the Clan Keith, and his first son, the 9th Earl, became Governor-General of South Australia in the 1890s. I stumbled across this fact when my wife and I visited Adelaide in 2005 and turned the corner into Kintore Avenue, a short distance from what has become the 'central business district', whose library also boasts a statute to Robert Burns.

Back to Ian. He had a penchant for bicycles, especially favouring one that stood 86 inches high, competing in a 42-mile race in 1875 and winning the National Cyclists' Union 2-mile race at Stamford Bridge in 1878, to be declared 'world champion'. In 1882, mounted on this ridiculously high bicycle, he rode from Land's End to John o' Groats in, according to his own account, a mere '13 days, less 45 minutes'. Bear in mind that this was in the days when the road system was primitive, most were in a poor condition, and many had an unmade surface. During the 994-mile cycle ride, Ian endured heavy rain, at least one misdirection (probably blaming this on poor signposting), an accident and constant pain in one of his feet. Even more incredible it is that the last 251 miles up through the northern part of mainland Scotland were covered in two days.

He was an advocate for cycling as a panacea for all social ills. In a letter to his friend Mr Charrington, dated 20 August 1881, he writes:

'It is an excellent thing to encourage an innocent sport (such as bicycling) which keeps young

fellows out of the public-houses, music halls and gambling hells and all the other traps that are ready to catch them. It is a great advantage to enter for a few races in public, and not merely to ride on the road for exercise, because in the former case one has to train oneself and this involves abstinence from beer and wine and tobacco, and early going to bed and early rising, and gets one's body into a really vigorous, healthy state. As to betting, nearly all Clubs forbid it, strictly… A bicycle race-course is as quiet as a public science lecture.'

There you have it. Once an evangelist, always an evangelist.

Fortunately, many have followed his sage counsel, if not to the extremes of total abstinence, then certainly reaping the benefits of a healthy pursuit and the opportunity to explore the countryside. Cycling touring clubs became very popular after the First World War, giving vent to a growing urban population who wanted to break free, if only temporarily, from the shackles of the workplace, the heavy industry of the Glasgow docks, and the sooty atmosphere of their homes and neighbourhoods. What an escape to cycle along country roads to explore the magnificent area around Loch Lomond or beyond, or head south to Ayrshire's rolling countryside or across to the Borders hills.

Glasgow Wheelers is acknowledged as the oldest cycling club in Glasgow, founded in 1923, to be followed two years later by the Glasgow Nightingale Cycling Club, and many more as the Roaring Twenties (together with its Great Depression) gave way to the 1930s. By 1934 the Scottish Amateur Cyclists' Association, in tandem with the National Cyclists' Union (NCU), was officiating at the Duntocher to Dunoon Race, a 75-mile route incorporating the Rest and Be Thankful, as a feature of the Cowal Highland Gathering.

In 1931 the Scottish Youth Hostel Association (SYHA) was formed, opening its first hostel at

Broadmeadows, near Selkirk in the Borders. A network of accommodation sprang up across the country, providing inexpensive overnight accommodation for bands of cyclists and walkers from the cities and towns, predominantly in the Central Belt. And the demand was there. Literally thousands of Scots took to their bikes or donned their hiking boots each weekend, or during holiday periods, 'the trades', including the Glasgow Fair, traditionally the last two weeks in July. I say 'traditionally', as this practice dates from 1190, when Bishop Jocelin obtained permission from King William the Lion to hold the festivities. As William the Lion, aka 'William the Rough', reigned Scotland for 49 years, the second longest serving Scottish monarch before the Act of Union in 1707, establishing this holiday as a precedent seemed a good move.

The Cycling Touring Club of Edinburgh had its own overnight accommodation in what became known as the Albert Watson Memorial Hut, in Tweedsmuir in the Borders. Its story is one that embraces all that can be achieved through collaborative and partnership working. A flourishing club in the 1930s, several of its members were active Cycling Messengers attached to the Civil Defence service in Edinburgh, so when one of them discovered a concrete base of what had been a workshop or hut beside the disused trackway of the Talla railway, it was considered an ideal opportunity for the Club to develop a base for what had become an extensive network of cycle routes across both public and privately owned estates in the Borders.

An approach was made to Edinburgh Corporation, as owner of the land, for the use of the base as a foundation for a hut. It was explained that the only income to cover upkeep, heating etc of the hut would come from bed-night charges and that it was essential to keep these as low as possible to encourage young people out into the county. The City Council, no doubt keeping in mind the Club's recent help and aware that the local section was part of a national body of high

repute, kindly granted rent-free use of the site without limit of time, subject to Peebles County Council, as planning authority for the area, granting permission. That was forthcoming and a hut was commissioned from a contractor, one of whose drivers was a Club member. Not only did the contractor, James Miller & Partners, provide a substantial discount, but also allowed free use of a lorry to convey the materials to the site at weekends.

Members, from all walks of life, rallied round and provided the labour to prepare the site and construct and fit out the hut, which was opened in May 1947. Fundraising was well orchestrated too, with members raising money from diverse sources, perhaps none as unusual as the 6 shillings raised by Bob Jeffrey, one of the volunteer builders, who raffled two onions. Mind you, he was the gardener at Oxenfoord House. The hut still stands today, a testimony to the cooperative spirit. It was named the Albert Watson Memorial Hall, in honour of Albert, a former Club member who had held several national records for tricycle and tandem bicycle races and who lost his life in Canada in 1943, while training to be a pilot.

By the 1940s there were 12 cycling clubs in Glasgow, and other cities followed suit. Edinburgh also had several clubs; Aberdeen Wheelers dates from 1929, and the Forres Cycling Club from 1938, which, together with newer clubs, such as the Deeside Thistle Cycling Club, established in the early 1950s, flourish to this day. The number of clubs appears to be growing, with several new ones established in the last 10 years. Among these is Team Ecosse Northboats (TEN), set up and chaired by Pete Lowson, son of my very close friend Mike Lowson. The club, based in Inverurie, Aberdeenshire, caters for all ages and abilities, with an emphasis on social cycling, and growing interest among youngsters leading to its Youths section being heavily oversubscribed. Sterling effort, chaps.

Special mention is merited of the visit by Pete Lowson and Lucy Ritchie to Inverurie's twin town,

Founder and chair of Inverurie cycling club Team Ecosse Northboats, Pete Lowson, with club member and accomplished international cyclist Lucy Ritchie.
Mike Lowson

Bagneres-de-Bigorre in the Pyrenees, in 2019. It coincided with the 12th stage of the world's most gruelling and famous bike race, the Tour de France, arriving in the town. Pete was there to build links with the cycling community, but Lucy was the only Scot in the 10-strong InternationElles team of women who spent three weeks cycling 3,460km (2,150 miles) across France to raise awareness of gender equality within cycling. The ladies mirrored the Tour de France route by completing every stage of the race one day ahead of the men's event. There is no equivalent women's Tour de France, yet … but more power to your pedalwork.

The National Cycling Network (NCN) boasts, quite properly, that of its approximately 2,371 miles of cycle routes in Scotland, 644 miles are traffic-free. The multiple routes include the northern section of Route 1, a long-distance route from Dover to Shetland. At 1,695 miles, it's difficult to get any longer than that in the UK, travelling along the eastern seaboard of Scotland, via Edinburgh, Aberdeen, Inverness, north to John o' Groats and across the Pentland Firth to Orkney.

To mark the Millennium, the Royal Bank of Scotland funded the provision of 1,000 cast-iron mileposts along the established routes, a wonderful gesture and something that is both functional and celebratory and should be a lasting legacy. There are 175 of these mileposts in Scotland.

Four designs were commissioned, one from an artist native to each of the four countries of the UK. They are somewhat unusual designs, but hey, the prosaic never inspires. Iain McColl, the Scottish sculptor, produced a design called 'The Cockerel', with 'Fossil Tree' being from the hand of Jon Mills, 'Tracks' by David Dudgeon, and the 'Rowe Type' from, well, Andrew Rowe. Iain was born in Glencoe in 1954 and graduated from the Glasgow School of Art. He's exhibited his prolific work in New York, Dublin and Heidelberg.

I've always been challenged by the thought of trying to reach inside the mind of artists and sculptors, which is probably a reflection on my own inadequacy. That doesn't mean I can't appreciate esoteric design for what it is – esoteric.

McColl describes the influences behind 'The Cockerel' as being Miro's 'The Fork' and Brancusi's 'The Cock'. The design incorporates additional space for partners to cast their own short message. Jon Mills's design takes the form of an abstract tree with relief imagery of fossils, depicting the passage of time from early primitive creatures to the ultimate demise of fossil-fuel-driven technology. The principal design on Dudgeon's post shows the tracks made in the landscape by cyclists, complemented by a piece of text exploring sensations and observations one makes while travelling through various environments. Rowe based his sculpted milepost upon the nautical and industrial heritage of his native Swansea. It can have up to four directional fingers.

When I looked up Constantin Brancusi's entry in Wikipedia, for his work as a pioneer of Modernism was unknown to me, I found this quote from the great man:

Each of the four styles of Millennium mileposts. From left to right they are by Mills at Findhorn Bay (Moray), Rowe at Coldstream (Borders), McColl at Douglas (South Lanarkshire), and Dudgeon at Falkland (Fife). *Cosmo Blake and Sustrans*

'There are idiots who define my work as abstract; yet what they call abstract is what is most realistic. What is real is not the appearance, but the idea, the essence of things.'

Now we know. I'm glad we cleared that up.

Each design was used in all four countries and the photographs illustrate each of the designs on a route in Scotland.

Each of the milestones contains a disk featuring symbols and text, in code. These are the clues to the Millennium Time Trail, a treasure hunt puzzle of mind-blowing ingenuity, devised for Sustrans in 2001 by Charlie Harrow, an arts and maths teacher. Now please pay attention – this gets a trifle complicated, for me at any rate…

Each milestone has a disc, on which one of six different themes is depicted. Theme 1 is the seasons – hence four different signs; theme 2 is the continents – hence six signs; theme 3 is The Ages of Man, of which there are eight if you've studied Shakespeare's *As You Like It*; theme 4 is signs of the Zodiac (12 – you must be getting the drift by now?); and theme 5 represents the 20 centuries of human history (e.g. the Industrial Revolution). Just to make it interesting, theme 6 has four special discs, each with a key piece of the 'jigsaw'. Competitors in the Time Trial take brass rubbings of the clues, which form three-dimensional shapes for each of the classic elements of water, air, fire and earth, and the universe. I'm led to believe that the symbols on each milepost build together to create a poem, *Utopia*, written by Thomas More in the early 16th century. Actually he wrote it in Latin, so there's a further double translation required to read the verse in English. But that's not even the answer.

Cut to the chase. In the 20 years since the Millennium Time Trial was launched, no one has yet solved the puzzle, so the rather elegant trophy remains unclaimed. Admittedly things got off to a slow start as the challenge was announced in the press on the same day as news broke of the outbreak of foot and mouth disease in 2001. The closure of certain parts of the countryside in the months thereafter didn't help. Unfortunate, but then again maybe it's just a step too far in terms of challenge, even for the hardiest of cyclists.

There's a name for everything, of course. Here's one you may have heard of – Semiotics – the observation and interpretation of signs. I bet you're impressed? In case you're wondering, I learned that from an episode of *The Chase*, the television quiz show presented by Bradley Walsh.

Anyway, enough philosophy – let's get back to exploring some of the great cycle routes on offer

A Rowe Millennium Milepost in Glasgow.
Cosmo Blake and Sustrans

and where you'll find some of these Millennium Milestones.

There have been several changes to the NCN recently, so to ensure you get up to date advice on routes, please consult the Ordnance Survey website. You need to click the layer button in the bottom right-hand corner and select 'National Cycle Network'.

The Lochs & Glens Route (No 7) is divided into two sections. The Northern part covers 214 miles from Inverness to Glasgow through Blair Atholl, Pitlochry and Lochearnhead, incorporating the Clydeside and Loch Lomond Cycleway. The Southern part covers 193 miles from Glasgow to Carlisle via the Ayrshire Coast, Kirkcudbright and Dumfries.

Route 73 starts at Lochranza on the east side of Arran and runs round to Brodick, where you catch the ferry to Ardrossan, making your way to Kilmarnock on the Cunninghame Gateway. There is a Southern section between Stranraer and Newton Stewart that connects with the primary Route 7.

Route 75 is also known as the Forth & Clyde Cycle Route and extends from Leith to Gourock, via Edinburgh, and the towpaths of the Union and Forth & Clyde Canals to Glasgow. From Gourock you can travel westwards on the ferry across to Dunoon to explore Argyll.

Extending from Campbeltown up the Mull of Kintyre to Oban, Route 78 takes you northwards on the Caledonia Way (Slighe na h-Alba) up the Great Glen to Inverness, via Fort William and Fort Augustus.

Catching the ferry from Oban, Uig or Ullapool to Stornoway provides the visitor to the Western Isles with the opportunity to cycle or walk the 185 miles of the Hebridean Way on Route 780 from the north end, or Butt of Lewis, southwards across ten islands including Harris, the Uists and Benbecula to Barra and Vatersay, the most westerly permanently inhabited place, not only in Scotland but in Great Britain. Although there is ample evidence of people having lived on Vatersay from

the 3rd Millennium BC, the 2011 Census shows a population of only 90.

These cycleways have captured something of the outdoors in all of us. According to a Sustrans Report in 2017, that year saw 4.4 million people enjoying the 16,575 miles of the National Cycle Network in the UK, undertaking 786 million walking and cycling journeys. I don't have individual figures for Scotland, but they are very popular. I'd very much like to boast that I'd cycled each of these routes in Scotland, but modesty – nae, sorry, honesty – precludes such a claim. To mark the 20th anniversary of the NCN, the Scottish Millennium Mileposts have received a paint and, in some cases, repositioning.

We've already seen some examples of the refurbishment projects when we caught up with some volunteer groups in Lanarkshire, but people of all ages have been actively involved throughout Scotland as part of the Festival in 2020. In Kingussie the Millennium Milepost was repainted in the colours of the local shinty team, Kingussie Camanachd. They are no mean team either, for according to *The Guinness Book of Records* in 2005 it is the world sport's most successful sporting team of all time. Kingussie Camanachd won 20 consecutive leagues and remained unbeaten for four years in the early 1990s – surely worthy of celebration on any milestone.

In addition, and partly coexisting with the National Cycle Network, there are 371 miles of National Byway in Scotland. These provide signposted cycle routes along quiet roads in the Borders and Dumfries & Galloway, extending into South Ayrshire.

Those wishing to explore rugged and beautiful scenery on foot or bike are well catered for in Scotland. It also offers exceptional, and exceptionally, long-distance footpaths, all assiduously waymarked. Distance markers are as important as directional markers when you are in remote countryside.

On Scotland's Great Trails website there are 29 routes listed. The shortest is the Dava Way, from

The Kingussie Camanachd Millennium Milestone.
Sustrans

In Troon a design competition organised by Ecoayrshire featured painting a Millennium Milepost.
Laura White and Sustrans

A painting project at St Joseph's School in Inverness brought colour to a Millennium Milepost.
Laura White and Sustrans

Forres to Grantown-on-Spey, at 24 miles, and the longest is the Southern Upland Way, at 214 miles. In addition to a good pair of boots, you need both stamina and resilience for that one.

It was always my ambition to walk the 96 miles of the West Highland Way, from Milngavie to Fort William, then proceed north-eastwards along the 78 miles of the Great Glen Way to Inverness. Apart from rambles along non-contiguous sections – interspersed by many years, I hasten to add – it's one of several 'bucket list' objectives I've failed to achieve.

An option on the Great Glen Way is to walk it in one direction, then do the reverse journey by canoe, for it's also one of Scotland's great canoe trails. Or you could swim it, as Alina Warren did in July 2012, when the marathon swimmer from Wales became the first person to swim the Great Glen. She achieved this massive effort by swimming the three lochs and the interlinking rivers, rather than making use of the Caledonian Canal. And for railway enthusiasts, in June 2017 the 'Biggest Little Railway in the World' was created, for that month only, with an O-gauge model railway constructed through 71 miles of spectacular scenery.

One of the shorter trails I have walked is the 13 miles of the John Buchan Way, from Broughton to Peebles, across the Borders hills by way of Stobo. The walk takes its name from the author of *The Thirty-Nine Steps* and many other novels, for John – or, as he became, Lord Tweedsmuir and Governor General of Canada – had a home in Broughton. The rather magnificent house occupying the property now is a much more recent structure, dating from the late 1930s, by the architect Sir Basil Spence.

Everybody has a favourite, often for different reasons. My friends Mike and Ann Lowson from Aberdeenshire introduced me to the Speyside Way, the 65-mile route from Buckie to Aviemore. You can go further south, to Newtonmore, if

The John Buchan Way at Broughton Place, where the Jacobite army camped on its march southwards in 1745. *Jim Barton*

The routes are very well signposted and waymarked these days. Here is an example of modern waymarking on the Great Glen Way, at the junction where the path from Braveheart car park meets the Peat Track to Cow Hill, in Glen Nevis. *Jim Barton*

stamina allows. Or you may choose to take the 15-mile spur known as the Tomintoul Extension, from Ballindalloch as it crosses the Glenlivet Estate to reach the 1,866-foot summit of Carn Daimh, lying within the Crown Estate. This is whisky country. There's a network of paths, including Smugglers' Way, publicly opened by the doyen of Scottish

People have been undertaking these challenges for much longer than the formal recognition of them as 'Great Trails'. Witness this old footpath sign on the West Highland Way, indicating the start of the path across the Lairig Mor, which is now part of the West Highland Way. *John Allan*

Right and below: Modern distance and waymarkers on the Tomintoul Extension and the Smugglers' Trail. *Both Mike Lowson*

hillwalking, Cameron McNeish, and tales to hear of the 500 illicit stills that covered this district, and distillers such as Robbie McPherson. It was risky but lucrative work. When he died in 1872, Robbie's estate was valued at £218 17s 9d, a not inconsiderable sum.

A couple of miles north-west of Killearn, the West Highland Way crosses Gartness Bridge. The modern bridge dates from 1971 and replaces the old masonry arched bridge. The date stone from the old bridge has been incorporated into the parapet wall on the north-western corner of the new design, an engineering fact recorded on the plaque that commemorates its opening. Also recorded was the engineer's name – J. F. Keith – who was the county road surveyor for Stirlingshire. He was also my Dad.

The old bridge was built in 1715, so earlier than Wade's major road and bridge construction projects. And it is not only part of the West Highland Way, but since 2014 it has shared this section with the John Muir Way, stretching 134 miles from Helensburgh to Dunbar.

I'd remembered this bridge when I was writing *Bridgescapes* in 2017, but couldn't recall its exact location. I'm grateful to friends John and Jayne Riddet who 'rediscovered' Gartness Bridge for me and took the accompanying photograph,

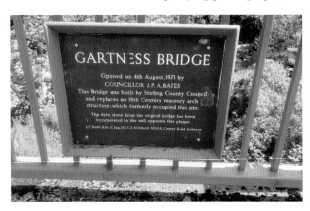

Gartness Bridge, a crossing point for two national long-distance walks. *John M. Riddet*

when they hiked the West Highland Way in June 2021.

I do recall, however, that the Saturday following the opening ceremony we visited as a family, and enjoyed a pub lunch in a hotel in Killearn. We'd just started our meal when a group of about six folk, dressed as cowboys and Indians, were ushered to the table some feet away. We were puzzled at first, my father suggesting that they must be members of the local country and western club, out for Saturday lunch. However, as the meal progressed it was clear that they were attracting more than passing attention from others too. It turned out that the group included Walter Carr and Una McLean, both very well-known Scottish actors, and they were taking a lunch break from filming a television comedy programme nearby. I hope you encounter such colourful characters on your travels along Scotland's highways and byways.

Another great trail in the north-east is the Formartine & Buchan Way (Buchan as in the home of the Doric rather than John Buchan). Following the line of old railways, this is both a cycle and walking route, stretching the 53 miles, including the spurs, from Dyce, near Aberdeen, to Fraserburgh via Peterhead.

New routes are being developed or opened up to new markets. A great example of a community-led local initiative is the Highland Perthshire Gravel Trails, where Highland Perthshire Cycling trustees Mike Stead and Kat Brown have worked with Markus Stitz of Bikepacking Scotland to develop 11 different routes across beautiful and remote countryside using old drove roads and forestry and windfarm roads. Launched in 2020, funding came from the Rural Perth & Kinross LEADER Programme and SSE Renewables' Community Fund to support the route design and promotional activity. Visit the website for details: perthshiregravel.com. Whatever your age or ability, you will not be disappointed.

There are many shorter, but equally interesting and attractive, walks available too. One such, the Gordon Way, is a waymarked hiking trail in

Aberdeenshire that runs for 11½ miles through the Bennachie Forest linking the hills of Bennachie and The Suie.

In total, the Great Trails cover a distance of 1,935 miles – that's the distance from Edinburgh to the Canary Islands as the crow flies. The total ascent for the 29 walks is calculated at 147,093 feet – that's five times the height of Mount Everest. Not bad for a country whose highest mountain, Ben Nevis, is 4,413 feet high. According to the guide, and it is only a guide, the time taken to walk all the trails would be 171 days, just shy of six months. You wouldn't do them all back-to-back, so to speak, of course. If you're exceptionally fit, or mad, or both, and did attempt this feat, and your companion asked you on Day 52, 'Are we nearly there yet?', you now know how to respond.

Creating routes that open up our history to modern generations is a feature of the tourism business. It's a major business for Scotland, worth £6 billion per annum to the economy. That's 5% of Gross Domestic Product, and it employs 207,000 people, equivalent to 1 in 12 of the workforce. Tapping into this market needs to be done with care, however – educating, informing, entertaining, enhancing, but always seeking not damage the heritage, either physically or reputationally.

'Faith tourism' is an area that has grown out of the custom and practice of the medieval pilgrimages, which we described in Chapter 5, and has captured an increasing focus, way beyond those whose interests are solely religious. My friend since our days at Stirling High School in the early 1970s, Donald Smith, describes the network of major pilgrim routes, past and present, in his book *Pilgrim Guide to Scotland*. And much of this active re-interest has been since the Millennium. St Cuthbert's Way, across the 62 miles from Melrose to Lindisfarne via Jedburgh, was inaugurated in 1999, followed by the Borders Abbey Way in 2005. This links to 12th-century abbeys, of which only four remain as ruins, through Kelso to Jedburgh, to Hawick, to Selkirk and to Melrose.

St Magnus Way runs for 55 miles across Mainland Orkney; the Fife Pilgrim Way extends for 64 miles from Culross to St Andrews and onwards to Abernethy; the Forth to Farne Way is 72 miles long and runs from North Berwick down the east coast to Holy Island; and the Whithorn Way runs 149 miles from Glasgow to Whithorn.

These are all complete. Others in development include the Northern Pilgrims Way, from Tain to Gills Bay, and thence to Orkney (95 miles); Deeside Way from Aberdeen to Ballater (44 miles); Iona to Killin, via Oban and Tyndrum (90 miles); Three Saints Way from Killin to St Andrews via Crieff (111 miles); St Conan's Way from Iona to Dalmally (63 miles); Dalriada Way from Tarbert to Lismore (102 miles); and Kentigern Way from Annan to Glasgow via Hoddom (the site of a 7th-century monastery, established by St Mungo), Moffat, Peebles and Lanark (150 miles). The joy of the majority of these routes is that they are predominantly off-road.

So there's plenty of choice. Moreover, and probably no surprise if you've reached this far in this book, there's a society to help you. There is a British Pilgrim Society, but, even more relevantly, the Scottish Pilgrim Routes Forum, established in 2012, provides a network of organisations and individuals committed to developing routes for off-road pilgrimage travel in Scotland. A Gathering was held in October 2019 in Girvan … in the Milestone Church. Contact the Scottish Pilgrim Society's website for further details.

Be you a motorist or cyclist, the options for scenic routes in Scotland are almost endless. Visit Scotland promotes six special scenic routes, each offering its own blend of experiences. They total some 1,374 miles, but who's counting these miles? On offer are:

- 'The Snow Roads Scenic Route' (90 miles): The road from Blairgowrie takes you past the Spittal of Glenshee and the now bypassed hairpin bends of the Devil's Elbow (but you can still cycle or walk it) to the Glenshee ski centre, by the highest public road in Britain (2,198 feet), down into Braemar and northwards, past Corgarff Castle, to The Lecht, the second highest road in Britain (2,113 feet).
- 'South West Coastal 300': Explore Dumfries & Galloway and South Ayrshire, stopping en route at the earliest known Christian site in Scotland at Whithorn, the book town of Wigtown and the Scottish Dark Sky Observatory on the edge of Galloway Forest Park.
- 'North Coast 500': An iconic driving route from Inverness to John o' Groats, along the northern tip of mainland Scotland to Durness and south along the deeply indented west coast, before turning inland along the Applecross Peninsula. It's actually 516 miles, if you want to be pedantic.
- 'North East 250': Discover Speyside, the Cairngorms, the Moray Coast, the Malt Whisky Trail, Royal Deeside and Aberdeen.
- 'The Argyll Coastal Route' (129 miles): Venture north from Glasgow along Loch Lomond, heading west at Tarbet, to Inverary and northwards to Fort William.
- 'The Borders Historic Route' (89 miles): From Gretna Green, north-eastwards to the land of Sir Walter Scott and the textile towns, and thence to Edinburgh.

And there's a new variant, 'The Scotland Route 666', added in 2020.

The best thing about these routes is that the choice is yours. My advice would be to give yourself plenty of time, hope for dry and sunny weather – May and September are the most reliable – and allow yourself the luxury of stopping where you want and deviate from the route as you please. Discovering Scotland off the beaten track may lead you to unearth some interesting milestones.

Our milestone heritage: The Western Isles

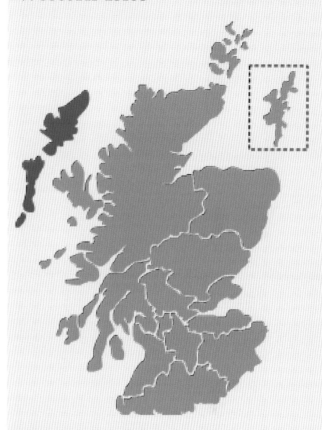

The Western Isles (The Outer Hebrides).
Wikimedia Commons

The Western Isles formerly lay within two county authorities. At the northern end, Lewis & Harris formed part of Ross & Cromarty, while the southerly islands of North and South Uist, Benbecula, Barra and the multitude of smaller islands in the archipelago were part of Inverness-shire.

Many of the former milestones marked on OS maps have sunk without trace, and not necessarily in the peat – mostly, I suspect, due to road

Modern eye-catching signage on North Uist at the junction of the A865 and C83 on the Lochmaddy road. It features a 'C' class road, which is most unusual. I hope this sign brings you 'solace'. *Christine Minto, The Milestone Society*

widening. Those that survive hold a fascination for the traveller.

Lewis had four stones in situ in 2011; although clearly old, none were very exceptional from a photographic perspective, so just for the database.

A granite column on the B888 near Daliburgh on South Uist. Christine Minto captured it during a cycle trip from south to north in 2011. *Christine Minto, The Milestone Society*

At the north end of Lewis we find Swainbost ('village/farm of the steading', from the Norse). In the early 1840s 17 families, cleared from their land at Uig on Skye, came to Swainbost. Their quest to find the 'land of milk and honey' in Canada by going west was foreshortened, arriving in what they described as a 'virtual wasteland' in Lewis, but the local landowner looked favourably upon them and, after an initial struggle, 40 new lots, each of approximately 6-7 acres, were created out of a reapportioned estate. In the early 20th century, following the construction of the Cross Skigersta Road, ten new 'fisherman's holdings' were detached from the common grazing land. Still, a life for those hardier than me.

The Western Isles also had a significant number of cast-iron mileposts, and we are indebted once more to Ken Diamond for capturing them on celluloid during his travels in his Triumph TR3A. The accompanying photograph showing 1 mile to Butt of Lewis was taken in the village of Eoropie, with its St Moluag's Church, or Teampall Mholuaidh in Gaelic, dating from the 13th century. It's a remote place by anyone's reckoning, but has long been held to be a place of healing. A

A milestone 3 miles from Swainbost in Lewis. *Christine Minto, The Milestone Society*

Captain Dymes, visiting Lewis in 1630, recorded that people who could not reach Eoropie due to its remoteness 'were wont to cut out the portion of their lame arms or leg in wood with the forms of their sores and wounds thereof and send them to the saint where I have seen them lying on the altar of the chapel.' I have been unable to trace any testimony of the success or otherwise of this somewhat bizarre practice, but perhaps it was an effective placebo.

This is wild country. The headland beyond Eoropie runs up to the lighthouse at the Butt of Lewis, the most northerly point on the Outer Hebrides. The rocks here are the oldest in Europe, having been formed in the Precambrian period, up to 3,000 million years ago.

A signpost for Butt of Lewis at Eoropie. *Ken Diamond collection, The Milestone Society*

Signposts at the junction of the A859 and the B887, north of Tarbert. *Ken Diamond collection, The Milestone Society*

13
'Paddy's Milestone': the story of Ailsa Craig

I couldn't resist some degree of writer's licence in including 'Paddy's Milestone' in a book on illustrious Scottish milestones.

Lying about 10 miles off the Ayrshire coast is the volcanic plug of Ailsa Craig, the home of the granite of which about 70% of curling stones are formed. Now uninhabited, the 240-acre island was a refuge for Catholics during the Scottish Reformation in the 16th century.

Kays of Scotland is one of only two makers of curling stones in the world. The firm has been making curling stones since 1851 and has exclusive rights to the granite quarried on Ailsa

Ailsa Craig, as viewed from the paddle steamer *Waverley*. *Mary and Angus Hogg*

Craig. The island's blue hone granite has the better water-resistant qualities, but the Ailsa Craig green granite is also highly valued. These stones have brought glory to Scotland's curling fortunes too. At the Winter Olympics of 1924, held in Chamonix, the Royal Caledonian Curling Club won Gold for its prowess, a feat not to be repeated until Rhona Martin and her team won in Salt Lake City in the winter of 2002. The resurgence in curling throughout Scotland is heartening, especially among the younger generation. Judging from what I've witnessed at the Dumfries ice rink, where my good friend John Riddet coaches local

schoolchildren in the techniques of the game, Scotland can look forward to a healthy future at world competition level. Gold and Bronze for the Scottish Ladies' team and Silver for the Men's team at the Winter Olympics in Sochi in 2014 underpins that revival in interest, which bodes well for the future success of the next generation, and a market for Ailsa Craig's granite.

Ailsa Craig stands proud in the outer Firth of Clyde, renowned nowadays as a bird sanctuary for large numbers of gannets and increasing populations of puffins.

However, the island earned its famous soubriquet of 'Paddy's Milestone' as it lies approximately halfway between Belfast and Glasgow on the route travelled by tens of thousands of Irish labourers emigrating to Glasgow and the West of Scotland to find employment.

The short distance between Scotland and Ireland meant that over the centuries there has been significant migration in both directions. The Ulster Scots would remind you, quite properly, that their pedigree lies in the Scots settlement in Ireland, which began in 1609. Aimed at confiscating the lands of the Gaelic Irish nobility in Ulster and settling the province with Protestant Scottish, largely drawn from the Lowlands and Scottish Borders, and English colonists, this was the Government-sanctioned Plantation of Ulster. To say that this division between a Protestant landholding minority and a dispossessed Catholic majority, stemming from the 17th century, lies as a cornerstone in the recurrent theme in

Ireland's troubled history is an understatement. But this book is about Scotland, so let's leave that discussion for another day.

By the early 19th century Irish immigration over the water was well-established. By the 1840s there were up to 25,000 economic migrants crossing the Irish Sea to Scotland, England and Wales, bound for seasonal agricultural work or other temporary contractual employment. The late 1820s witnessed a boom in construction in Scotland. New houses, factories, canals, roads and bridges were built to facilitate the burgeoning coal, steel and textile industries. New towns grew up to house this workforce, many with significant Irish communities, who had moved permanently to reside in Scotland. In 1831, for example, three-quarters of the 6,000 population of Girvan in Ayrshire had been born in Ireland.

The first Scottish census, in 1841, recorded that some 125,321 (4.8%) of the 2.6 million population were Ireland-born. By way of comparison, only 1.8% of the population of England was of Irish descent, and less than 0.8% in Wales.

The greatest surge in migrants passing 'Paddy's Milestone' en route to Glasgow happened in the late 1840s and early 1850s, fuelled by the Great Famine exodus. The repeated failure of the potato crop in Ireland led many to seek pastures new in Scotland. 'Pastures new' was seldom a rural idyll, however. They came to heavy industry, manufacture and railway construction, and often lived in overcrowded accommodation, but it sure was an improvement on the poverty and starvation they left behind. By 1851 the Irish population of Scotland had reached 7.2% overall, heavily concentrated in Glasgow and Dundee (with Irish-born populations of 18.9% and 18.2% respectively) and the mining communities of Mid and West Lothian, and in Airdrie, Coatbridge and Motherwell.

So 'Paddy's Milestone' is a natural monument to much social and economic migration – journeys that spelled new milestones in the lives of so many.

Our milestone heritage: The Northern Isles

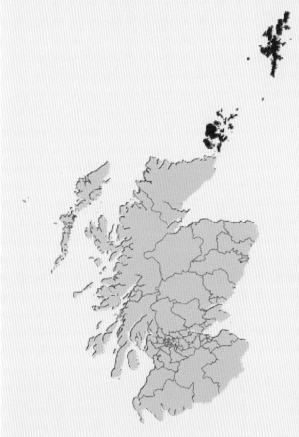

The Northern Isles. *Wikimedia Commons*

Orkney

If you have never been to Orkney, then go! Although I've a cousin who was born in Stromness, my only sighting of the archipelago had been from travels along the north coast of Caithness while visiting the Department of Agriculture's office in Thurso, until my trip to the Northern Isles in 2016. I will return.

Not only is Orkney absolutely steeped in archaeology and what I might term 'more modern history', but it also has a vibrant farming and fishing community with a 'can-do' approach to business, an oil industry that has made every effort to blend with its environment, outstanding wildlife, and spectacular coastal scenery. In a nutshell, it has much to commend it, which it would benefit others to emulate. And the Orcadians are a decent bunch too, very down to earth and genuine.

As well as witnessing many historic milestones since our Neolithic ancestors ran a highly organised and successful society here in days of yore, Orkney has a few physical milestones, too, which are worthy of note.

Near Lyness, on Hoy, there are a couple of Listed milestones – the first is a segmental-headed stone slab milestone, bearing the marks 'N[orth] Ness 2' and 'Hoy 9'. The other is a sandstone milestone showing 'Hoy 11' and 'S[outh] Ness 5'. In both cases, the lettering looks suspiciously akin to the influences of the Arts & Crafts movement, which was popular in the early years of the 20th century. It may be a coincidence, but the prominent English architect W. R. Lethaby had been commissioned by the owners of Melsetter Estate, the Middlemores, to rebuild the mansion house. The Middlemores, who had made their fortune manufacturing bicycle saddles, of all things, in Birmingham, purchased the estate on Hoy in 1898, so the timing works well for an association with the design on the milestone. Interestingly, however, the first milestone is not recorded on the 1903 2nd Edition OS map. Does it post-date 1903, or was it missed by the surveyor?

While on Orkney, marvel at Scapa Flow, one of the greatest natural harbours in the world, a safe haven for the longboats of seafaring Vikings and host to the British Navy during both World Wars. Beneath its waters lie 53 of the 74 ships of the Imperial German Navy's High Seas Fleet, interned here at the end of the First World War and scuttled by German Rear Admiral Ludwig von

Reuter on 21 June 1919 to avoid the vessels being used by the British.

Staying within Scapa Flow, the island of Flotta is home to the oil terminal, the huge tanks constructed in the 1970s for the burgeoning North Sea oil industry. Their colour merges perfectly with the grey of the water and the skyscape, the visitor's eye only drawn by the ring of red around the top circumference of each tank. This, the architect, whom I heard lecture on his design at a seminar in Edinburgh in the early 1990s, advised the audience, was because the regulations require fire extinguishers to be placed at regular spacings atop each tank, and the fire authority insisted that all fire equipment be painted red. History is still being made here. In 2007 Flotta witnessed the world's first ship-to-ship transfer of liquefied natural gas (LNG).

In Stromness there is a plaque on the walls of the Parish Rooms with a table showing distances to 26 places. It replaced an earlier wooden one.

The Stromness distance marker. *John Higgins, The Milestone Society*

On the B9057 in the village of Dounby in the north-west of Orkney Mainland stands an ancient milestone. There aren't many milestones recording sixths of a mile.

The Dounby milestone. *The Milestone Society*

But Orkney's original milestones probably date from the early 1870s. A report of a meeting of the Orkney Road Trustees was published in *The Orkney Herald* on 12 April 1871. It included the surveyor's report that:

'The milestones authorised by the Trustees to be placed along the roads, were supplied by the contractor, in terms of his offer, and they have been set along the constructed lines of road. The

cost of these milestones, 93 in number, including cartage, amounts to the total sum of £31, which is little more than the estimate.'

Beside it, the unified parish of Birsay, Harray and Sandwick has built a modern community church. The symbolism of the milestone as a marker on a journey is not lost on the local congregation, as the community building provides a space for people to mark milestones through their lives, be it births, marriages or deaths. However, it's meant for all the community, of whatever faith, as a meeting place for social communion and a very wide range of activities. It is very good to see this type of development acting as a cohesive force, and a transformation for the better from the traditional church hall available, in days gone by, only to those whose creed too rigidly espoused 'Three Gods in one, but only for one day in seven'.

Near Crunbrecks on Mainland Orkney is a milestone that looks at first glance to be a '10', transposed. Actually, the '0' is an 'O' and stands for Orphil.

The milestone near the junction of the A964 and an unclassified road on Mainland Orkney near Crunbrecks. *The Milestone Society*

TABLE of DISTANCE from STROMNESS			
	Miles		Miles
KIRKWALL	16	BURWICK	36
FINSTOWN	8	STANDING STONES	6½
DOUNBY	9½	MAESHOWE	5½
STENNESS PO	4	SKARA BRAE	8
ORPHIR PO	11	BY SEA	
RENDALL PO	12	GRAEMSAY	2
EVIE PO	17	MOANESS	5
SANDWICK PO	6½	BY LAND (from Moaness)	
TWATT PO	18½	LONGHOPE	17
PALACE BIRSAY	14	LYNESS	9½
YESNABY	5½	OLD MAN OF HOY	6
BLACK CRAIG	2½	DWARFIE STANE	3
WAREBETH	1½	BERRIEDALE	3
HOUTON	7	RACKWICK	5

Orkney boasts a distance record too. The 738-yard, par 6, third hole on the Westray golf course is officially recognised as the UK's longest golf hole. At more than two-fifths of a mile, its length isn't the only challenge for the golfer. Bill Turnbull, a former club captain who is now the greenkeeper, commented that 'on a windy day a bogey is a good score, but it can be parred. There are even a couple of members who have birdied it.' Situated beside the village of Pierowall, the nine-hole course has spectacular coastal views and since 2005 has been in community ownership, thanks to a contribution from the Scottish Government's Land Fund.

Shetland

At the very southern tip of the Mainland of Shetland we encounter another Robert Stevenson lighthouse, Sumburgh Head, dating from 1821. Since 2014 it has also functioned as a modern visitor centre, hosted by the Shetland Amenity Trust, in collaboration with the RSPB and the

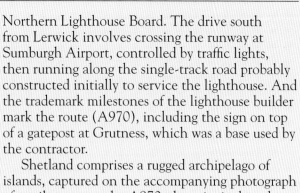

Northern Lighthouse Board. The drive south from Lerwick involves crossing the runway at Sumburgh Airport, controlled by traffic lights, then running along the single-track road probably constructed initially to service the lighthouse. And the trademark milestones of the lighthouse builder mark the route (A970), including the sign on top of a gatepost at Grutness, which was a base used by the contractor.

Shetland comprises a rugged archipelago of islands, captured on the accompanying photograph of a milestone on the A970, the principal road through the mainland.

Above: A Shetland milestone.
Christine Minto, The Milestone Society

Right: A Millennium Milestone at Voe. *Deborah M. Keith*

Left: The milepost atop the gatepost at Grutness. The inscription reads 'To Lighthouse/1 mile/1033 yards'. *The Milestone Society*

The Milestone Society's logo. *The Milestone Society*

14
The Milestone Society

There's a collective human instinct to wish to belong to a club or society whose members share a common interest with your own. That's all perfectly reasonable. It's part of society in most parts of the world, although I suspect the British display a particular disposition towards such groupings. Bill Bryson more than hints at this in his excellent reflections captured in *The Road to Little Dribbling – Adventures of an American in Britain*. It's even true across the globe. 'Wherever you travel,' someone once remarked, 'the Scots have been there first,' and you can still witness the collective presence of the diaspora, with Caledonian Societies and Burns Clubs worldwide.

One outstanding feature of this societal bond is that no matter what your interest, there's almost certainly a 'club' that caters for it, no matter how distinctive it might be.

It was with little, if no, surprise therefore that when I started my quest to research milestones, a quick web search revealed the existence of The Milestone Society.

When I approached the honorary secretary and the editor of the Society's excellent journal, *Milestones and Waymarkers*, to enquire further, they without hesitation – and I should say graciously – expressed an interest in my project and generously offered their support. Further, although I'm oft guided by Groucho Marx's comment on such matters – 'I don't want to belong to any club that will accept me as a member!' – I did join.

It's proved fruitful.

The Society is UK-wide, but there is a keen Scottish contingent and the Journal has featured articles on Scottish milestones on many occasions. Moreover, there is a wealth of material and photographs to hand, and I was expertly supported and enthusiastically embraced as a fellow devotee.

I have paid tribute to particular Society members in the Acknowledgements, but special mention must be made of Christine Minto.

Christine has spent a lifetime enjoying exploring Scotland on her bike, travelling the length and breadth of the country, including the Northern and Western Isles. She and her late husband Frank, natives of South Yorkshire, developed a strong passion for cycle touring, observing the fabric of Scotland's countryside along their routes and, when The Milestone Society was formed, assiduously visited and recorded thousands of examples on their frequent visits north of the border. Christine is the Scottish Representative on the Society's Committee.

Christine was instrumental in 'getting the show on the road', so to speak, with this book, and I would still have been ferreting around Scotland's highways and byways looking for milestones had she not been so generous in her support.

I want to include some details of the Society in this chapter, so that if you've been sufficiently engaged by the subject matter of this book, perhaps you might also wish to join.

Established as a specialist interest group in 2001, one of its founding fathers, Terry Keegan (1931-2012) was of Scottish and Irish parentage. Born in Dublin, he lived throughout the UK and Ireland, but evacuation to his uncle's farm in Kinross during the Second World War gave him a lifelong love of all things Scottish. He served the Society as both Honorary Secretary and Vice Chair and, although firmly established in Worcestershire in later life, he was a frequent visitor to Scotland. Organised by Nigel Bishop from Doune, Terry chaired the Society's Scottish Conference held in the David Marshall Lodge in Aberfoyle in May 2009, and compiled the 'Scrapbook of Information on Scottish Milestones and other waymarkers'.

The Society's purpose is to encourage people, from individuals to Highways and Local Authorities, Parish Councils, Civic Societies, local history groups and others, to look after their local milestones and protect them from the risks of neglect, vandalism, vehicle impacts and road works. As a means of recording information on milestones, volunteers have logged 31,230 such artefacts with 21,250 images, available to view on Google Earth and on Geograph.org.uk.

It is easiest, perhaps, to quote the Aims and Objectives of the charity, so I can't be accused of misrepresentation. The Aim is:

'To identify, record, research, conserve and interpret for public benefit the milestones and other waymarkers of the British Isles.'

The Objectives spell out the hows, for what purpose and for whom in more detail:

1. To publicise and promote public awareness of milestones and other waymarkers and the need for identification, recording, research and conservation for the general benefit and education of the community at large;

2. To enhance public awareness and enjoyment of milestones and other waymarkers and to inform and inspire the community at large of their distinctive contribution to both the local scene and to the historic landscape in general;

3. To represent the historical significance and national importance of milestones and waymarkers in appropriate forums and through relevant national organisations;

4. To organise and coordinate relevant practical projects at both national and regional/local levels, thereby enhancing public access;

5. To protect, preserve and restore milestones and other waymarkers through the planning process, representing their significance to appropriate authorities locally and nationally; and

6. To manage the Society's affairs in ways which maintain effective administration and appropriate activity, including the establishment of regional groupings through which to delegate and devolve the Society's business.

For more information, please consult the Society's website. The Society looks forward to hearing from you.

15
Journey's end

Well, that's us nearly at the end of our journey through Scotland's milestone heritage. Along the way we've encountered how distance has been measured, and signalled, over the centuries, and ghosted several significant journeys by our forefathers. We've also witnessed how our fellow countrymen, and women, have gone that extra mile in establishing speed and distance records and flown the Saltire at national and international events.

'Are we nearly there yet?' Well, almost. It only remains to wonder how future journeys will measure up and where they will take us. One thing is for sure – increasingly sophisticated IT will play a major part in how we plan and execute our travels. The milestones of yesteryear have, to a large extent, already given way to satellite navigation – on our mobile phone as we walk, strapped to the handlebars of our bike, or as an integral component of the instrumentation of the dashboard in our car. Satnav not only shows you the journey on a digitally derived map, but also speaks to you! It gives you directions, it alerts you to speed cameras and traffic diversions necessitated by road works and accidents, guides you to your destination, and advises you of your arrival. Before my old grey cells become too diminished, I hope that the technology will evolve to include, upon arrival, a gentle reminder of the purpose of my visit.

The childhood query 'Are we nearly there yet?' is replaced with the enquiry 'Why am I here?'

But the end of the writing phase of this project is also a chance to catch one's breath and reflect upon the journey.

Although I have 'resided' in England for a quarter of a century, my visits to Scotland have been frequent. There's a strong magnetic attraction to both country and friends, as well as a familial link with my daughter, Lauren, who has followed my career footsteps in the Scottish Government. A pride in one's country is imbued in all who have studied its history, been nurtured by its culture and enriched by its humour, and have explored its beauty. That doesn't mean that any of these four aspects are without blemish, but rather that one feels 'at home' in its ambience. Nor does it mean that if you leave, as so many Scots have done over the centuries, that you are any less an integral part of the Scottish psyche. 'You can take the man out of Dundee, but you'll never take Dundee out of the man,' as my friend and fellow member of the Scots diaspora, Blyth Morris, reminds me often. Or, as Mike Lowson expresses it, 'You get it,' the inference being that others may not.

A favourite tune of mine is one that has its pedigree in the pibroch, an ancient tune played on the Scottish bagpipes. Entitled 'The Dark Island', it is actually much more modern, composed in 1958 by Iain MacLachlan as a pipe lament for a departing local doctor, one Dr Mackay of Creagorry on Benbecula. In 1963 it was used as the theme music for the BBC TV series of the same name, filmed on South Uist. My Dad met the producer, Gerard Glaister, while on a bridge inspection tour of the Hebrides. Namedropper! One version of the lyrics was written by Stewart Ross of Inverness, and recorded by Calum Kennedy and his daughter Fiona, and is particularly evocative to us Scots diaspora:

'In the years long gone by
When I first left my home
I was young and I wanted
The wide world to roam.
But now I am older and wiser you see
For that lovely dark island
Is calling to me.'

When *Bridgescapes* was finally completed and rolled off the press in 2017, it offered the opportunity to visit history and heritage societies, Civic Trusts and Rotary and Probus clubs all over Scotland, and a few Caledonian societies south of the border, too. For the next almost three years I gave more than 150 talks, meeting an eclectic mix of different folk, but all of them sharing a keen interest in Scotland's heritage. From Stranraer to Brora, from Oban to Aberdeen, my own knowledge of Scotland's road network was brought up to speed. Then the Covid-19 coronavirus pandemic arrived! My last talk to date was in Hawick on 12 March 2020.

Confined to barracks in Peterborough with all remaining talks rescheduled to resume in September 2021, I needed a project to keep me out of mischief. Hence the milestone project evolved, and once this book is published I'm hoping the legacy will include a 'second lap' of all these friendly clubs and societies to give my new, illustrated, talk.

I've acknowledged already the very significant help from members of The Milestone Society and others in enabling me to reach this point. Throughout the past year my close friends who contributed the Foreword have been hugely supportive, too. We have not, of course, managed a physical Boys Walking Weekend, but we have kept in touch via a weekly virtual meeting, and each week I've updated them on progress with the book.

They have therefore experienced a sense of deja vu, having been subjected to the *Bridgescapes* evolution, but, as we all reach retirement age, have also been reflecting on some of the times we've shared together.

I'm honoured indeed that they've offered to finish the book for me, so I'll leave the concluding remarks, almost an epilogue, to each of them.

Memories are made of this…

Mike Hogg: a seasoned railwayman who has never lost his passion for buses. *Lyndsay Hogg*

Smoking was still allowed. The air was pretty thick as we stood in the packed pub in Keswick for the 1997 Jazz Festival. We'd arranged that weekend as a walking weekend, not realising that the nation's jazz glitterati were also going to be in town. The tempo was quick, the saxophones swinging, the double-basses strumming, the band leader's brow laced with sweat, when he made the mistake of asking the crowd for suggestions for the next number. Sure enough, Bruce placed his pint of Jennings on a nearby shelf and made his way to the stage. I tensed. A quick conversation, a glimpse of a puzzled look, an 'OK…' look from the leader,

then, once the current foot-stomping number was complete, the change to Bruce's request, the slowest of the slow – a Dean Martin number, covered by many singers, including Bruce's hero Val Doonican. Never have I witnessed the atmosphere in a pub change more quickly. Suddenly watches were being consulted, the exit door looked at, pints drained, ladies heading for the Ladies and the band leader wondering how quickly he could politely bring the number to an end and thus get his audience back and regain the previous magic.

So, Bruce is good at making his mark in all sorts of unexpected ways. His mark is part of an indelible friendship going back 40 years and

MEMORIES ARE MADE OF THIS
Words & Music by Terry Gilkyson, Rich Dehr & Frank Miller

Recorded by
VAL DOONICAN
on Decca

MONTCLARE
MUSIC CO. LTD.
Sole Selling Agents:-
CAMPBELL CONNELLY & Cº Ltd
10, Denmark Street, London W.C.2.

3/.

Val Doonican rocks, but gently. *Wikimedia Commons*

rekindled as the 'boys' do their 'walking weekends', now generally, post-retirement, mid-week and having tea shop visits as a feature replacing the longer walks of yore. Long may they continue as we continue our gentle amble past the milestones of friendship.

Mike Hogg

Man on a mission...

Bruce is a man on a mission, mounting sustained forays into Scotland from his Peterborough retreat. This man thinks nothing of criss-crossing the

Colin Shearer: a true and fervent 'gutterbluid' and Bruce's first tenant, which mercifully didn't ruin a wonderful friendship. *Yvonne Sheppard*

nation in what might seem a totally erratic fashion to meet any and all requests to give a talk. One fine morning while headed south, we spotted the light blue Jaguar headed north, swinging smoothly along the graceful curves of the A701 approaching the Devil's Beef Tub. There was a steely glint in his eye as he passed by, oblivious to our frantic waves as he headed for Fife, or was it East Lothian? That passion to share knowledge and understanding is the most worthy of pursuits.

I thought back then, as I do now, to the numerous fish, chip and beer nights we'd shared in pubs in the King's Cross area, always choosing places where Bruce could make use of a discount voucher. I well remember the secretive way he whispered plans for this new book. Much furtive debate on milestones and nautical measures followed, before he caught the last train back to Peterborough calling at all 23 stations, armed with his cheap day return.

The lads have clubbed together to buy you a year's subscription to a car breakdown service, so concerned have we been about the extended stays in Moffat and Blair Atholl, when punctures and red dashboard lights gleamed and the only hire vehicle available for you to use was a 13-seater minibus.

I'll be flicking through the pages of this book to solve the mystery of why the mileage to Huntingdon is boldly imprinted on Dumfries town hall, and will expect a refund if it hasn't been explained. We rail lads are demanding, for we have been brought up on travel and the endless fascination of measuring time and distance to anticipate late, early and on-time arrivals. It was a pastime I took to extremes when, aged about 14, I maintained timekeeping records of Western SMT buses on the old Peebles to Lanark route.

I jest. We are proud and delighted that this best of friends for 40 years has come up trumps with another insight into Scotland's heritage. I, for one, hope to become a roadie on a forthcoming adventure to share this new book. I recall attending a *Bridgescapes* talk one very wet

night in Melrose where most of the audience subsequently retired to the pub together. I know what is needed from a friend on such occasions: to prompt applause, ask questions and take down any hecklers. And now and again to suggest a new joke to go with the talk. Bruce I'm there for you.

Colin L. Shearer

A view from the armchair critic

Tim Roebuck: reputedly the only lifelong fan of both English cricket and British Railways in the US state of New Jersey – photographed on one of his walkabouts at the Kennedy Space Center in Cape Canaveral. *Tim Roebuck*

I was trying to recall early memories and I probably didn't meet Bruce until 1980 in Guthrie following a memorable trip with the lads to Islay. Certainly, a fiercely contested three-a-side England v Scotland football match in the public park in Friockheim, followed by a pint in the village's Balmoral Hotel, is an early recollection. Sadly, the result is lost in the mists of time. Our friendship is much like my favourite chair – certainly needs a bit of upholstery, the covers are probably dated (especially in some areas), it's dangerous to move it too far, and it has that comforting aroma that some visitors find utterly mystifying. But you know what you are getting, it's pretty well impossible to fall off, and you have had that inevitable warm feeling before and can often predict what's coming next.

Tim Roebuck

A passion shared

The friendship that has drawn us together over many years to explore some part of the British Isles, and indeed sometimes further afield, is partly rooted in a common and shared curiosity about the places and things that we see.

That might be some long-forgotten industrial archaeology, a disused railway, a canal, an interesting building, a national monument, a fine example of our built heritage, or simply an expanse of glorious and often unrivalled scenery, from mountain to coast.

So it is entirely natural that Bruce has harnessed that curiosity and written this illuminating book about milestones and their unique role in history. In doing so, we all contributed in some way – the topic of railway milestones, for example, would in itself generate a significant volume of its own.

But as Bruce has done his research, we have all come upon interesting snippets and discovered that there is a great deal to be learned about milestones, as I hope you discover, gentle reader.

Charles Devereux

Charles Devereux: a man whose boundless enthusiasm for railways worldwide is matched by his endless enthusiasm for his beloved dogs. *Charles Devereux*

Light relief

The affection with which Bruce is held and the respect and admiration we have for him as a friend, colleague and now as an accomplished author is universal. He is a one-off.

To my mind, one memory in particular typifies his character. Some years ago our group spent its annual get-together in Scotland's beautiful North West Highlands. The six of us stayed at a small hotel that could offer only three small rooms: one single, one double and one three-bedded example, each with bathrooms arguably bigger than the bed spaces. Two of us shared the tiny triple-bedded room with Bruce, lying side-by-side like Apollo astronauts awaiting blast-off. We had no fears of disappearing into the blackness of space, though. Instead, we feared who would be first to head into the darkness to answer the inevitable nocturnal call of nature. Fortunately, perhaps, it was Bruce.

We heard him struggle out of bed, mercifully avoiding tripping over any bags, beds or bodies,

Mike Lowson: a man of a' the airts and many parts, some of which are still reported to be in working order. *Ann Lowson*

but pause at the bathroom door. On the wall were three adjacent switches – one for the bathroom lights, a second for the bathroom fan and a third for main room lights. Solicitously aware that choosing the latter and switching on the lights would awaken his sleeping colleagues, he paused, unaware that we weren't actually asleep but silently witnessing his discomfort.

With his need to visit the facilities swelling to

seriously uncomfortable levels, he faced a Russian roulette-style choice lest disaster strike. Eventually he chose the middle switch – it was the bedroom lights and instantly turned our room into a Highland version of the Blackpool Illuminations.

Before we could laugh out loud, he rapidly switched it off again, plunging us back into darkness before making his next choice. It turned out to be the fan. By the time he finally selected the bathroom light switch, not only was he almost helpless in desperation but we were helpless with laughter.

It was typical of him. Careful, considerate, concerned for colleagues yet constantly creating comedy gold along the way.

As I said, Bruce is a one-off. We are all very fortunate to know him.

Mike Lowson

The Last Post

'They say life is a highway and its milestones are
    the years.
And now and then there's a toll-gate where you
    can buy your way with tears.'

Alfred Joyce Kilmer (1886-1918)
Killed by a sniper's bullet at the Second Battle of the Marne

Glossary

Chain A unit of linear measurement of 66 feet; a surveyor's measuring tool.

Circumferentor A surveyor's compass, used to measure horizontal angles. It was superseded by the theodolite in the early 19th century.

Dr Slop A character from Laurence Sterne's *The Life and Opinions of Tristram Shandy, Gentleman*, published in 1759, the year of Robert Burns's birth. He is the village doctor, described as 'a little squat, uncourtly figure … about four feet and a half perpendicular height, with a breadth of back, and a sesquipedality of belly.' And that's his appearance; he's also incompetent.

Ell A unit of linear measurement. In Scotland an ell was 37 inches, but it varied significantly across European countries. In England it was usually 45 inches; in Holland 27 inches; in France 54 inches; in Poland 31 inches; and in Denmark 24 inches. In Germany the length varied considerably depending whether you were in Frankfurt, Cologne, Leipzig or Hamburg. Imagine what that did for international trade – and trust.

Fall A unit of linear measurement, equating to 6 (Scots) ells.

Finial Usually used in architectural terminology, in the context of this book it is a small, ornamental or decorative terminal feature on top of a milepost.

Furlong A unit of measurement used in linear distances; a length of an eighth of a mile, or 660 feet, 220 yards, 40 rods or 10 chains.

Grig A lively, jovial fellow.

Ordnance Datum Newlyn (ODN) A vertical datum for use in topographical mapping throughout the UK, including throughout the Scottish mainland and the Inner Hebrides, but excluding the Outer Hebrides, Orkney and Shetland. It is the Mean Sea Level at Newlyn in Cornwall between 1915 and 1921. From 2002 it was redefined through OSGM geoid models.

Raip, fall or rod A unit of linear measurement that equates to 5½ yards or 16½ feet; therefore 4 rods equals 1 chain.

Spelter A commercial form of zinc.

Stereoscope A device for viewing a stereoscopic pair of separate images depicting left-eye and right-eye views of the same scene, as a single three-dimensional image; a key to interpreting aerial photographs.

Sympiesometer A device that combines a traditional mercury thermometer and a barometer, widely used on ships in the 19th century, but also used to measure altitude.

Theodolite A precision optical instrument for measuring angles between designated visible points in the horizontal and vertical planes.

Bibliography

A History of Scotland, Neil Oliver

A History of the Scottish People, W. W. Knox;
    Chapter 9: *Transport and Scottish Society 1840-1940*

A Journey to the Western Isles of Scotland, Dr
    Samuel Johnson (published 1775)

*A Project to Identify, Survey and Record
Archaeological Remains in Strathconnon, Ross-*
    shire, Reports 2008/09: North of Scotland
    Archaeological Society

A Tour in Scotland 1769, Thomas Pennant

A Tour thro' the Whole Island of Great Britain,
    Daniel Defoe

A Voyage Round Great Britain, William Daniell

Armadale: Past and Present, R. Hynd-Brown;
    Chapter IV *Reminiscences of the Coaching Days –
    Robbery of £5,000 and a Hanging* (1906)

*Assessment of the Impacts of the Road Equivalent
    Tariff* Pilot, Halcrow Group Ltd (July 2011) to
    the Scottish Government

Battles of the '45, Katherine Tamasson and Francis
    Buist

Boundary Stones Trail, Aberdeen City Council

*Britain's Scenic Railways – Exploring the Country by
    Rail from Cornwall to the Highlands*, Julian
    Holland and David Spaven (*The Times*)

Calum's Road, Roger Hutchinson (2006/08)

*Charting the Nation – Maps of Scotland and
    associated archives 1550-1740*, Charles W. J.
    Withers (Edinburgh University Library, 2014)

*Cobbett's Tour in Scotland; and in the four Northern
    Counties of England: in the autumn of 1832*,
    William Cobbett

*County Road Books by Nicholas Oddy and R.
    G. Inglis in Cycling History 9*; Proceedings,
    9th International Cycling History Conference,
    Ottawa, Canada, 19-21 August 1998, pp79-92

Freedom Lands and Marches of Aberdeen, 1319-
    1929, James Cruickshank (1929)

Historic Argyll – 2011, article on mileposts by
    Martin Petrie

Journal of a Tour of Scotland in 1819,
    Robert Southey

*Journal of the Marches by His Royal Highness the
    Prince Regent's Army, From the Time they
    entered England the 8th November, till their Return
    to Scotland, the 20th December 1745'*, Historical
    Papers 1699-1750, Vol 1, Appendix XXLL,
    1894-95 of the New Spalding Club

London coach departures 1819 in *Wicked William*,
    Greg Roberts (28 April 2016)

Marking the Miles: A History of English Milestones,
    Carol Haines

Milestones, article by Nigel Bishop in 'The Scottish
    Local History Journal', Issue 79, Summer 2010

Milestones, Ayrshire milestones from the
    Ayrshire History website: 'Catalogue of
    Ayrshire Milestones', David McClure

Milestones and Waymarkers Journal:
    Vol 3 (2009) *Morvern Milestones – preservation
        in the Lochaber district of* Scotland, Mervyn
        Benford, Ian Jolly and David Viner
    Vol 4 (2010) *Scotland*, Christine Minto
    Vol 4 (2010) *Western Isles* in Spring,
        Christine Minto
    Vol 5 (2012), article by Diane Burns
    Vol 6 (2013) *Military boundary stones at
        Hannahfield, Dumfries*, V. E. Weighill
    Vol 8 (2015) *The Roads to Auchenstroan Toll,
        Dumfries and Galloway*, A. B. Hall and V.
        E. Weighill
    Vol 11 (2018/19) *Thomas Telford's milestones*,
        David Ellis-Williams
    Vol 12 (2020) *Wayside markers in Eastern Fife*,
        Elizabeth and Michael Spencer
    Newsletter 37 (August 2019) *Scotland*,
        Christine Minto and *Melrose milestone*,
        David Viner
    Newsletter 38 (February 2020) *Scotland*,
        Christine Minto
    Newsletter 39 (Summer 2020) *Scotland*,
        Christine Minto

Milestones and Wayside Markers in Fife, W. Stephen,
    Proceedings of the Society of Antiquarians of
    Scotland, Vol 100 (1967-68)

Milestones of the Union Canal, Jim Lonie (2020),
    Union Canal Society

New Statistical Account for Carluke, Vol VI (1845),
    Rev John Wylie

Old Edinburgh Trams, Kenneth G. Williamson

'Old Roads of Scotland' website

Ordnance Gazetteer of Scotland, Vol I (1882),
    Francis H. Groome (Ed)

Pilgrim Guide to Scotland, Dr Donald Smith

Pilgrimage in Medieval Scotland, Peter Yeoman

Railway Signs and Signals of Great Britain, Section
    28, Distance Markers

Railway Mileposts: Second Revised Edition,
    Tim Petchley (Railway Antiques Gazette)

Recollections of a Tour Made in Scotland AD 1803,
    Dorothy Wordsworth

Road Furniture in the Countryside, Transport
    Scotland (2006)

Robert Burns, Dr Ian Grimble (1986)

Scotland from the Sky, James Crawford (BBC
    Scotland TV series)

Scottish Transport Statistics, No 38, 2019 Edition
    (Transport Scotland)

*Scrapbook of information on Scottish Milestones and
    other Waymarkers*, compiled by Terry Keegan
    from various members of The Milestone Society

*Some Notes on the Old Military Roads in Dumfries
    and Galloway*, Alex D. Anderson, Transactions
    of the Dumfries & Galloway Natural History
    and Antiquarian Society, No 72 (1997)

Survey of the roads of Scotland on an improved plan,
    G. Taylor and A. Skinner (1776)

Sustrans Report: Scotland Review 2019
    (www.sustrans.scotland)

Telford, Man of Iron, Julian Glover

*The construction of Aberdeenshire's first turnpike
    roads*, Thomas Day, *The Journal of Transport
    History*, 3rd Series, Vol 24 (2003), pp154-76

The Finest Road in the World: The story of travel and transport in the Scottish Highlands, James Miller (2017)

The Glasgow Story (Glasgow Libraries/Mitchell Library)

The Historylinks Trail of Dornoch, produced by The Historylinks Trust and the Dornoch Heritage Society

The Kingdom of Fife: An Illustrated Architectural Guide, G. Pride (1990)

The Milestones of Arran, Ruth and Alan Thompson (2000)

The Milestones of Fife, Alex Darwood and Dr Paula Martin, East of Fife Preservation Society (2005)

The Milestones of Morvern, Dr Paula Martin in *Exploring Morvern*, Vol 2 (Morvern Heritage Society, 2010)

The Military Roads in Scotland, William Taylor

The Northern Antiquarian (9 December 2018)

The Public Roads and Bridges in Dumfries-shire 1650-1820, J. Robertson, Cromwell Place, Wiltshire (1993)

The Roads of Fife, Owen Silver (1987)

The Roman Milestones of Britain, Jeffrey Sedgley, Archaeology Reports, Oxford, No 18 (1975)

The secret history of the milestone, from Roman Britain to Industrial Revolution and beyond, Matthew Dennison, *Country Life* (13 January 2019)

The Turnpike Road to Cramond and Queensferry, Book of The Old Edinburgh Club, New Series, Vol 4, 1997 (pp23-31)

The Wicker Basket, Eric Sinclair

Transport and Economy: The Turnpike Roads of Eighteenth Century Britain, Eric Pawson

50 top sporting Scots who went the extra mile

Archibald, Katie
Baillie, Ian
Beaumont, Mark
Blyth, Chay (Sir Charles)
Budgett, Richard

Campbell, Donnie
Chambers, Thomas
Clark, Jim
Cook, Stephanie

Di Resta, Paul
Dumfries, Johnny
Duncan, D. S.

Findlay, A. P.
Fleming, Philip
Flockhart, Ron
Franchetti, Dario

Gillan, Angus
Graham, Jenny
Grainger, Katherine

Haswelle, Wyndham
Harvie, J.
Hawkins, C.
Hoy, Sir Chris

Kinnear, Wally

Liddell, Eric
Lindsay, Andrew
Lindsay, Robert

McCallum, James
McColgan-Nuttall, Liz
McDonald, Gary
McIntyre, Michael
McNabb, James
McNeill, George
McNish, Allan
McRae, Colin
Moore, Isabella
Muir, Laura
Murray, Yvonne

Pattinson, Rodney

Quigley, Josh

Robertson, Arthur James
Robertson, Shirley

Scott, Duncan
Skinner, Callum
Stewart, Jackie

Twell, Stephanie

Wardell, Rab
Wells, Allan
Wilkie, David
Williamson, Graham

Index

Places

Aberdeen 46, 54, 73, 75-81, 92, 99, 114, 121, 128, 145, 150, 151
Aberfoyle 64, 108, 157
Abington 54, 63
Aberfeldy 43, 117
Abernethy 72
Aboyne 126
Addiewell 96
Ailsa Craig 59, 65, 153
Alford 44
Alloa 79
Alyth 17, 18, 115
Annan 37, 40, 78, 128, 151
Antonine Wall 9-11, 13, 18, 45, 111, 114
Arbroath 27, 42, 76, 79, 119, 121, 122
Ardentinny 106
Ardgour 67
Ardnamurchan 142
Arrochar 44, 69.80
Athelstaneford 48
Auchenblae 128
Auchtermuchty 43, 99, 104, 106
Aviemore 7, 47, 106, 122, 149
Ayr 15, 48, 50, 56, 58, 63, 78, 96
Ayton 28, 32, 33, 124
Balfron 64
Ballantrae 38
Balquhidder 108, 109
Banchory 73
Banff 79, 80
Barrhill 38, 39
Bathgate 35
Bearsden 64
Benbecula 20
Ben Nevis 23, 24, 150
Berwick-upon-Tweed 28, 29, 32, 33

Bishopbriggs 20, 112
Blair Atholl 7, 147, 160
Blairgowrie 44, 49, 118, 151
Braemar 44, 151
Brechin 79, 119
Bridge of Feugh 36
Broadford 80, 138-140
Brodick 61, 147
Broughton 74, 148
Bo'ness 78, 96, 110, 124
Bonnybridge 103, 108-110, 112
Bowling 111
Buckie 149
Burntisland 53, 100, 101, 121
Bute 71, 98
Butt of Lewis 147, 152
Callander 108, 124
Camelon 112
Campbeltown 65, 130, 147
Cape Wrath 135, 136
Carlops 48, 94
Carluke 11, 18, 19
Carmuirs 9
Carnoustie 119, 121, 122
Carnwath 63
Carrbridge 7, 141
Castle Douglas 37, 38, 45
Clackmannan 104
Clydebank 112
Cock Bridge 126
Cockenzie 120
Coldbackie 136
Coldstream 29, 78, 146
Contin 138
Corgarff 44, 126, 151
Coulport 25
Coupar Angus 115, 119
Craill 101
Cramond 9, 53, 82, 83

Crianlarich 117
Crieff 42, 43, 75, 151
Crinan 46
Cromarty 137
Cullen 142
Culloden 14, 18, 73-75, 78
Cumnock 50, 80
Cupar 79, 99, 101-103
Dalbeattie 38, 39
Dalkeith 33, 84, 86
Dalwhinnie 7, 43
Dingwall 76, 137
Dounby 155
Draffan 27
Drimnin 67
Dull 117
Dumbarton 44, 141
Dumfries 27, 38, 40-42, 45, 48, 78, 94, 128, 147, 153
Dunbar 32, 78, 93, 150
Dundee 79, 81, 92, 99, 101, 105, 115, 119, 11, 125, 126, 154
Dunfermline 72, 79, 101, 103,
Dunglass 28
Dunkeld 14, 43, 47, 72, 79, 118, 126
Dunlop 21
Dunnet Head 135
Dunoon 70, 144, 147
Duns 29, 30, 78, 131
Duntocher 144
Dunvegan 139
Durness 135, 151
Easdale 69
East Fortune 95
Ecclefechan 11
Edinburgh 9, 13, 18, 22, 23, 28, 34, 47, 48, 53, 63, 76, 77, 80-82, 89, 91, 94, 96-98, 101, 111, 112, 120, 124, 125, 128, 145, 150

Edzell 15
Elgin 80
Eyemouth 78
Falkirk 34, 42, 48, 98, 107, 109, 112
Falkland 43, 146
Fettercairn 14, 44, 127
Fochabers 44
Forfar 48, 76, 115, 119, 125, 128
Forres 80, 145, 148
Fort Augustus 18, 26, 43, 44, 80, 141, 147
Fort William 43, 44, 81, 147, 148, 151
Friockheim 119
Garve 137
Girvan 38, 50, 122, 151, 154
Glasgow 13, 22, 34, 48, 53, 60, 63, 72, 75-77, 80, 81, 92, 98, 99, 112, 114, 115, 120, 121, 124, 144, 145, 147, 151, 153
Glenluce 38
Golspie 137
Gourock 53, 147
Grangemouth 109
Grantown-on-Spey 44, 45, 142, 148
Grantshouse 28, 124, 125
Greenock 63
Gretna Green 27, 40, 45, 60, 121, 151
Haddington 48, 78, 92, 93, 110
Haugh of Urr 39
Hawick 29, 128, 151
Haymarket 123-125
Helensburgh 150
Hownam 29
Hoy 154
Huntly 44, 127
Inverary 44, 79, 97, 151
Invercauld 44
Invergarry 141
Invergordon 138

Invermoriston 141
Inverness 43, 44, 53, 54, 75, 76, 79-81, 105, 141, 145, 147, 148, 151
Inverurie 114, 145
Irvine 50, 56, 57, 78
Islay 67, 68
Jedburgh 17, 29, 78, 128, 150, 151
Jemimaville 138
John o' Groats 28, 135, 144, 145, 151
Johnstonebridge 27
Joppa 92
Jura 68, 69
Keith 75, 123
Kelso 17, 29, 73, 74, 79, 128, 151
Kilconquhar 101
Killin 117, 151
Kilmarnock 55, 56, 58, 60, 76, 120, 143, 147
Kilmuir 139
Kilsyth 124
Kincraig 45
Kinghorn 99-101
Kingshouse 108, 109
Kingussie 43, 45, 147, 148
Kirkcaldy 79, 99, 101-103
Kirkcudbright 47, 78, 81, 147
Kirkintilloch 112, 120, 124
Kirknewton 96
Kirk o' Shotts 35, 95
Kirkwall 72, 128
Knowe 39
Kyle of Lochalsh 141
Ladybank 125
Lagg 61
Lamberton 21, 28
Lamlash 61, 62
Lanark 48, 78, 95, 128, 151
Largs 56, 57, 59
Laurencekirk 121, 127, 128
Ledmore Junction 136
Leith 53, 77, 91, 101, 106, 111, 147
Lerwick 135
Lilliesleaf 29

Linlithgow 34, 78, 96, 98
Lintrathen 118
Livingston 48, 95, 97
Lochaline 67
Lochearnhead 116, 147
Lochgilphead 69
Lochmaben 14
Lochmaddy 139, 152
Lochranza 61, 147
Lockerbie 40
Lost 117
Machrihanish 65
Mallaig 121, 139
Maryculter 73
Maybole 48, 49
Meigle 115
Melrose 9, 33, 79, 128, 150, 151
Menmuir 118
Mid Calder 42, 96
Milngavie 64
Minto 29, 48
Moffat 27, 49, 74, 151
Monkland 120
Montrose 79
Morebattle 43
Moscow 59
Mull 66, 67, 133, 180
Mull of Kintyre 65, 79, 114, 147
Musselburgh 78, 89, 128, 131
Nenthorn 33
Newbridge 10, 35
New Galloway 39
Newport-on-Tay 100, 110
Newstead 9, 11
Newtonmore 7, 23, 49
Newton Stewart 38, 39, 45, 147
North Berwick 110
Oban 69, 80, 114, 147, 151
Orphil 155
Paisley 63, 76, 78, 114, 120
Peebles 31, 43, 48, 74, 78, 128, 145, 148, 151
Penicuik 94

Penpont 73, 143
Perth 13, 14, 27, 43, 48, 49, 54, 76, 79, 99, 104, 115, 119, 125, 126
Pettycur 72, 100, 101
Pitlochry 7, 147
Pittenweem 101
Polmont 98, 113
Port Downie 112, 113
Port Ellen 12, 67
Port Glasgow 25, 111
Port Hopetoun 112, 113
Portmahhomack 137
Portobello 92, 106
Port of Menteith 108
Portpatrick 37, 38, 45, 50, 78, 122
Portree 76, 140
Portsonachan 69
Prestonpans 74, 78, 125
Pultneytown 46
Queensferry, North 48, 49, 72, 99, 100
Queensferry, South 48, 81, 83
Raasay 80, 81, 140, 141
Ratho 113
Riddell 29
Rothesay 71
Royal Mile 78, 82
Rumbling Bridge 101, 103, 104
St Abb's Head 25, 26
St Andrews 72, 79, 81, 101, 102, 110, 151
St Fillans 116
Salen (Ardnamurchan) 142
Salen (Mull) 66
Sannox 61
Selkirk 128, 145, 151
Skelmorlie 25, 56
Stirling 34, 48, 76, 107, 114,
Stonehaven 73, 127, 128, 136
Stornoway 50, 147
Stow 30, 31, 144
Stranraer 38, 45, 76, 78, 122, 147
Strathdon 126
Strathyre 45

Stromness 154, 155
Strontian 142
Sumburgh Head 156
Swainbost 152
Swarkestone 75
Tain 72, 73, 79, 137, 151
Tarbert (Argyll) 65
Tarbert (Harris) 139, 152
Tarbet 80, 97, 151
Thurso 53, 121, 154
Tighnabruaich 70
Tobermory 66, 142
Tomatin 141
Tomintoul 44, 45, 126, 149
Tranent 120, 131
Troon 60, 120, 148
Tyndrum 44, 151
Uig 139, 147, 152
Ullapool 50, 136, 137, 147
Upper Largo 102, 103
Wallyford 125
Wanlockhead 41
West Calder 96
West Linton 43
Westruther 33
Whithorn 72, 73, 151
Wick 46, 81, 121
Wigtown 38
Winchburgh 113

People

Abercrombie, Charles 46
Adair, John 17
Adam, William 44
Adie, Alexander 22
Agrippa, Marcus Vipsanius 13
Anderson, Andy 50
Arrol, Sir William 53
Bartholomew, John George 20
Blaeu, Joan 17
Boswell, James 78-80
Bouch, Sir Thomas 101, 121

Bridges, Robert 110
Brown, James 101
Bryson, Bill 157
Burns, Robert 15, 46, 63, 78, 80, 106, 144
Cameron, Ewen 116
Caulfeild, William 44-46
Cavendish, Henry 23
Chalmers, James 78
Close, Sir Charles 22
Cobb, John 26, 97, 129
Cobbett, William 81
Coleridge, Samuel Taylor 78, 80
Craigie, Charles 89, 90
Crawford, James 20
Crowe, Dame Sylvia 36
Cumberland, Duke of 14, 18
Dalzell, Gavin 143
Danielle, William 78, 80
Defoe, Daniel 78
Douglas, Robert 102, 103, 110
Dudgeon, David 146
Dunlop, John Boyd 144
Ferrie-Mabon, Alexander 22
Fforde, Lady Jane 61
Forbes, William 113
Gibbon, Lewis Grassic 128
Grahame-White, Claude 20
Grandison, L. 31
Groome, Francis H. 11
Gunter, Edmund 14
Hay, Colonel Lord Charles 45
Harrow, Charlie 146
Hemmings, Angus 23
Hutton, Charles 22, 23, 27

Inglis, Harry R. G. 27
James, Colonel Sir Henry 21, 23
Jefferson, Thomas and Peter 14
Johnson, Dr Samuel 78-80, 140
Johnston, George 53
Keith, William 73
Keith-Falconer, Ian 147
Kelly, Michael 98
Kennedy, Calum 105, 158
King Alexander III 101
King Charles I 13
King David I 14
King George II 18
King James V 17
King James VI 76
King Malcolm III 137
King Robert II 81
King William IV 22
Knox, John 45
Lauder, Sir Harry 106
Linklater, Andro 14
Lyndsay, Alexander 17
MacGregor, Rob Roy 108
Mackintosh, Brigadier William 73
MacLean, Sorley 140
MacLeod, Calum 140
MacMillan, Kirkpatrick 143
Marquis of Montrose 73
Maskelyne, Nevil 22, 23
McAdam, James Louden 46, 48, 61, 77, 144
McAlpine, 'Concrete Bob' 121
McCall, Thomas 143
McColl, Iain 146
McConnell, John 49

Metcalf, John 46
Miller, John 22
Mills, John 89
Minto, Christine 28, 157
Mitchell, John and Joseph 46, 49
Munro, David Scott 26
Murray, Lord George 74, 75
Murray, Sir John 74
Murray, Sarah 80
Napier, Robert 24, 25
Neilson, James B 96
Noble, Iain 140
Ogilby, John 17
Orwell, George 68, 69
Paterson, James 120
Pennant, Thomas 78, 79
Pittock, Professor Murray 75
Playfair, William 23
Pont, Timothy 17
Queen Victoria 22, 53, 66, 81, 108
Ramsden, Jesse 22
Reith, Lord John 37, 127
Rennie, John 114, 115
Robertson, Brian 50
Robison, Sir John 110
Rowe, Andrew 146, 147
Roy, Major-General William 18, 19, 21
Russell, Alexander 101
Russell, John Scott 120
St Joseph, J. K. 9
Sayers, Ben 110
Scott, Sir Walter 80, 81, 90, 109, 151
Scott, Tavish 141
Sherratt, Brenda 26
Sibbald, Sir Robert 9, 10, 17, 83

Simmons, Professor Jack 124
Skinner, Andrew 19
Smeaton, John 111
Smith, Adam 46, 111
Smith & Wellstood Ltd 103, 108-110
Smith Patterson & Company 30, 39, 66, 67, 110
Smith, Thomas 65
Southey, Robert 78, 81
Stephen, Walter M. 100-103
Stevenson, Robert 40, 53, 65, 67, 135, 137, 156
Stevenson, Robert Louis 90
Stewart, Andy 105
Stuart, Prince Charles Edward 74, 75
Stukely, Rev William 10, 11
Taine, Hippolyte 81
Taylor, George 19
Telford, Thomas 46-49, 61, 76, 81, 83, 101, 114, 115, 137, 138, 142
Tite, Sir William 125
Thomson, Robert William 144
Thomson, Sir William (Lord Kelvin) 22
Wade, General George 43-46, 74, 75, 79, 80, 141
Watson, David 18
Watt, James 120
White, James 22
Whitworth, Robert 111
Wills, Francis 20
Wordsworth, Dorothy and William 78, 80
Wylie, Rev John 11
Young, 'Paraffin' James 96, 97